Landscapes and Birds of Scotland

an Artist's View

Leo du Feu

Leo du Feu

Published by Northern Arts Publications
an imprint of Jeremy Mills Publishing Limited
www.jeremymillspublishing.co.uk

113 Lidget Street
Lindley
Huddersfield
West Yorkshire HD3 3JR

First published 2013

ISBN: 978-1-909837-00-3

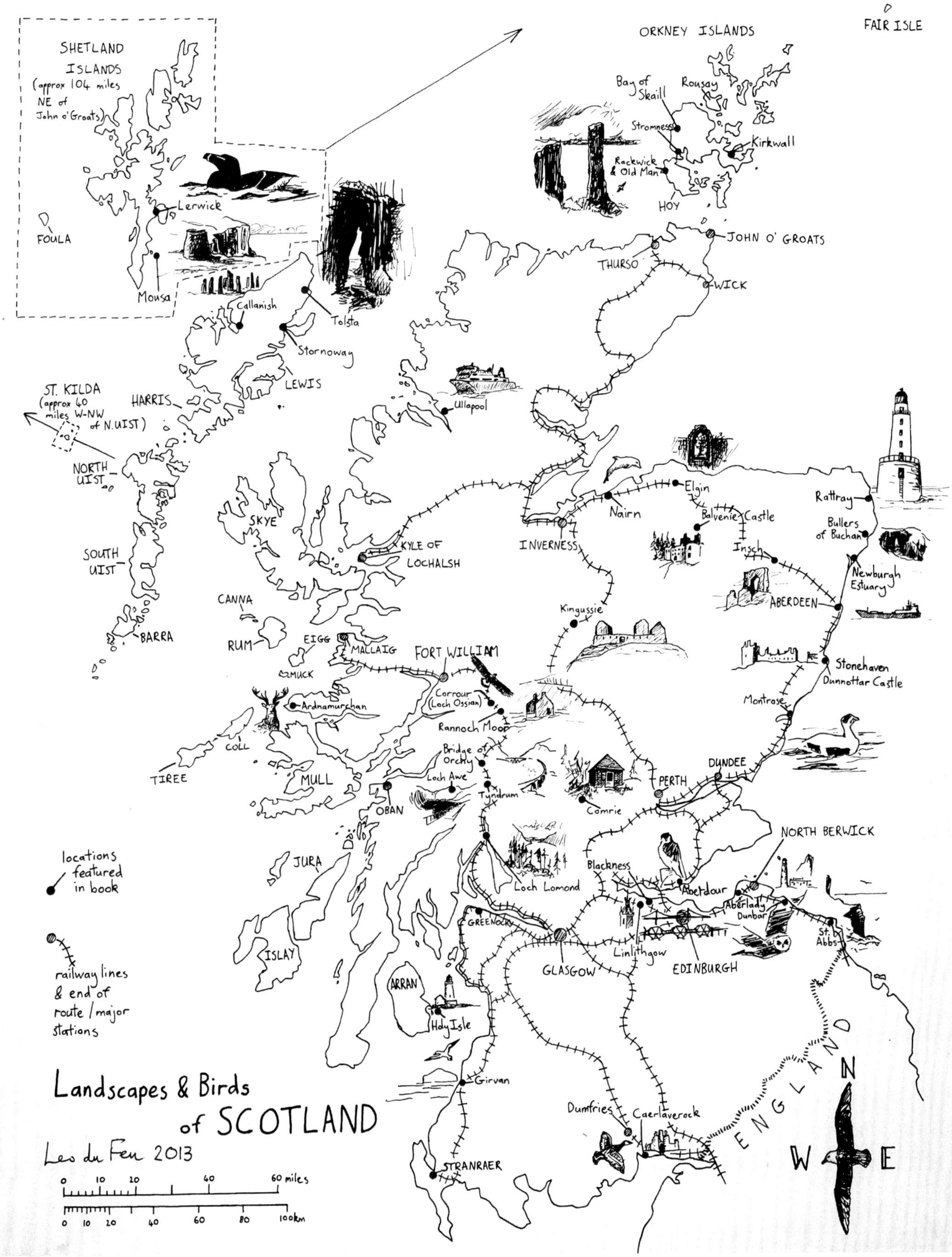

SHETLAND ISLANDS (approx 104 miles NE of John o'Groats)
Lerwick
FOULA
Mousa
ORKNEY ISLANDS
FAIR ISLE
Bay of Skaill
Rousay
Stromness
Kirkwall
Rackwick & Old Man
HOY
JOHN O' GROATS
THURSO
WICK
Callanish
Tolsta
Stornoway
LEWIS
HARRIS
ST. KILDA (approx 60 miles W-NW of N.UIST)
NORTH UIST
SOUTH UIST
BARRA
Ullapool
SKYE
KYLE OF LOCHALSH
CANNA
RUM
EIGG
MALLAIG
MUCK
FORT WILLIAM
Ardnamurchan
COLL
TIREE
MULL
Corrour (Loch Ossian)
Rannoch Moor
Bridge of Orchy
Loch Awe
Tyndrum
OBAN
JURA
ISLAY
ARRAN
Holy Isle
Girvan
STRANRAER
Loch Lomond
GREENOCK
GLASGOW
Nairn
Elgin
Balvenie Castle
INVERNESS
Kingussie
Insch
Rattray
Bullers of Buchan
Newburgh Estuary
ABERDEEN
Stonehaven
Dunnottar Castle
Montrose
DUNDEE
PERTH
Comrie
NORTH BERWICK
Blackness
Aberdour
Aberlady
Dunbar
St. Abbs
Linlithgow
EDINBURGH
Dumfries
Caerlaverock
ENGLAND
N
W
E
locations featured in book
railway lines & end of route / major stations
Landscapes & Birds of SCOTLAND
Leo du Feu 2013
0 10 20 40 60 miles
0 10 20 40 60 80 100km

Contents

Forewords

Michael Palin

Leo du Feu's paintings capture many moments I've experienced when travelling through Scotland, more often than not from passing trains, across Rannoch Moor or the cliff-tops of the East Coast – moments when the light and the landscape combined to produce images that I wanted to freeze for ever, but which flashed by, out of time and out of vision.

It's Leo's great skill to have captured such evocative glimpses, to have given me the chance to enjoy them all over again without them being snatched away by the onward hurtling of the train. The space and scale of the Scottish scenery is all here, caught with swift brushstrokes and bold colours that convey immediacy and permanence at the same time.

This is Scotland as I want to remember it.

MICHAEL PALIN CBE
TRAVEL WRITER, PRESENTER, COMEDIAN
JUNE 2013

John Busby

Leo's travels along the railways of Scotland bring new life to the view seen through the window. The walks that follow from his destinations take him into the heart of Scotland's great 'Outside'– its glens and lochs, sea cliffs and castles. Leo's paintings and drawings have all the excitement of these moments of discovery – images seen which must be captured.

There is a joy evident in the spontaneous way he uses his brush and applies colour, which looks effortless – a great achievement, knowing how all artists struggle to find this. These works have that vital freshness of colour and movement that makes paintings memorable.

Leo responds especially to the drama of sea cliffs and ruined castles: Slains, standing serene above the red cliffs and dark pounding sea; the Old Man of Hoy on fire with sunlight; Ailsa Craig standing on the horizon like a distant dream – all wonderful images. The birds live as part of their surroundings, often adding a touch of humour to the scene.

Leo says that a train journey used to be a time to enjoy a good read: not any more, there is far too much to see. His book is sure to open our eyes as well, and stimulate the urge to explore.

JOHN BUSBY
WILDLIFE ARTIST
JUNE 2013

Stuart Housden

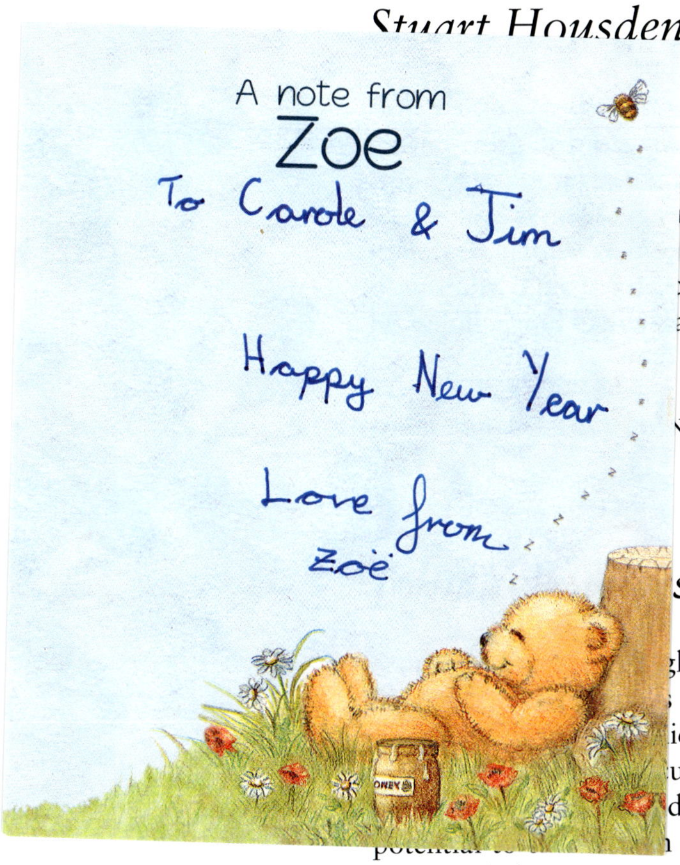

ds and seascapes of Scotland can't fail to see birds – a
eeling over rocky stacks or gliding over the swell of the
places, and it is wonderful to see them through the eyes
Feu. His depiction of Hoy, where the RSPB has one of
s, including the 'Old Man', captures its rugged essence
cinating journey brought to life by someone who knows
athy with the wild places of Scotland's dramatic coastline.

ND

s

ghted to support Leo du Feu's travels by train throughout
provide refreshing images which we believe can help
ic routes to a new generation of travellers.

ulous eye for detail, and the way in which he captures
dlife and other features in the passing landscape has the
the most seasoned of our customers to see their journey
in a new light.

JOHN YELLOWLEES
SCOTRAIL
MAY 2013

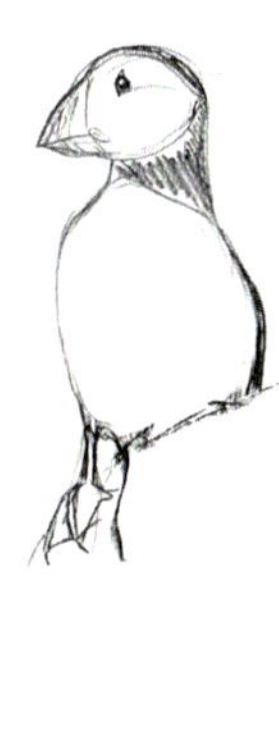

Introduction

Born and brought up in Scotland, with holidays and weekends spent walking, cycling, or in the garden at home, it's little surprise that Scottish landscape and nature is what inspires me. My mum is an artist and art teacher so creativity was a major part of childhood. Back then I loved to draw flowers (pansies were my favourite!) but nowadays my focus is as the title of this book suggests.

Upon graduating from Edinburgh College of Art in 2006 I wanted to find ways of exploring my country through my art. I wrote to train operator ScotRail and the response was positive; they've been supporting my explorations of Scotland ever since.

Armed with binoculars and sketchbook, pencil, pen, and watercolour box, I walk the main streets of whichever station town I've chosen before setting off into the surrounding countryside. Usually I have an anticipated route or endpoint but I try to allow myself to deviate if I encounter an enticing footpath or hear an unknown bird call. If inspiration strikes I stop to sketch. If it doesn't I choose a place to stop anyway and wait to see what happens, normally in a spot that looks good for birds. A privilege known to those who spend a lot of time sitting outdoors, as I do when sketching, is that the longer you sit quiet, the more used to your presence birds and animals become. That's when you start to see things. Humans often only find time to look quickly then move on; we forget to study and to wonder. Drawing forces you to absorb your subject and subsequently you learn a lot.

Once back in the studio after a railway trip I write about it on my blog, including any work that I've produced. Many of these sketches will never become finished paintings, but every drawing made is a valuable experience.

Not everywhere can be reached by rail of course, so some trips have to be by car; I don't yet drive so I'm mostly generously chauffeured by my lady Jennifer or my stepdad Ian. Other sketching excursions are on foot from my studio in my dad's house in Linlithgow, or from the home of whichever kind friend or relative I'm staying with at the time.

Possibly the most exciting of all ways to travel is by ferry, to islands! I can't not mention Scotland's islands here, given that they comprise a fifth of this book. In his excellent book, *The Scottish Islands*, Hamish Haswell Smith counts Scotland as having 162 un-bridged islands of forty hectares (approx 100 acres) or over, and hundreds of smaller ones. I've found great inspiration on the handful that I've visited so far.

Within the natural world, my passion is birds. I volunteer on and off for the Royal Society for the Protection of Birds (RSPB) Scotland, and undertake regular voluntary survey work for the British Trust for Ornithology (BTO). Volunteer surveys and observations are vital for understanding, educating and lobbying about the extremely worrying trends seen in many of our UK bird populations; it's really satisfying to be so easily able to contribute to such important and useful science. Anyone in the UK can get involved in BTO surveys, be it up in the mountains, on your walk to work, in your local park, or from your kitchen window. I find it a great motivation to spend more time outside, enjoying and learning about the fauna of Scotland. The more I learn, the more I learn there is to learn, if you see what I mean.

In this book I bring together my three passions – birds, art, and being outside. It was difficult knowing how best to present the content: by council region? by rail route? by habitat type? All have advantages and disadvantages. In the end I've chosen to divide Scotland into three sections – Highlands, Lowlands and Islands. A final fourth section shows a few of the many sketches I make from train windows whilst travelling.

I intend the reader to open this book at any page and enjoy what they find there. Anyone wishing to be more exact in their reading can find page numbers of all the locations covered on the Contents page. The map gives a general idea of where each location lies within Scotland, but I strongly suggest that it be used in conjunction with an Ordnance Survey! At the end of the book are acknowledgments and a short list of organisations, names and links that may be of interest.

To finish, I hope this scattering of drawings, paintings, and writings will encourage people to get out and explore nature, especially to know the satisfaction of discovering new places by rail and bike and foot. Scotland is a wonderful country, with a wealth of landscape and wildlife that needs to be understood, appreciated and protected. Perhaps start by getting to know your own local patch, then see what else you can find.

LEO DU FEU
APRIL 2013

Lowlands: Central & South

Dumfriesshire

CAERLAVEROCK WETLAND CENTRE

From Glencaple village I spent a few days exploring the area around Caerlaverock on the Dumfries & Galloway coast. The Wildfowl & Wetlands Trust's (WWT) Caerlaverock reserve sees the winter arrival of tens of thousands of Svalbard barnacle geese and hundreds of Icelandic whooper swans. The birds come to forage on the plentiful fields and wetlands and the birdwatchers come to sit in hides and watch. There are numerous hides and you get really close-up views.

I was especially taken by the teal – our smallest British duck – which bobbed on all the pools and ponds. Their head is bright rust-orange with metallic green eye bands (teal, in fact!). An intricate delicate patterning covers the rest of the body. Also the shoveler ducks: I watched them swim in tight circles, bodies floating on the surface but heads underwater, stirring up sediment and dabbling for weed. The head rises momentarily, just enough to glimpse a golden eye and the top of a black beak before it plunges back down, over and over. Their huge spade-like beaks made my drawings look like comic sketches.

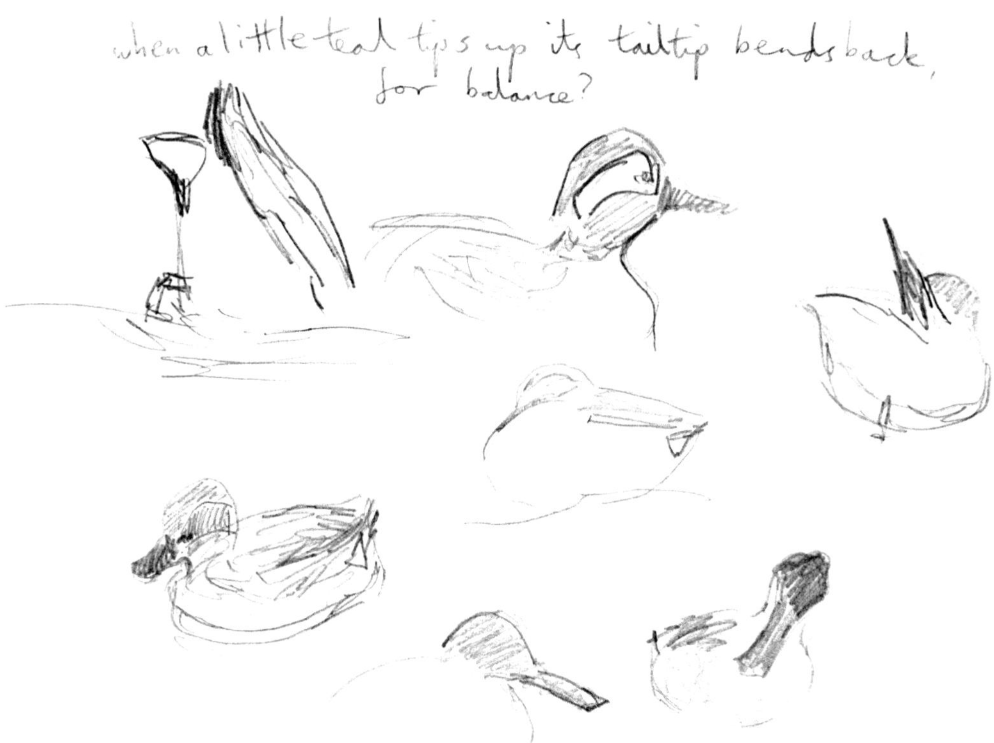

teal studies
pencil
14.5 x 20.5cm

***right:* shoveler sketch**
pencil
14.5 x 20.5cm

***below:* little egret studies**
pencil
14.5 x 20.5cm

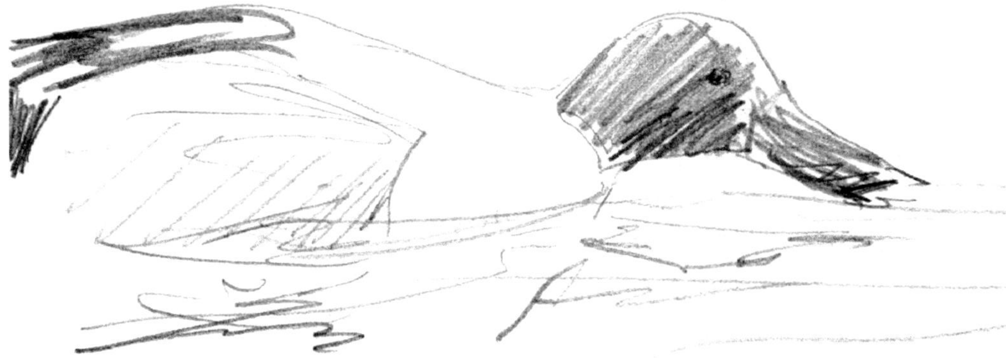

Leaning on top of one of the original low-roofed 'Presco' hides from the 1970s I sketched three little egrets that stalked purposefully amongst a large group of wigeon. Their pure white plumage shone brightly beside the ducks and dull grassy wetland.

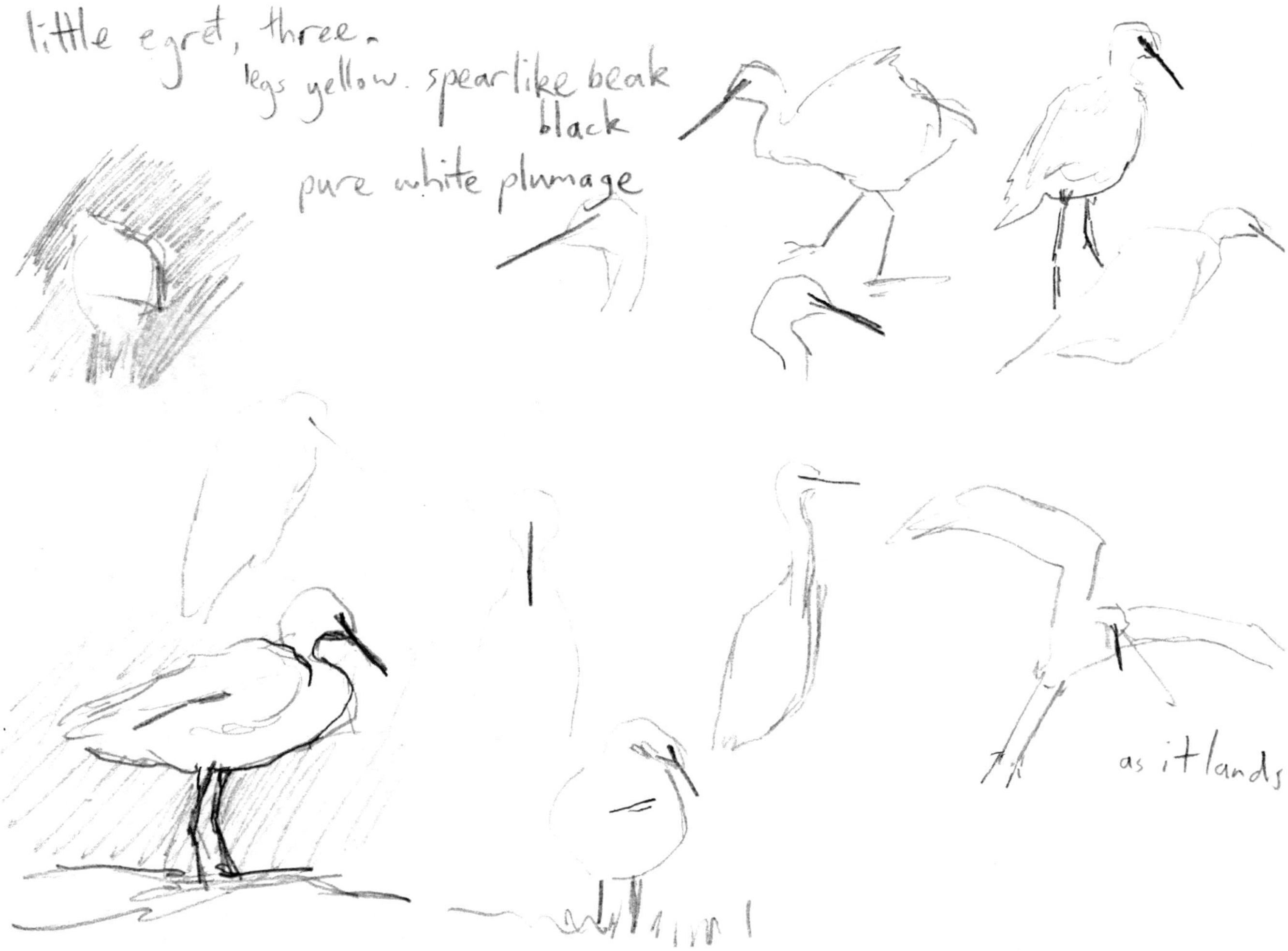

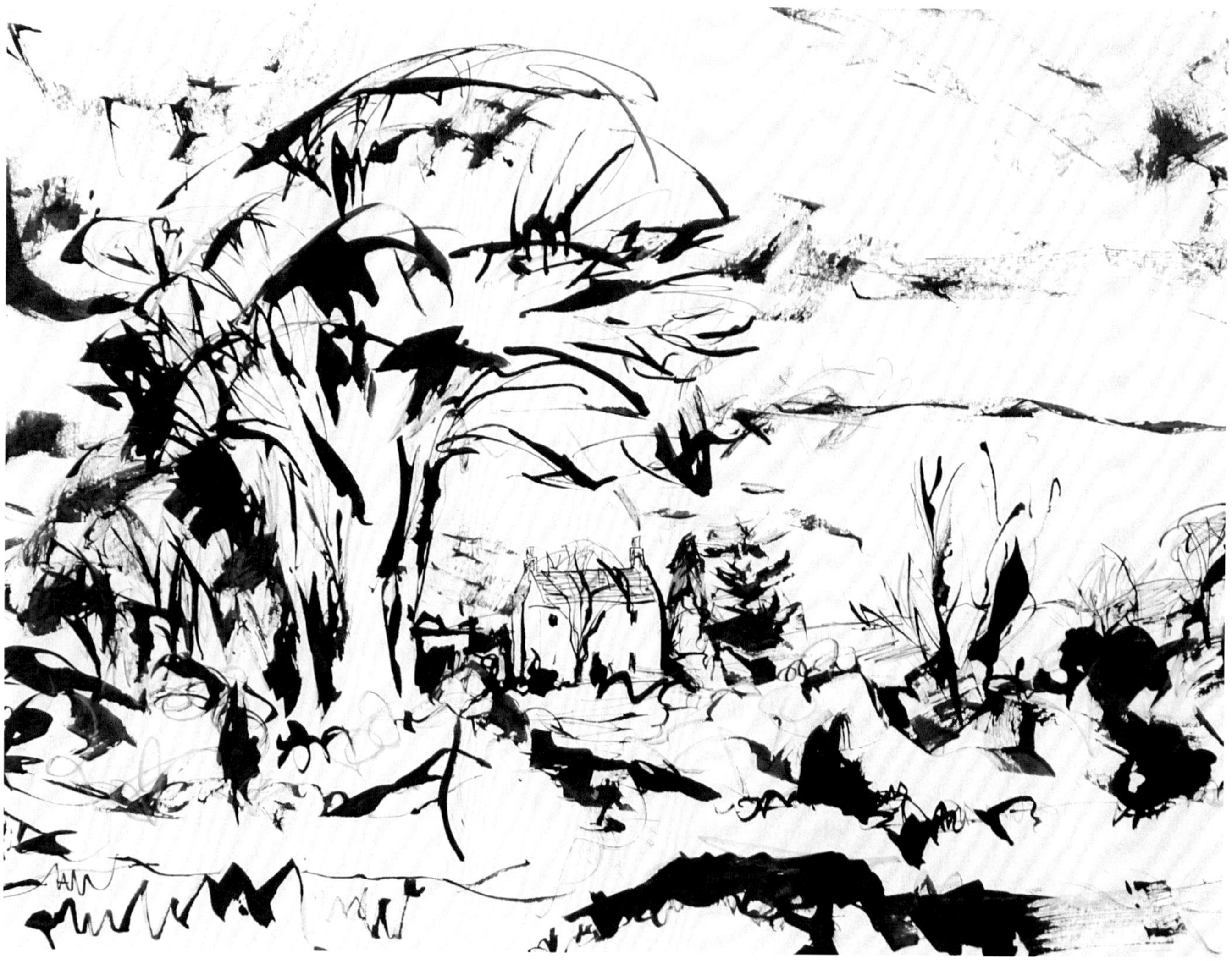

farmhouse from Caerlaverock wetland
pen & ink
25 x 35.5cm

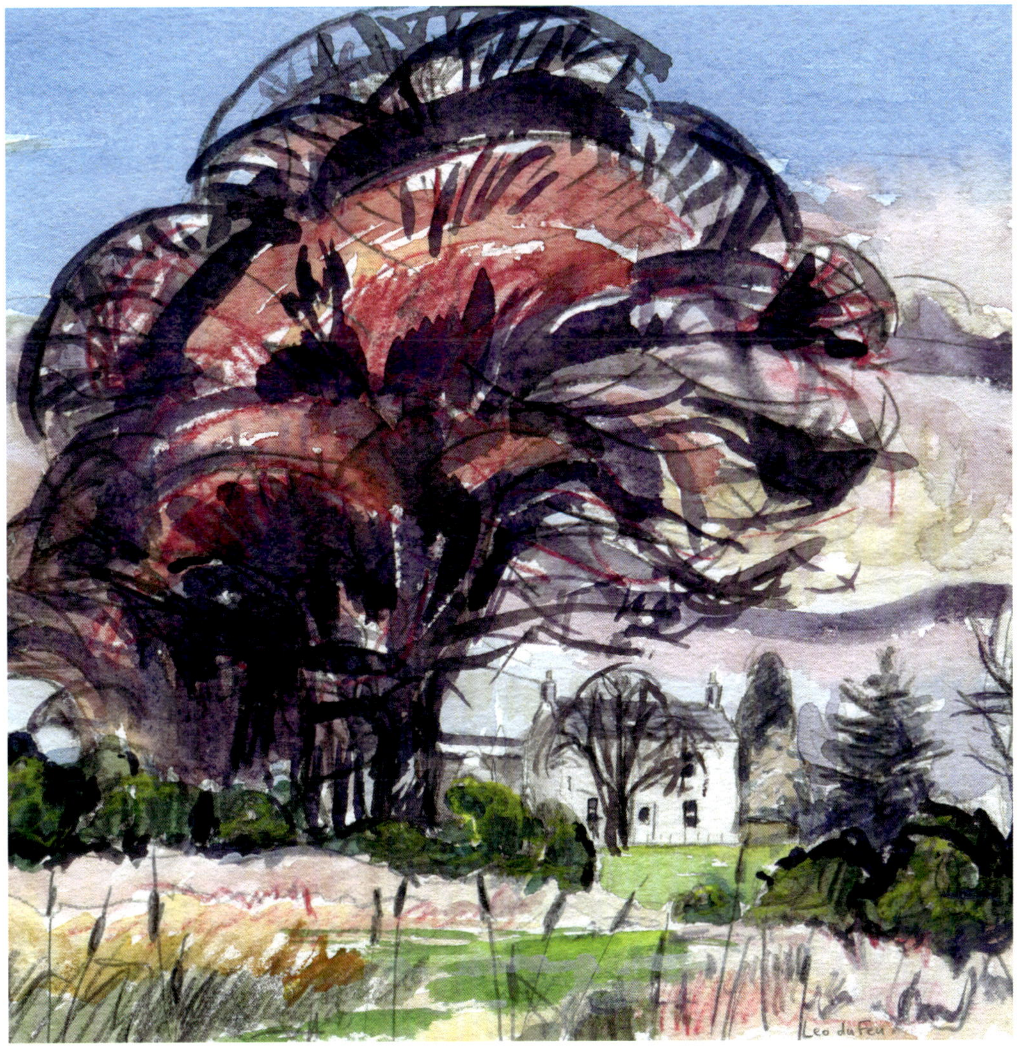

farmhouse from Caerlaverock wetland
watercolour
14.5 x 15cm

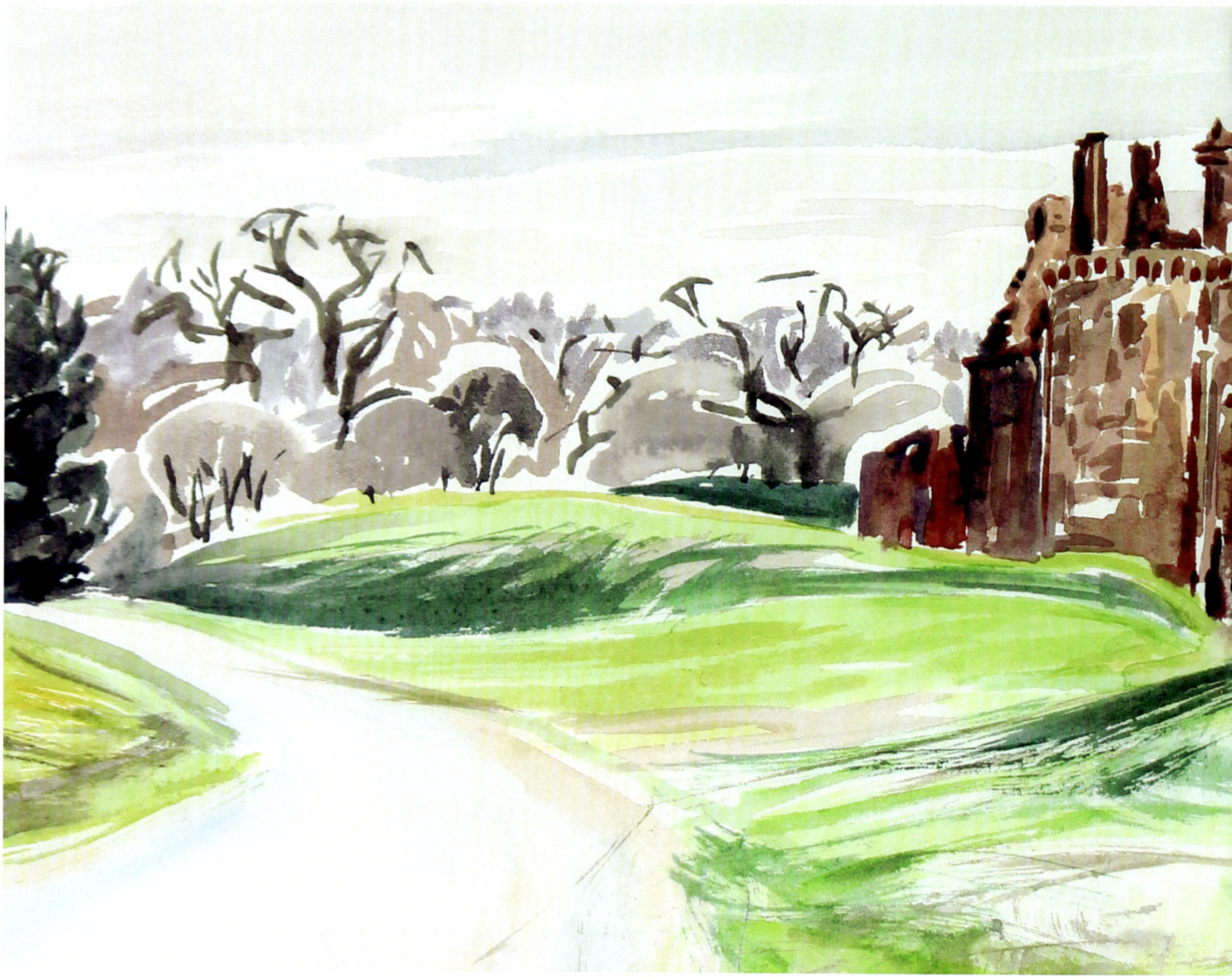

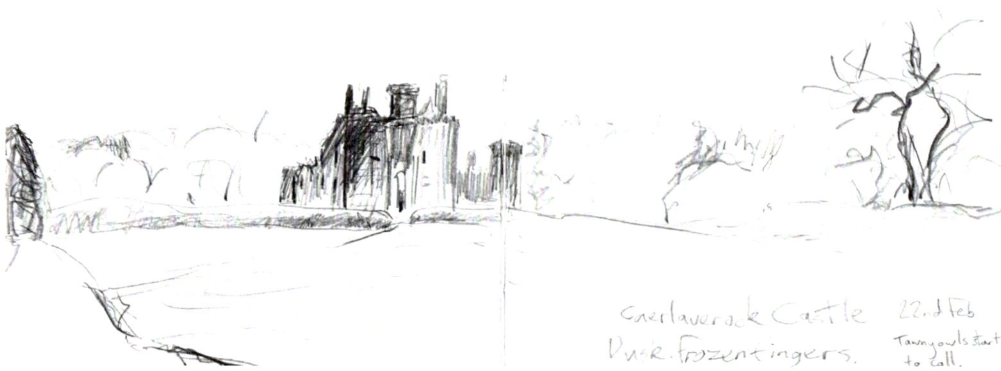

***above:* Caerlaverock castle**
watercolour
14.5 x 35cm

***left:* Caerlaverock castle**
pencil
14.5 x 41cm

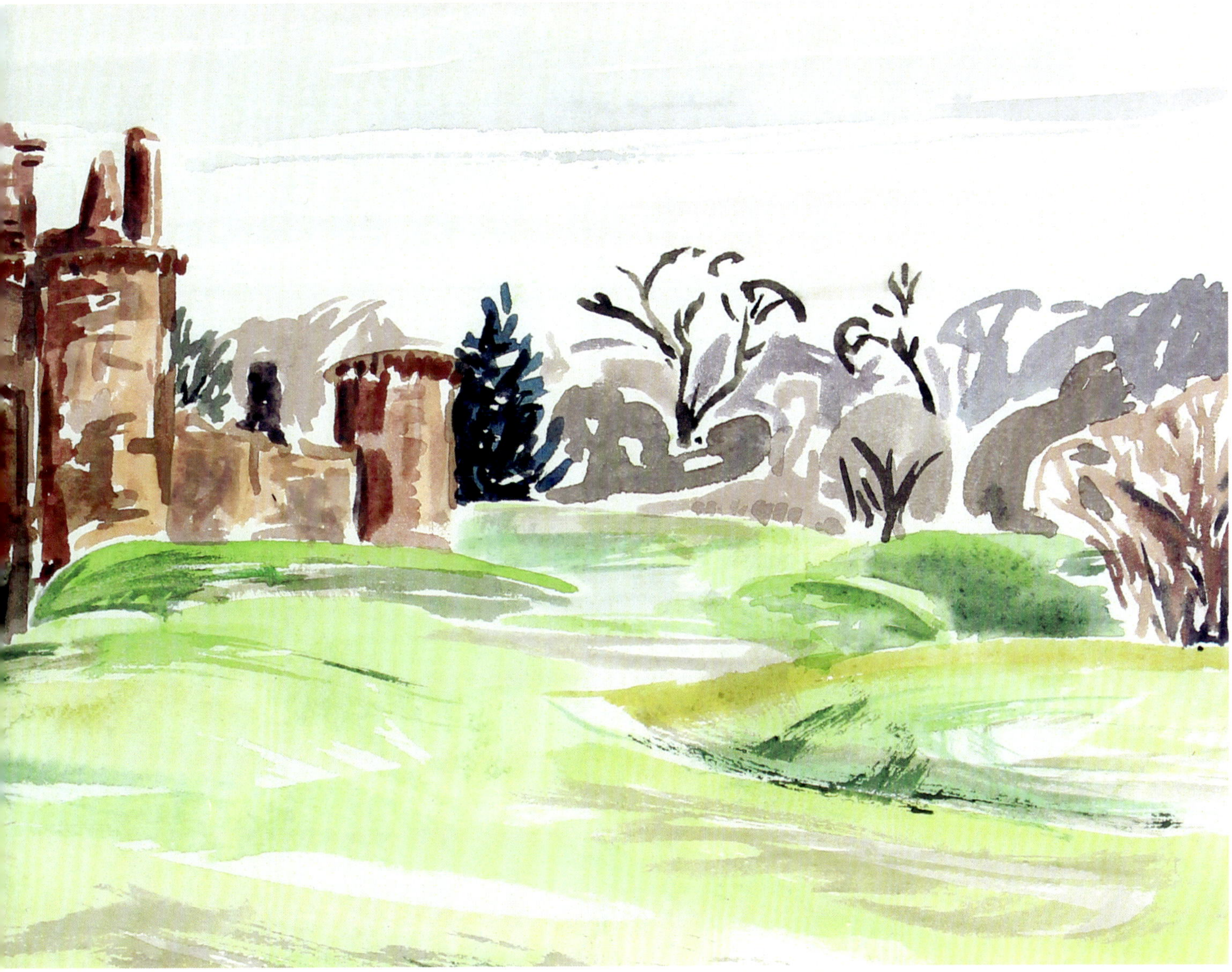

CAERLAVEROCK CASTLE AND WOODS

Set in lichen-festooned woodland and surrounded by a still-full moat is the triangular, red sandstone Caerlaverock Castle. On my way to the castle I stopped on reedy marshland and made an ink drawing and two watercolours of an impressive whitewashed farmhouse framed by an avenue of tall beech trees. As dusk fell at the castle I painted again in watercolour and watched crows, rooks and jackdaws start to settle for the night (meaning they become noisier than ever!). I heard tawny owls calling and the distant clamour of thousands of barnacle geese as they congregated to roost. Every few minutes small skeins of barnacles flew over, heading towards the noise.

Beside the Historic Scotland shop is a tearoom. Perfect to warm up in if you're there during opening hours.

GLENCAPLE

Each morning before breakfast I sat overlooking the River Nith, seeing what birds were around and making sketches in watercolour. A leucistic redshank was there every day – white plumaged, but without the pink eyes of an albino. Although completely unexpected in appearance, its behaviour seemed perfectly normal as it probed the muddy sandbanks alongside other redshanks.

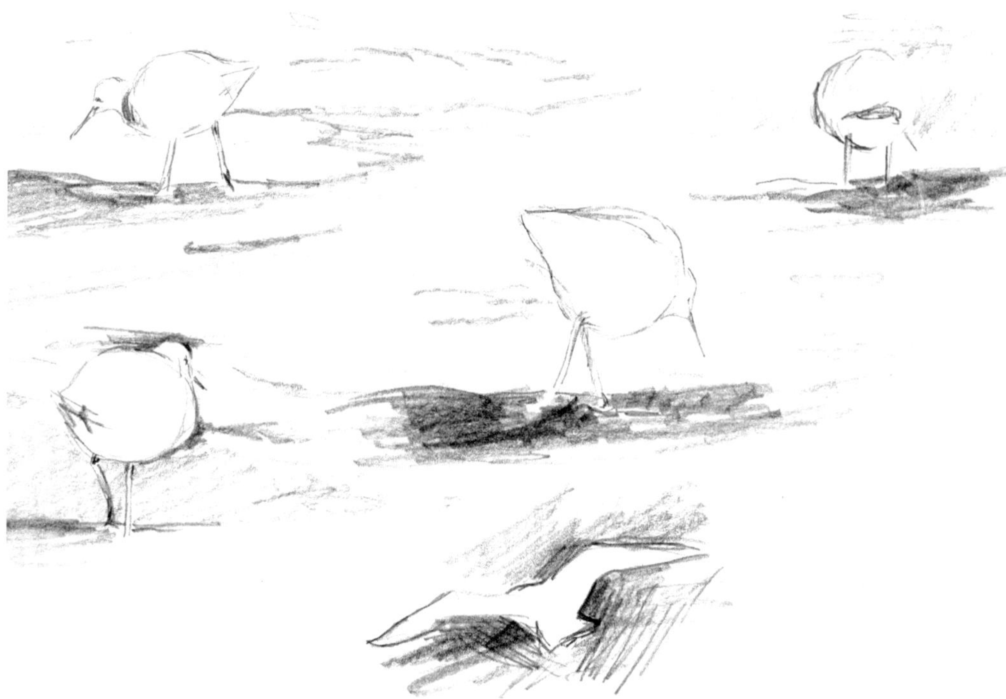

leucistic redshank, Glencaple
pencil
14.5 x 20.5cm

views to Ailsa Craig
watercolour
13 x 20.5cm

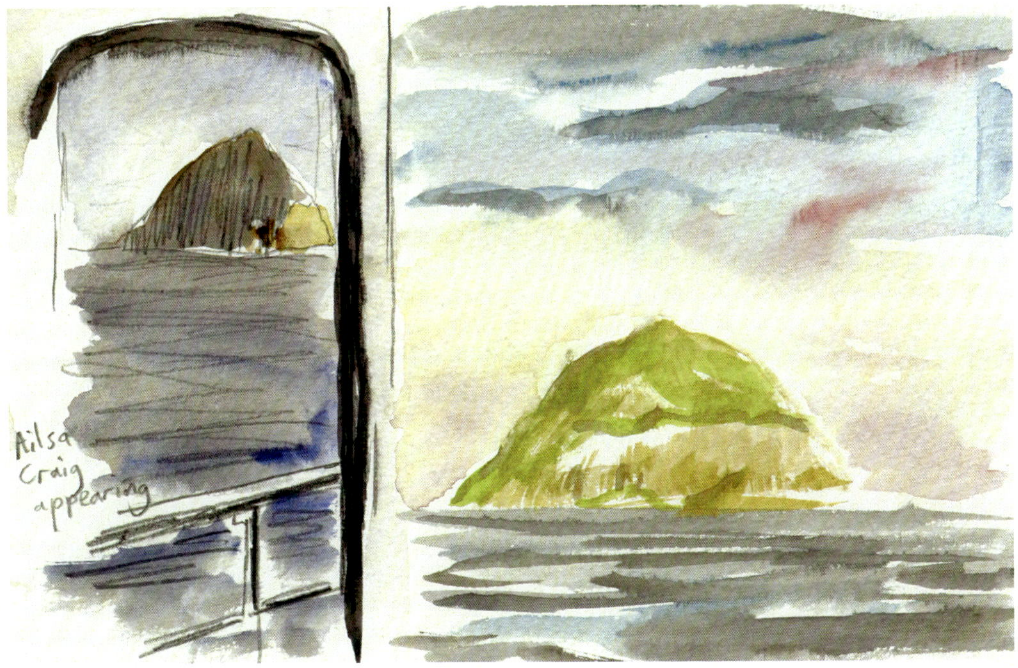

Girvan

As with the line itself, a lot of towns on the Glasgow-Stranraer line are much undervisited. I've done good walks from most of the stations at which the train stops.

From Girvan you get great views across the Firth of Clyde to Ailsa Craig, a domed island famously quarried for curling stones. I've sketched Ailsa Craig from Girvan's shore as it appeared and disappeared through sheets of sea mist. One day I hope to visit.

On the beach were oystercatchers, and while I was drawing, several hundred mixed finches and sparrows flocked down into a car park near to me, foraged briefly, then twittered off again.

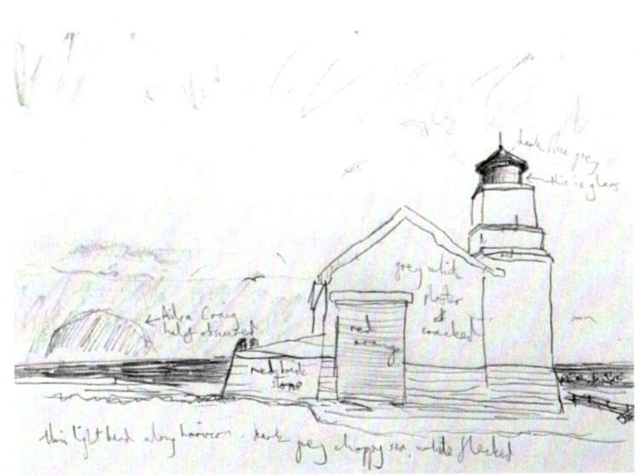

Ailsa Craig from Girvan shore
pencil
14.5 x 20.5cm

Linlithgow & Blackness

It's important not to overlook one's home territory. Mine is Linlithgow, on the railway line between Edinburgh and Glasgow. We don't have remote or 'wild' landscape here, but it's a great place to have grown up. There's mature woodland at Beecraigs and Muiravonside country parks; the Union Canal runs through the town with a well-surfaced towpath all the way from Edinburgh to Glasgow; there are lots of shore birds at Blackness and Bo'ness. All this is within a few miles' walk of my home. Even closer is Linlithgow Palace, overlooking Linlithgow Loch with its thriving breeding populations of coot, moorhen, swans, assorted ducks and both little and great crested grebes.

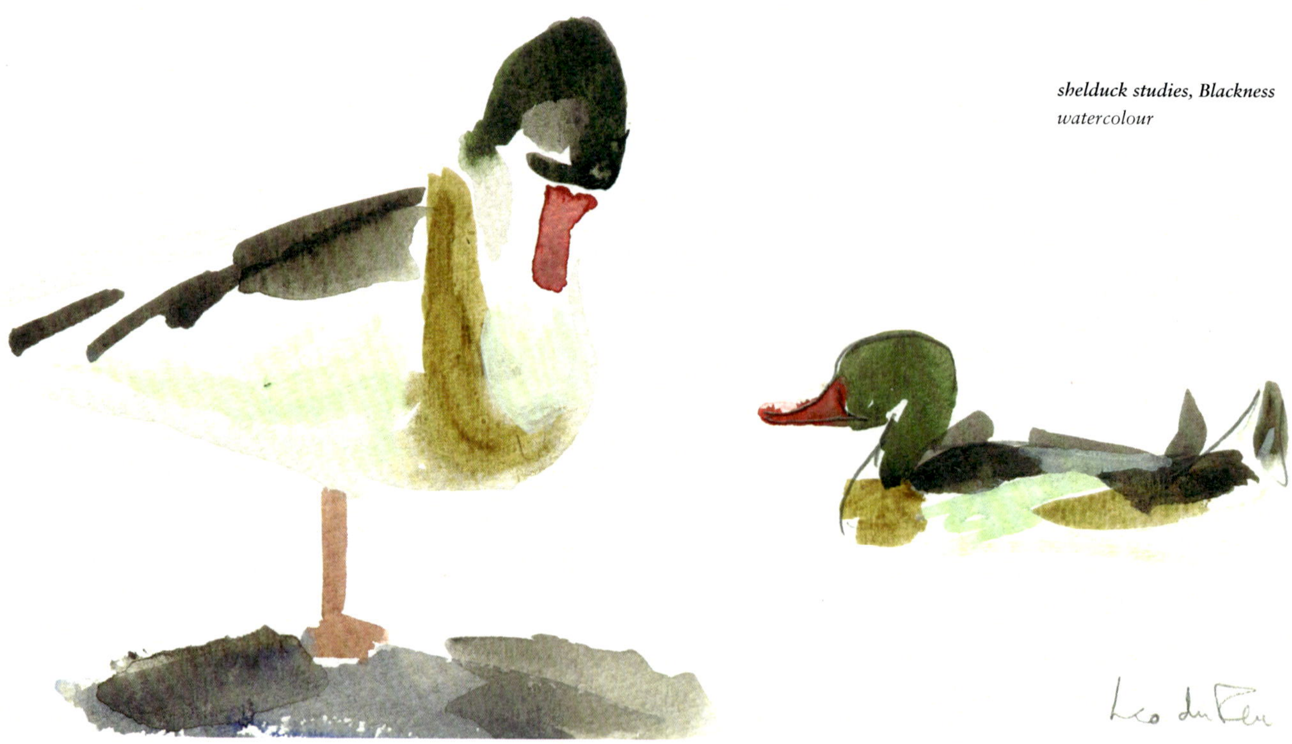

shelduck studies, Blackness
watercolour

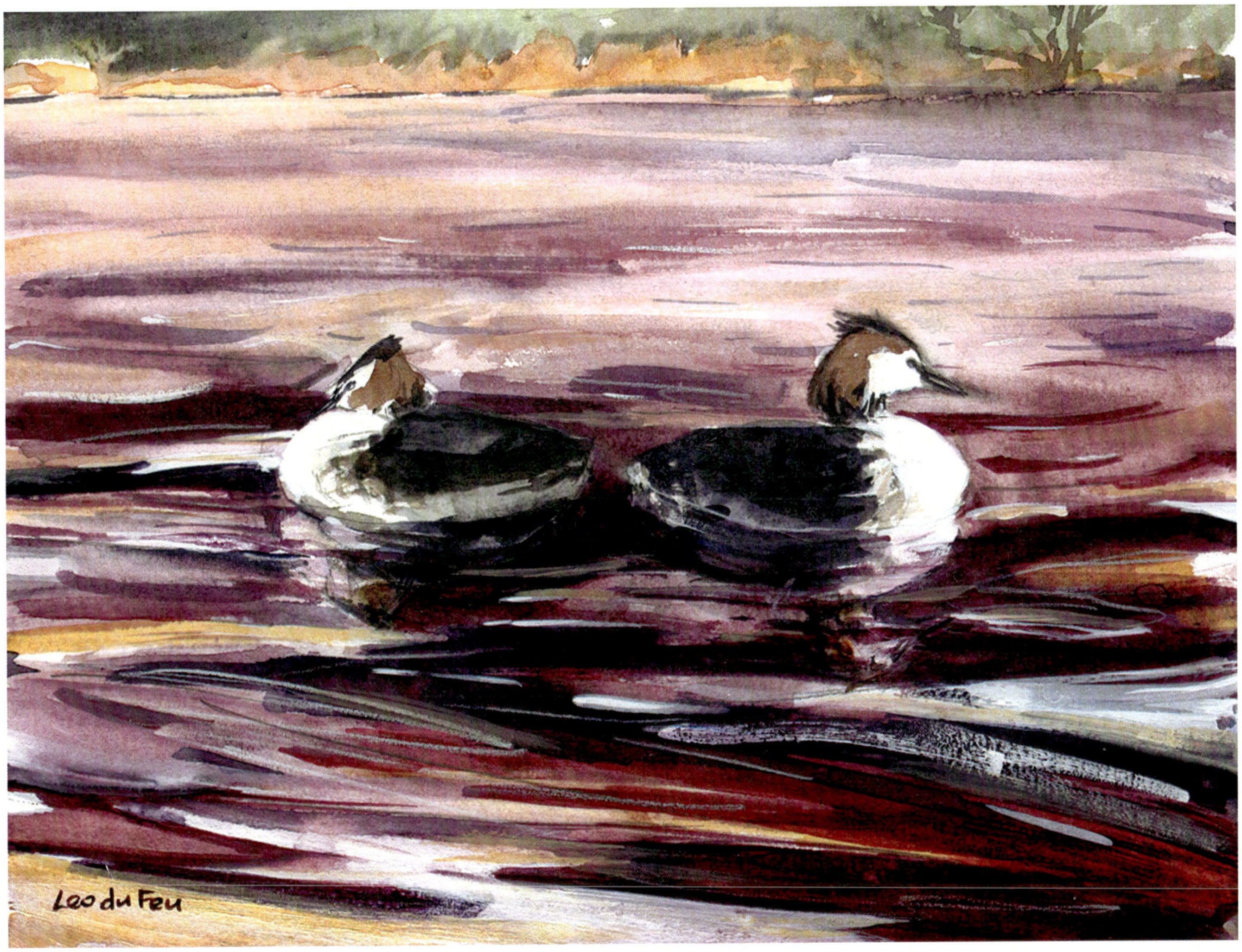

great crested grebes,
Linlithgow Loch
watercolour & acrylic
14.5 x 20.5cm

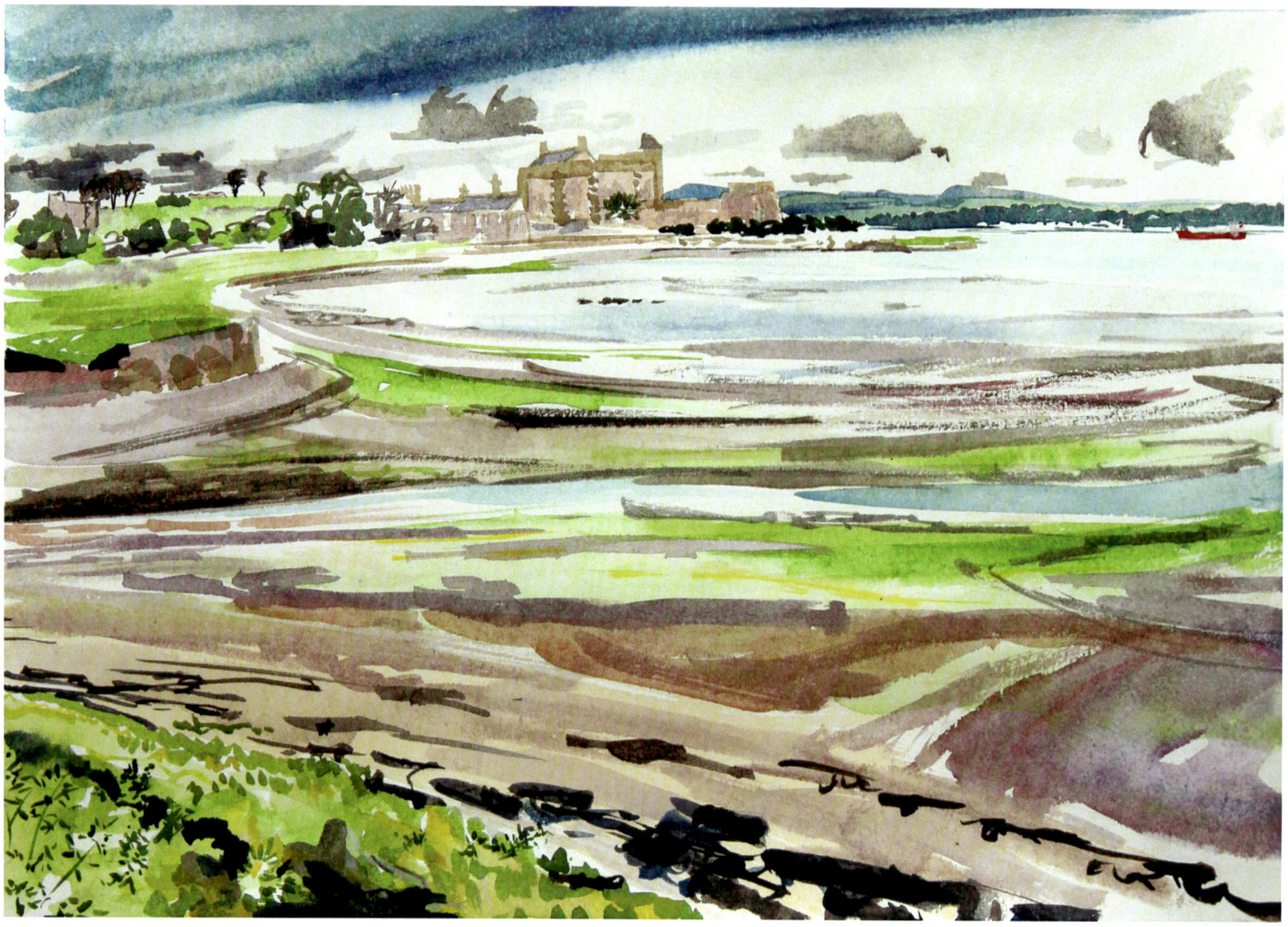

above: Blackness Castle
watercolour
26.5 x 38cm

right, top: shelduck, Tadorna tadorna
acrylic
14.5 x 21cm

right: shelduck studies
pencil

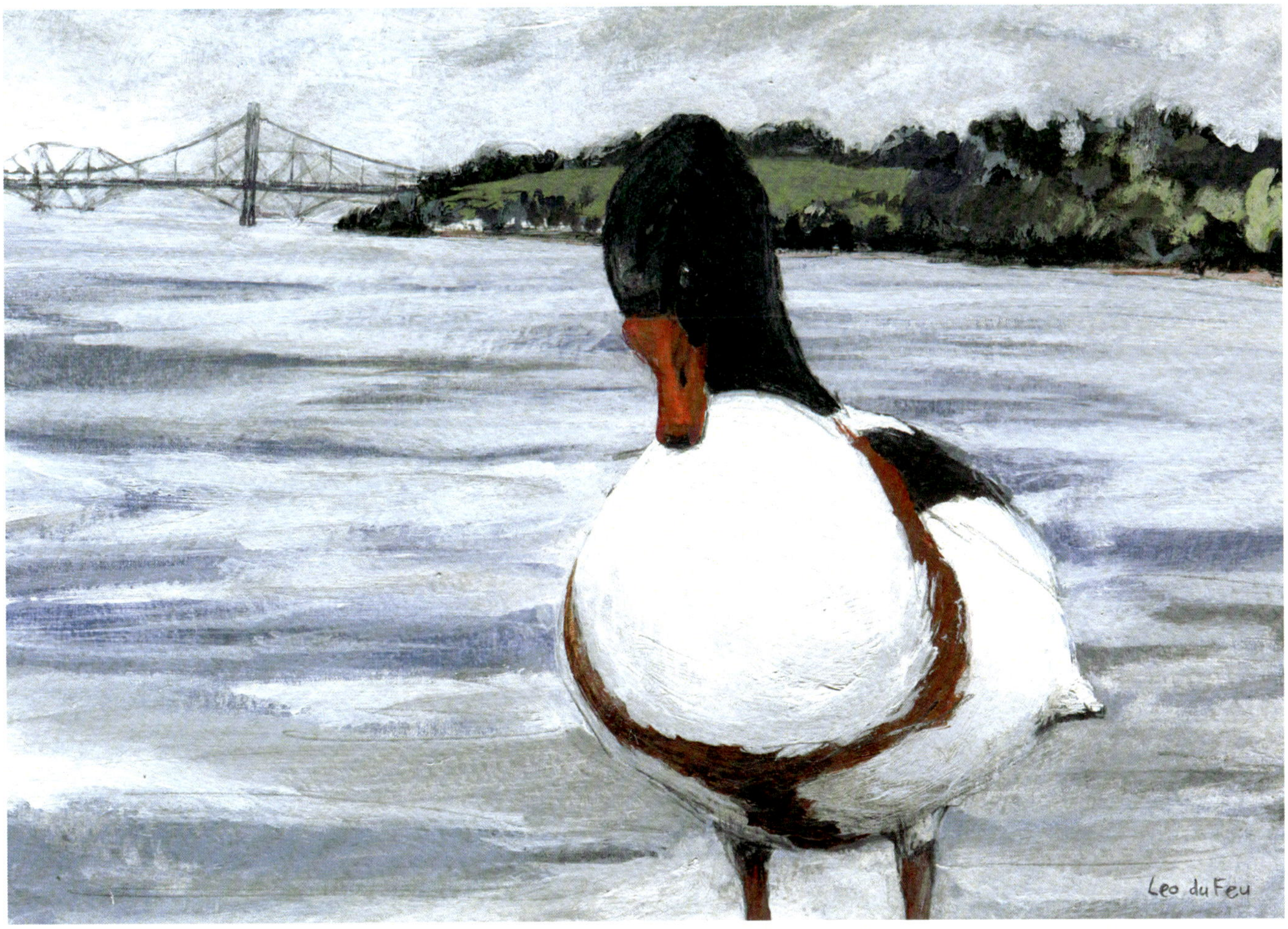
Leo du Feu

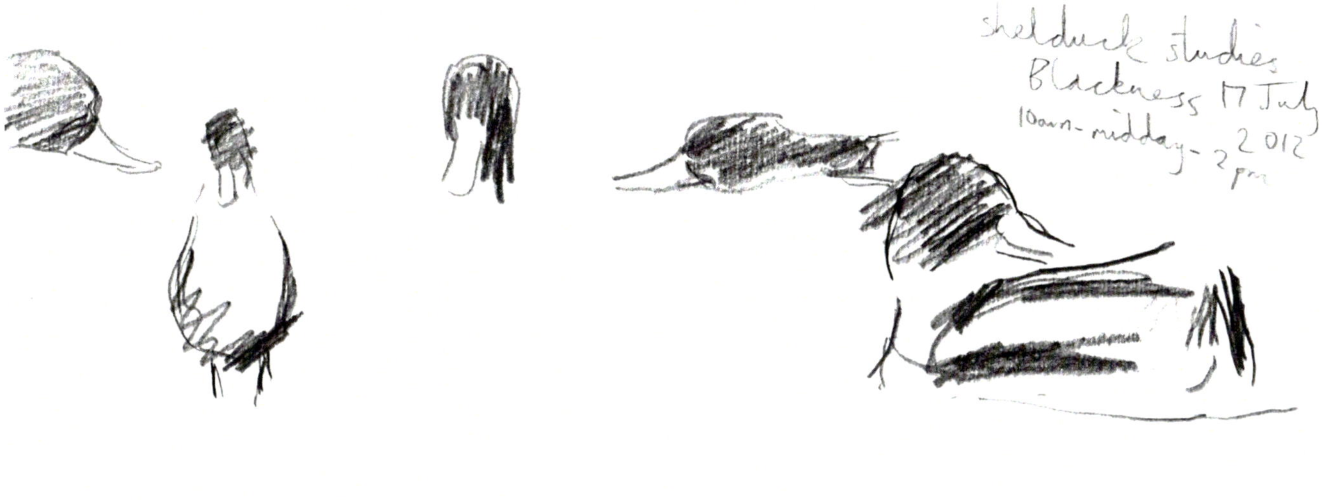
shelduck studies
Blackness 17 July
2012
10am - midday - 2pm

My friend, retired wildlife film-maker and photographer Chris Mylne, lives locally and is probably largely responsible for my interest in birds. I gardened for him as a holiday job from school and eventually his enthusiasm caught me. Now when we find time we wander together through Fiddler's Croft at the east end of the loch or we take Chris's telescope and go by bus to scan for waders on the Blackness mudflats. In just an hour at Fiddler's Croft on January 10th 2013 we saw these 32 bird species:

carrion crow, jackdaw, blue tit, great tit, chaffinch, greenfinch, bullfinch, goldfinch, redwing, mallard, tufted duck, swan, moorhen, coot, goldeneye, goosander, cormorant, black-headed gull, common gull, herring gull, woodpigeon, magpie, mistle thrush, little grebe, great crested grebe, greylag goose, starling, wren, blackbird, grey heron, cormorant and kingfisher.

Once as I stood looking towards the regular kingfisher spot, a snipe flew zig-zagging in and disappeared, completely camouflaged, into the reeds before me.

Linlithgow Loch – pochard, tufted, coot, goosander
pencil
25 x 35.5cm

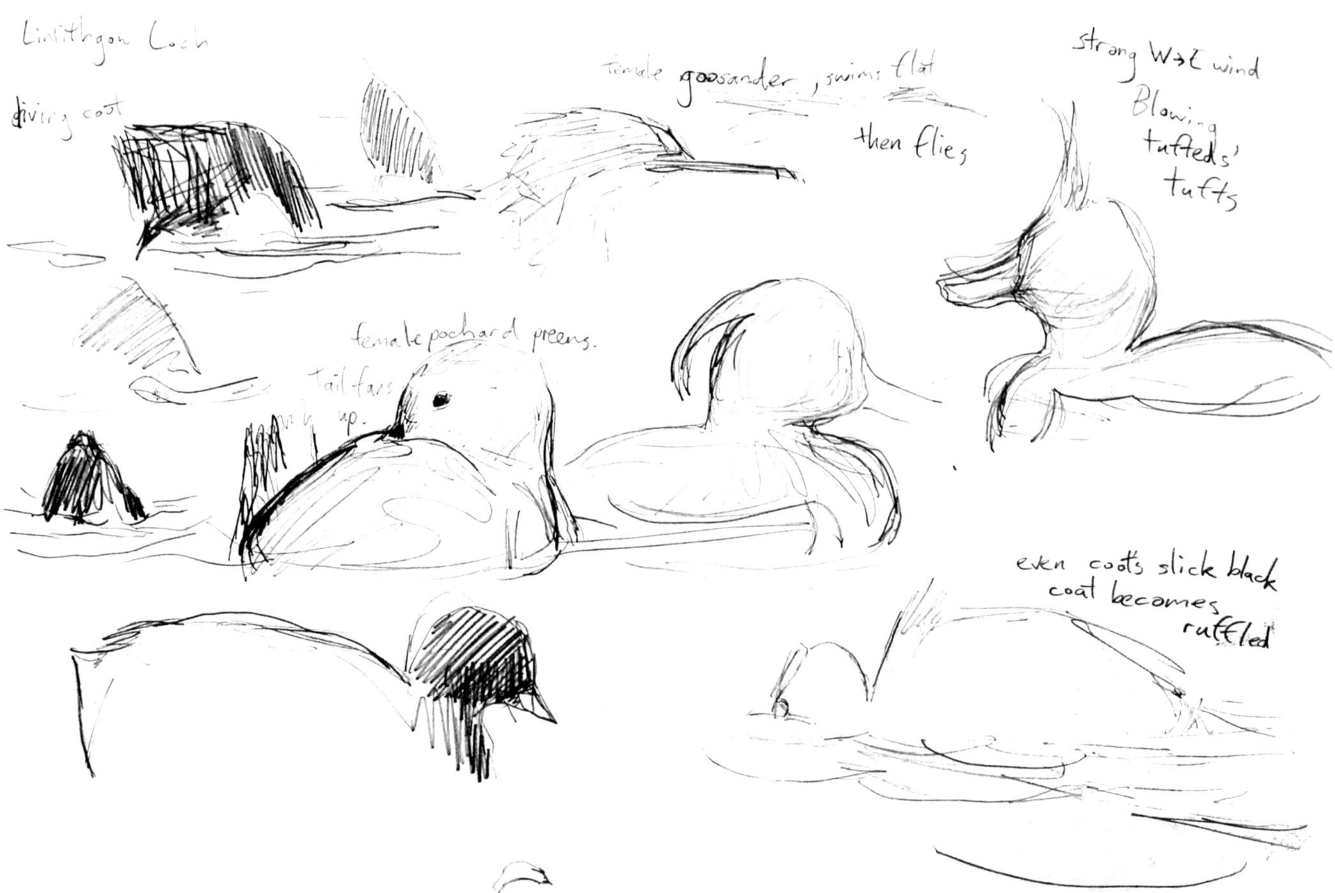

kingfisher studies
watercolour
25 x 17cm

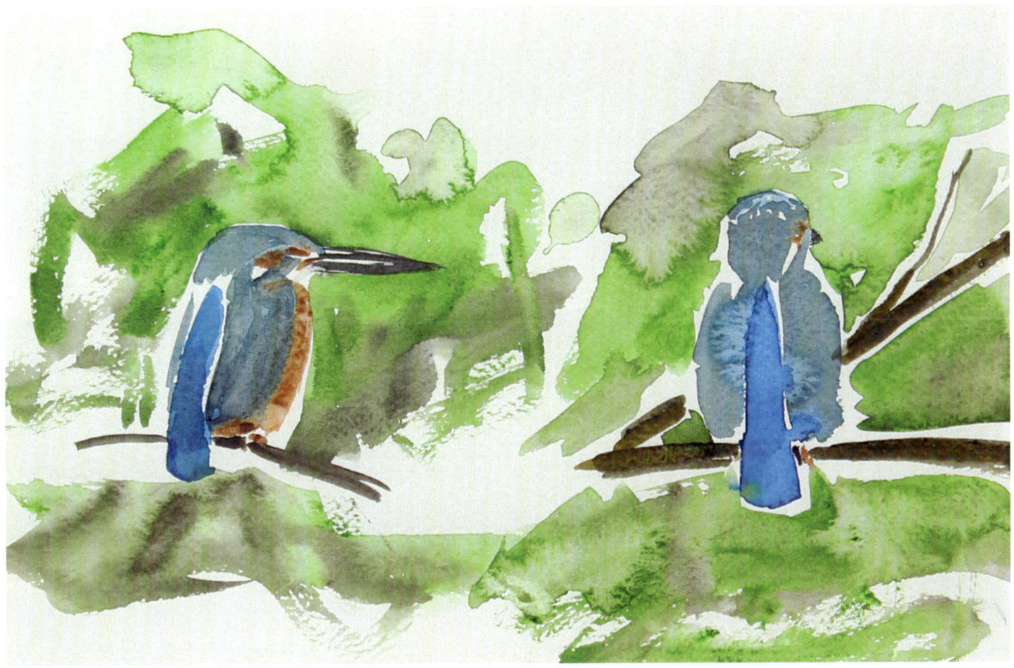

sparrowhawk & prey
acrylic
20 x 19cm

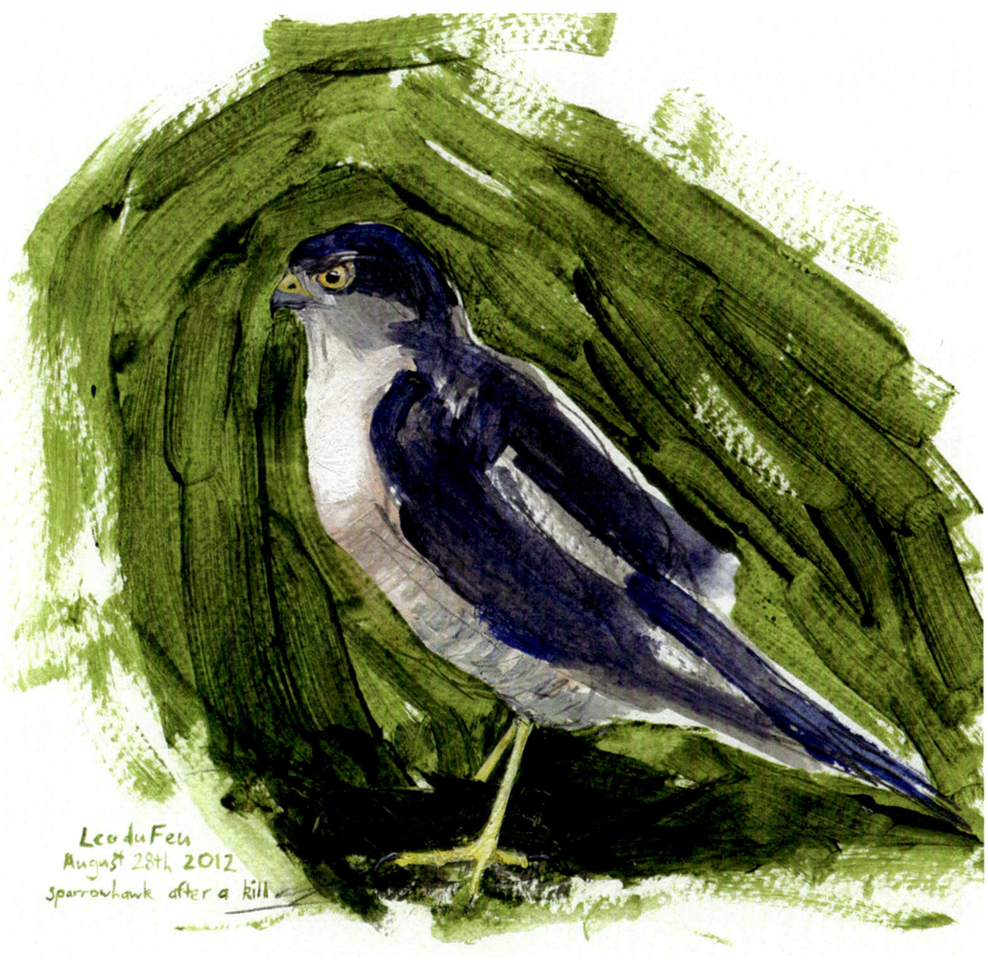

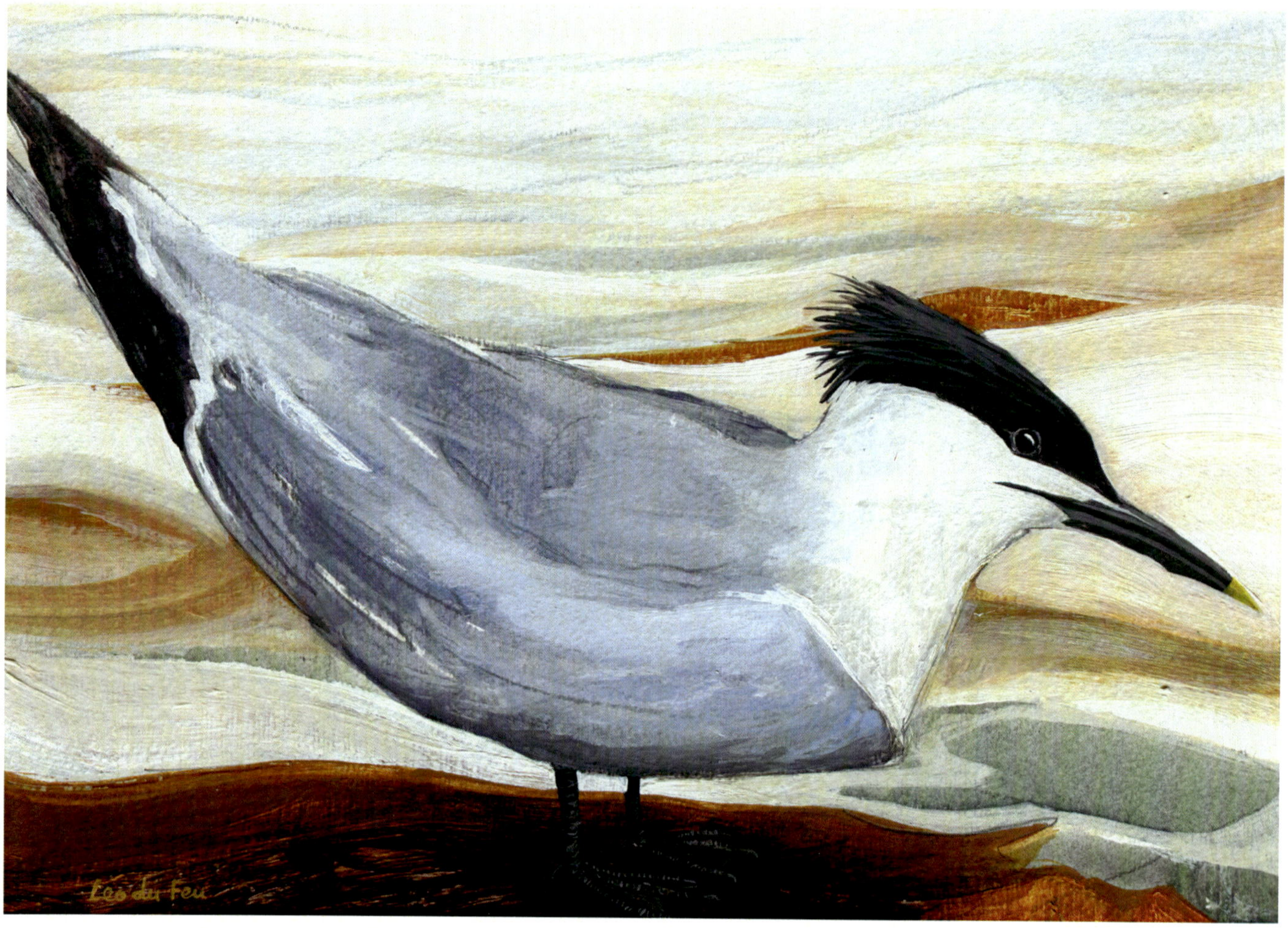

sandwich tern,
Sterna sandvicensis
acrylic
14.5 x 21cm

right: lapwings on canal flood field
pencil
14.5 x 20.5cm

I also carry out a monthly count of wetland birds for the BTO along the three-and-a-half-mile stretch of canal between Linlithgow and Philipstoun. Walking a route regularly is the only way to get to really know it. I've been doing this count for three years and now have a fairly good idea of how the land changes through the seasons and of which birds I'm likely to see in which locations.

There's an often-flooded field halfway along my route that attracts oystercatchers, curlews, wigeon, mallards, wagtails and gulls. I made my first lapwing sketches here and if I sit on the banking and use knees to steady binoculars I usually spot snipe, so small and so hidden at the edge of the water. In winter there can be up to several hundred geese – pink-footed and greylag.

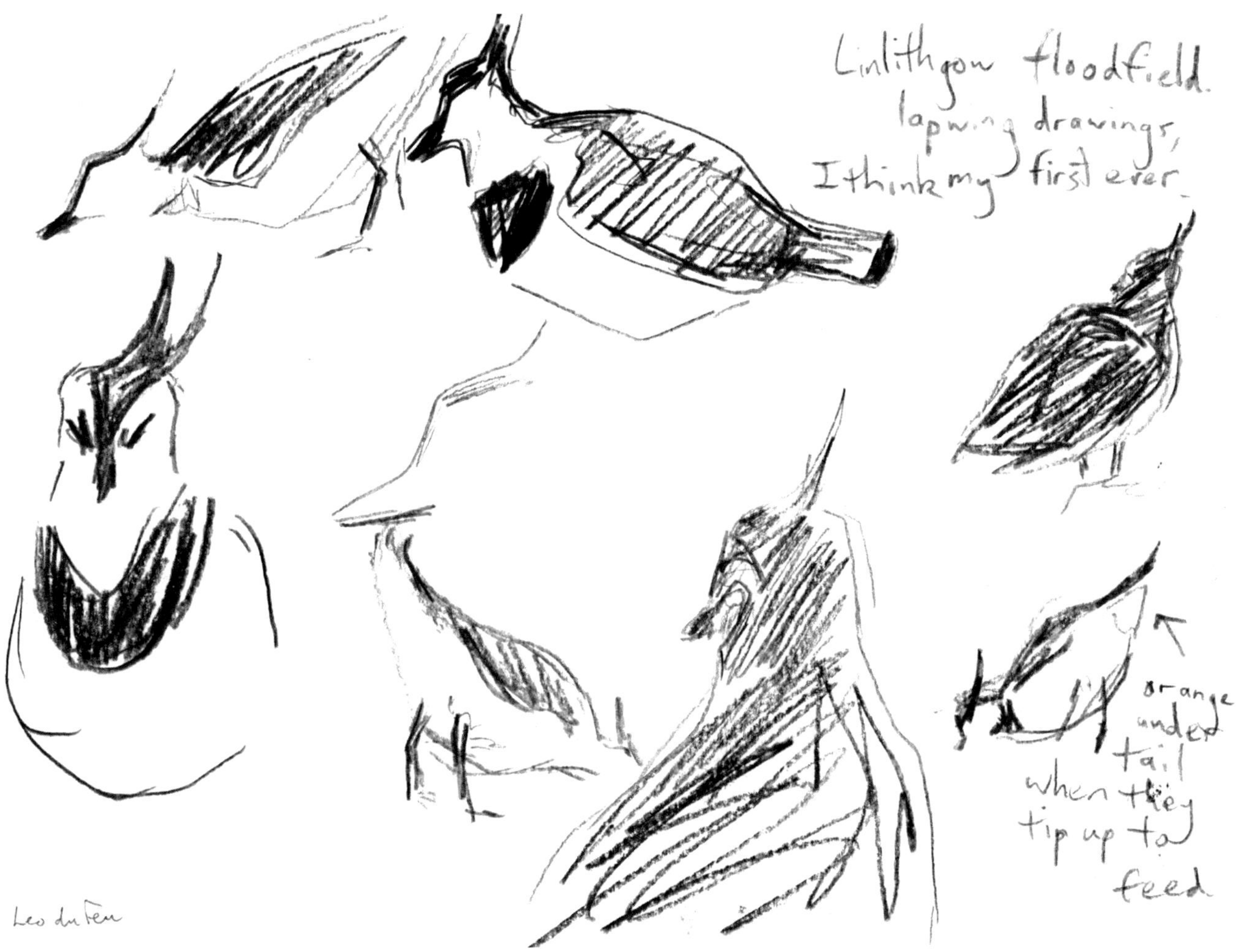

East Lowlands

St Abbs

The cliffs here support one of the most easily accessible seabird colonies in mainland Scotland. Access is so good that wheelchair-users can get close enough to look down from the heights at thousands of nesting guillemots, kittiwakes, razorbills and more.

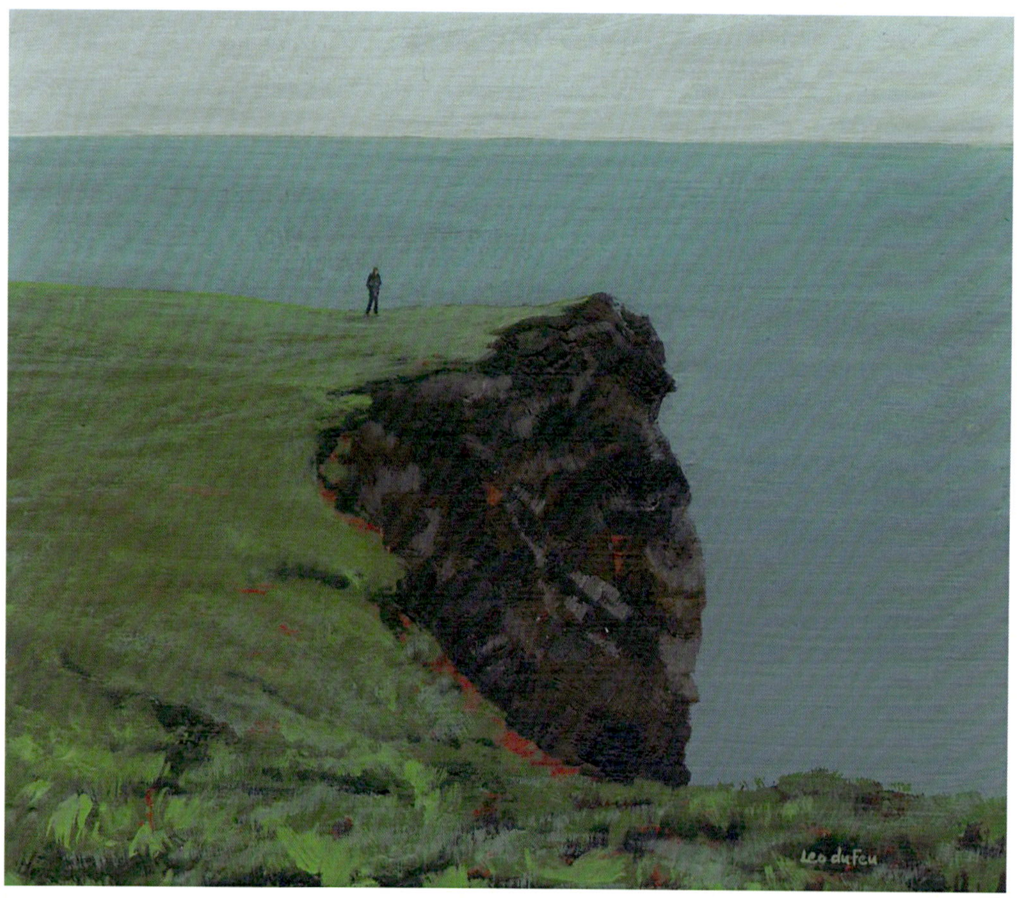

a walk at St. Abbs
acrylic
11.5 x 10.5cm

This miniature painting won me the Alexander Graham Munro Travel Award from the Royal Scottish Society of Painters in Watercolour (RSW). The award funded my first trip to Orkney.

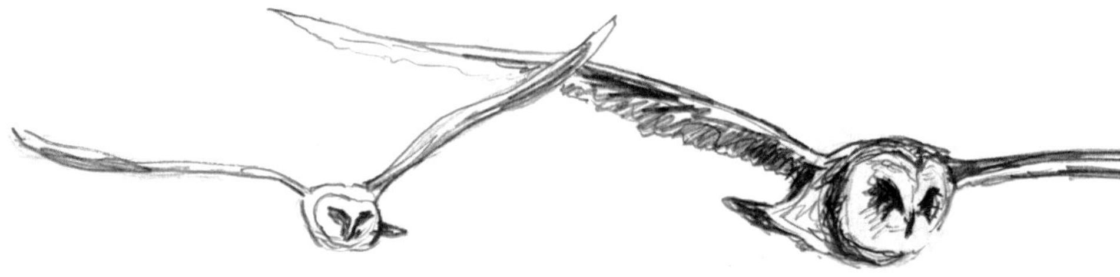

short-eared owl sketches
pencil & pen

Dunbar

Following regular reports one February of short-eared owls near Dunbar quarry, my friend Kittie and I made a trip there by train. Every bird is exciting but, for me, owls beat any other. Being chiefly active at night they're also among the most frustrating. Short-eared owls are a bit easier to see; they're diurnal so also hunt in daylight.

From Dunbar follow the John Muir Way east along the shore, being sure to watch for airborne golf balls and seaborne ducks: eider, mergansers, perhaps scoters and long-tailed. Turning inland at the arcing sweep of Whitesands Bay you come to a substantial lagoon that attracts many wildfowl. In winter we've seen whooper swans and geese; teal, wigeon and mallard ducks.

Above and beyond the flooded quarry is the scrubland where we saw the owls. Our hands became numb as we sketched and took photos of the birds hunting to and fro, flying low. Sometimes one of the owls would drop down into the grasses in an attempt at a vole or some other prey. Two birds came together, seeming to touch talons in mid air before tumbling apart. One shrieked a shrill, hoarse cry.

Two finished paintings have resulted from this encounter. The larger is a view across Whitesands to D.A. Stevenson's 1901 lighthouse, Barns Ness. An owl is close-up on the left but doesn't dominate.

The smaller painting was auctioned for charity at RSPB Scotland's 2012 Nature of Farming Awards in the Balmoral Hotel, Edinburgh.

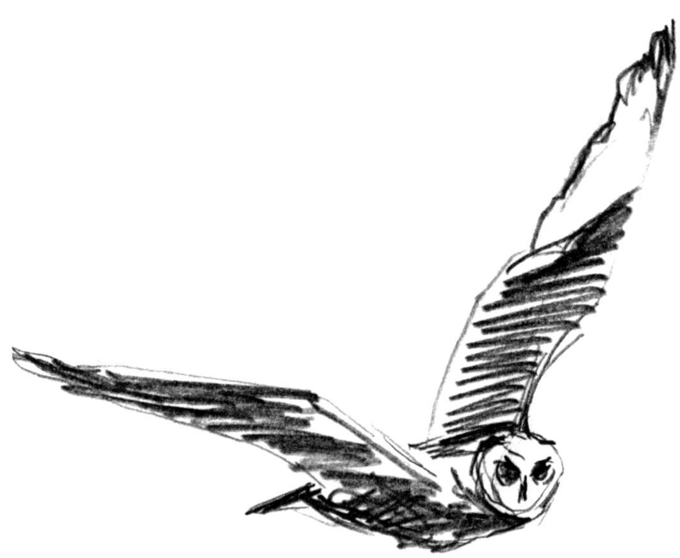

short-eared owl
pencil

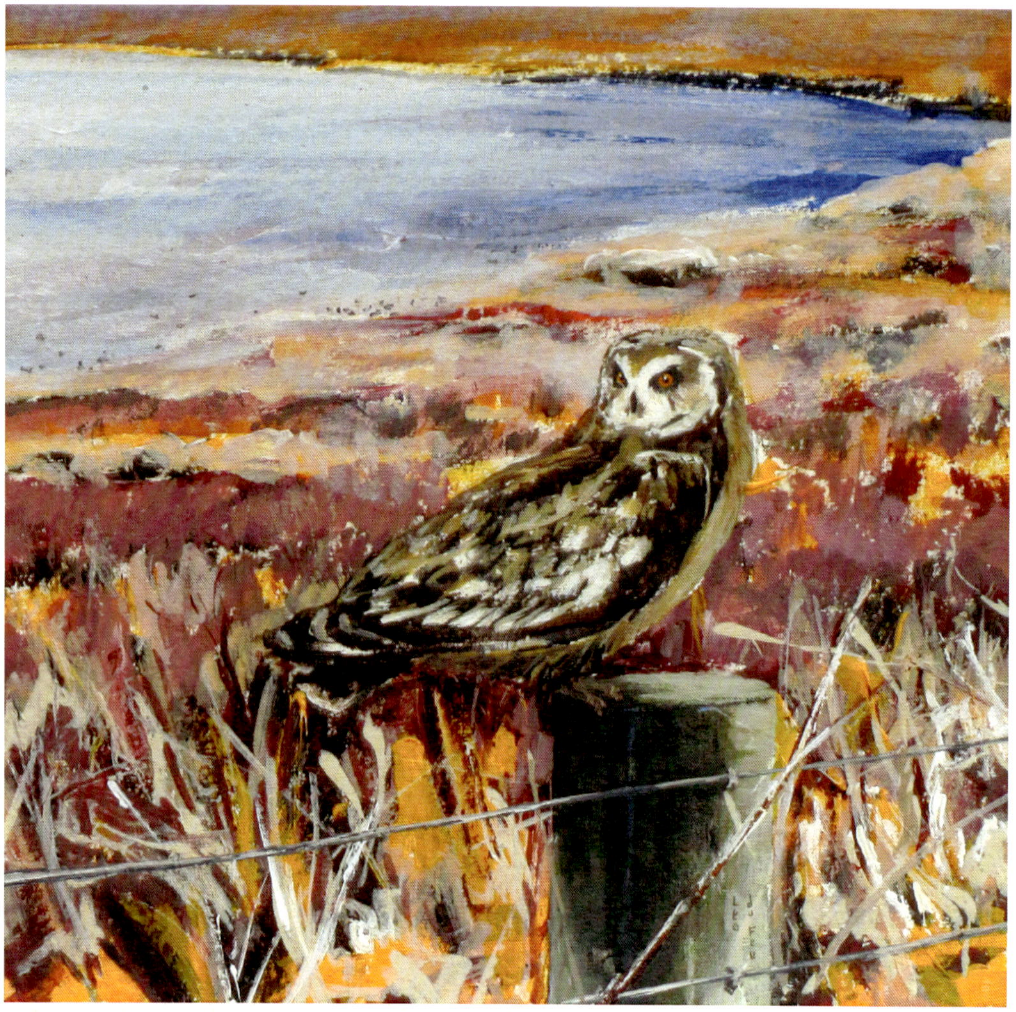

short-eared owl
acrylic
15.5 x 16.5cm

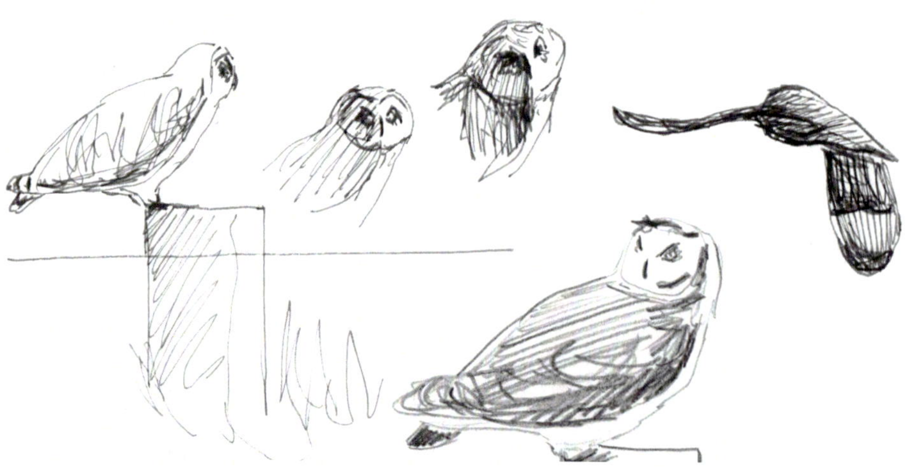

short-eared owl sketches
pencil & pen

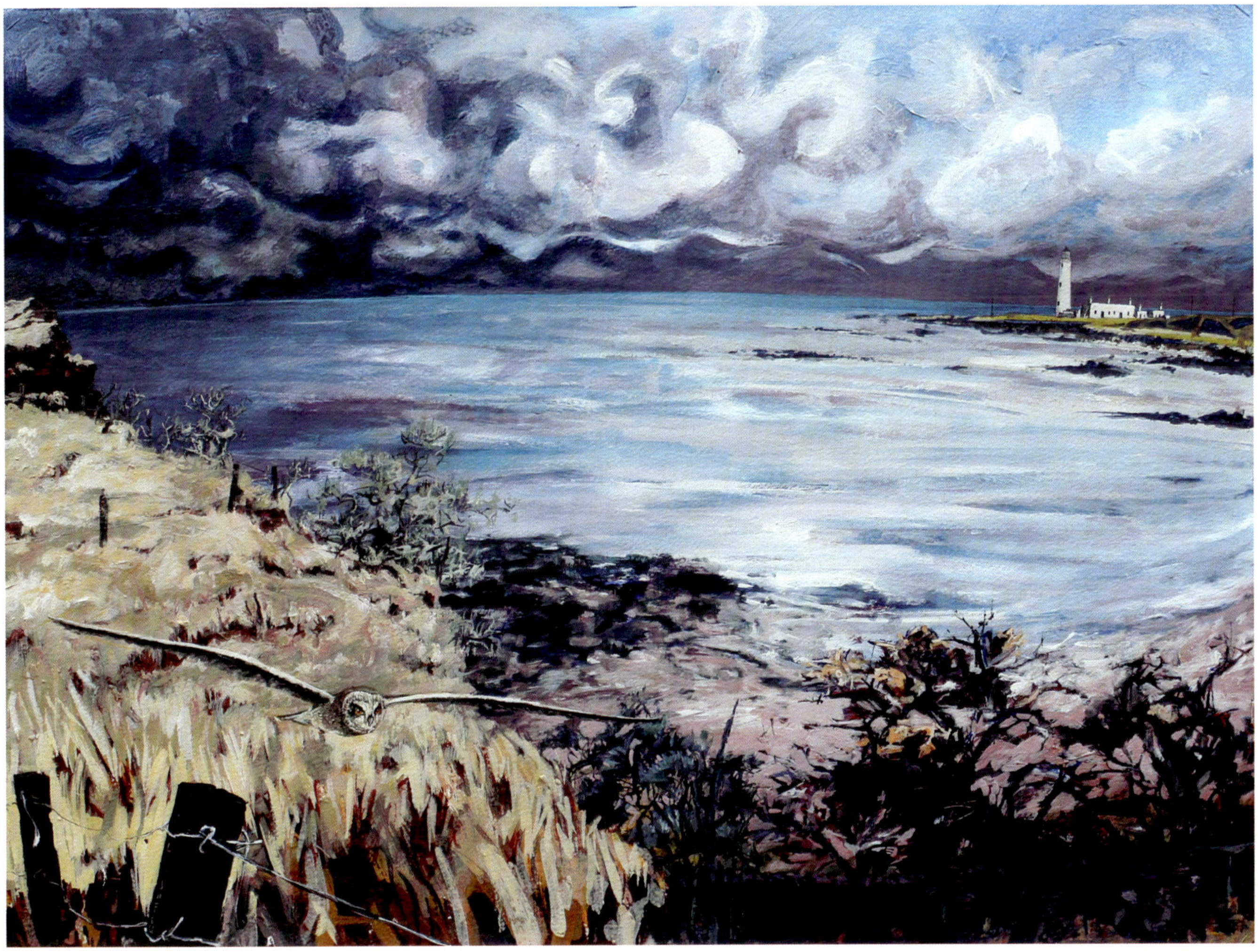

Whitesands, short-eared owl
acrylic
56 x 76cm

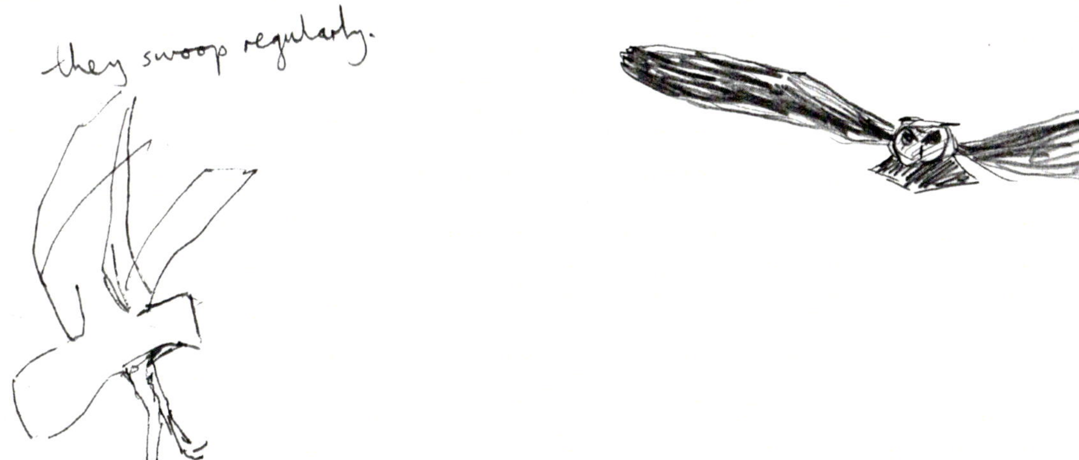

short-eared owls
pencil & pen

Aberlady

Start at Waterston House, the beautifully constructed wooden home of the Scottish Ornithologists' Club (SOC). There's a great exhibition space as well as the most comprehensive ornithological library in Scotland, and it's all open to all. There are books, binoculars, and telescopes for sale, and tea or coffee to warm you. Someone is always on hand to tell what the latest interesting sightings have been.

Walk from Waterston House to the edge of Aberlady village and turn left, passing beside the church graveyard, to the shore. Now you're in bird territory; look especially at the waders and ducks as you follow the shoreline east. After a mile, cross a long wooden footbridge over the tidal river (the Peffer Burn) into the nature reserve proper. Owls are sometimes seen hunting over the fields and once a water rail ran across our path here.

A roughly straight line north through grassland and orange-berried sea buckthorn takes you eventually to rocky Gullane Point and the sea. In winter on the water are ducks and divers and grebes. One stormy afternoon, in spitting rain, I quickly made a pencil and watercolour sketch that became this finished acrylic.

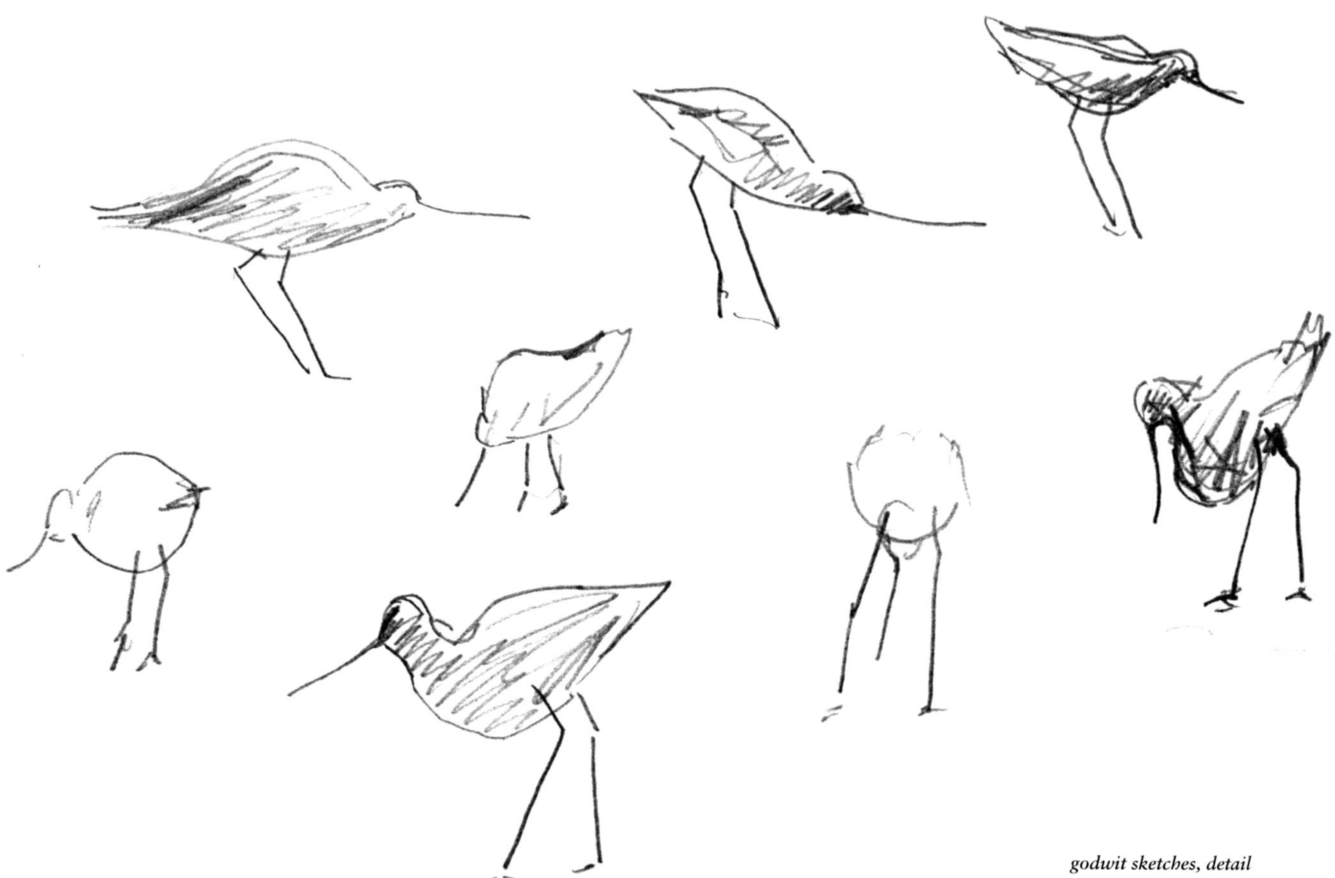

godwit sketches, detail
pencil

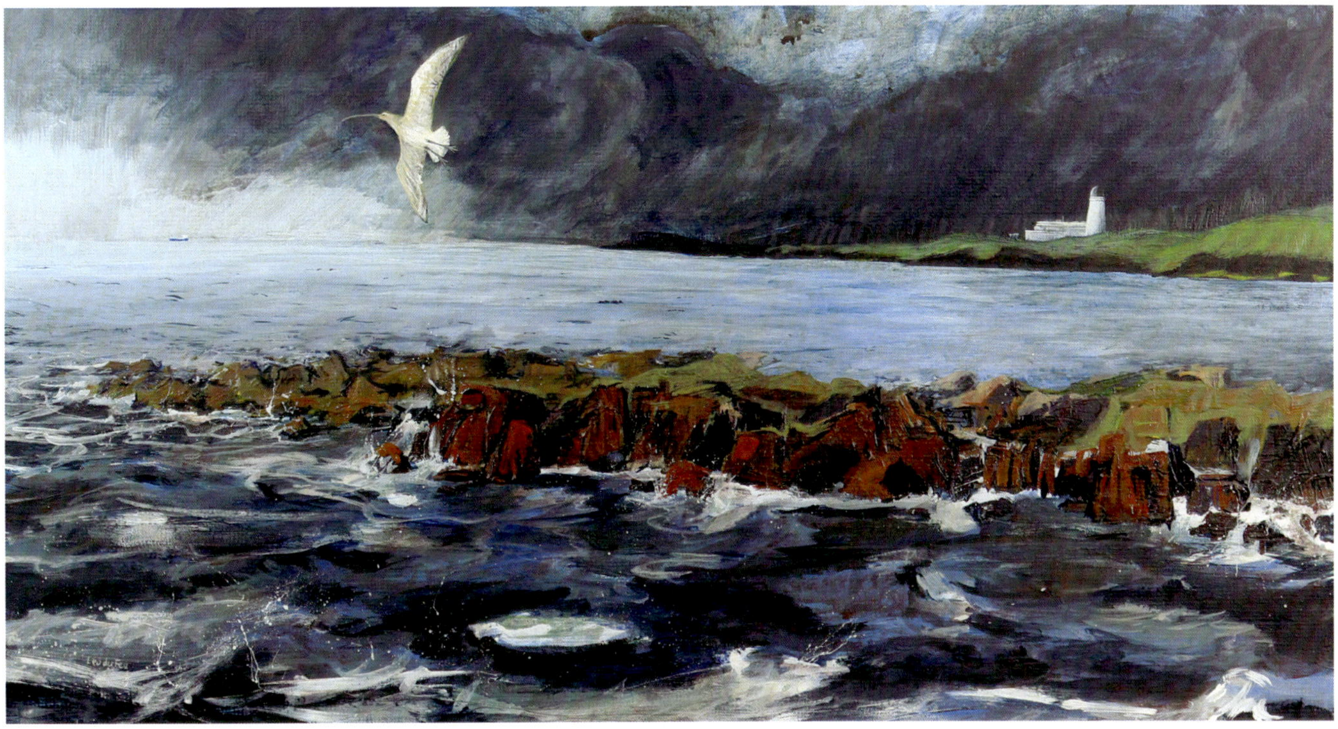

Aberlady curlew
acrylic
33 x 62cm

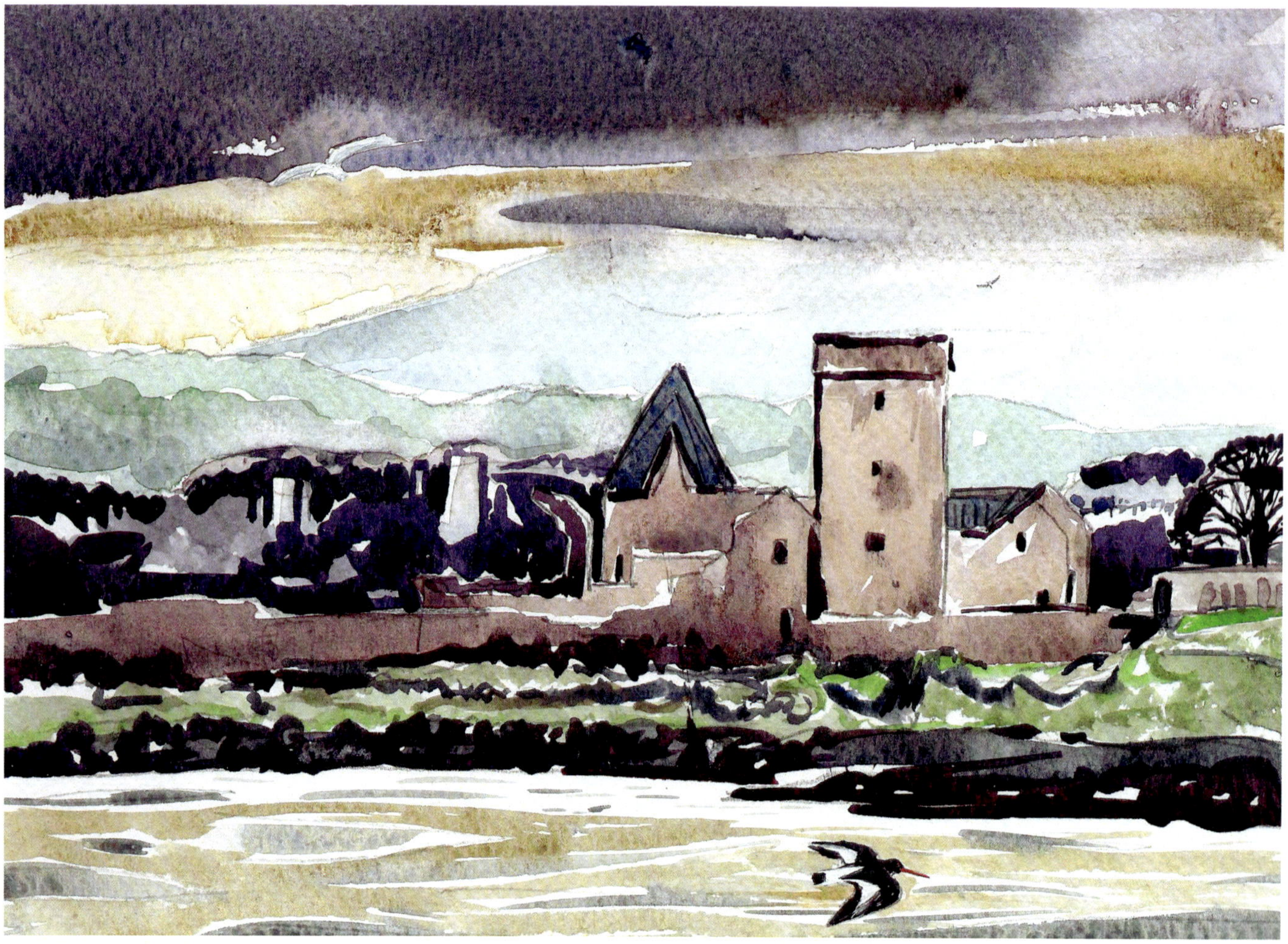

Inchcolm oystercatcher
watercolour
14.5 x 21cm

Aberdour

It's very useful to go sketching with fellow artists. You can offer advice and encourage each other to get on with work. I often go drawing with printmaker-painter friend Kittie Jones. Our style is very different but our subject matter is similar: me – landscape and birds; she – birds and landscape.

A favourite spot is a little peninsula a mile or so south-west of Aberdour on the Fife coast. It's near farmland but feels remote and unused and has lots of great wildlife habitat. There are wartime gun emplacements to use as hides or to shelter in if weather is poor. Views are across the Forth to Inchcolm Island and the higgledy-piggledy outline of Edinburgh.

At the right time of year there are stonechats in the scrubland and shrubland, godwits probing the sheltered sand-beach shores, guillemots and razorbills in the two bays and gannets diving further out to sea. One October day we saw a group of twenty or more goosanders or mergansers sheltering in the northern bay.

There's almost always a kestrel, sometimes two. Magpies fly up to try to chase them off. The kestrel hovers as it hunts, head perfectly stationary, wings and tail flapping to keep airborne. It well deserves its old English name – the windhover.

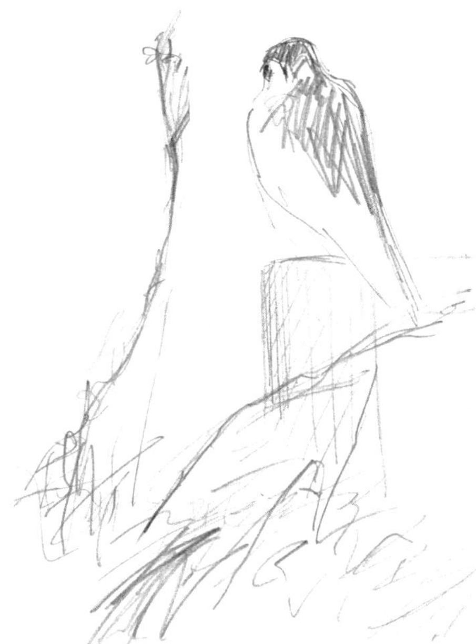

kestrel
pencil

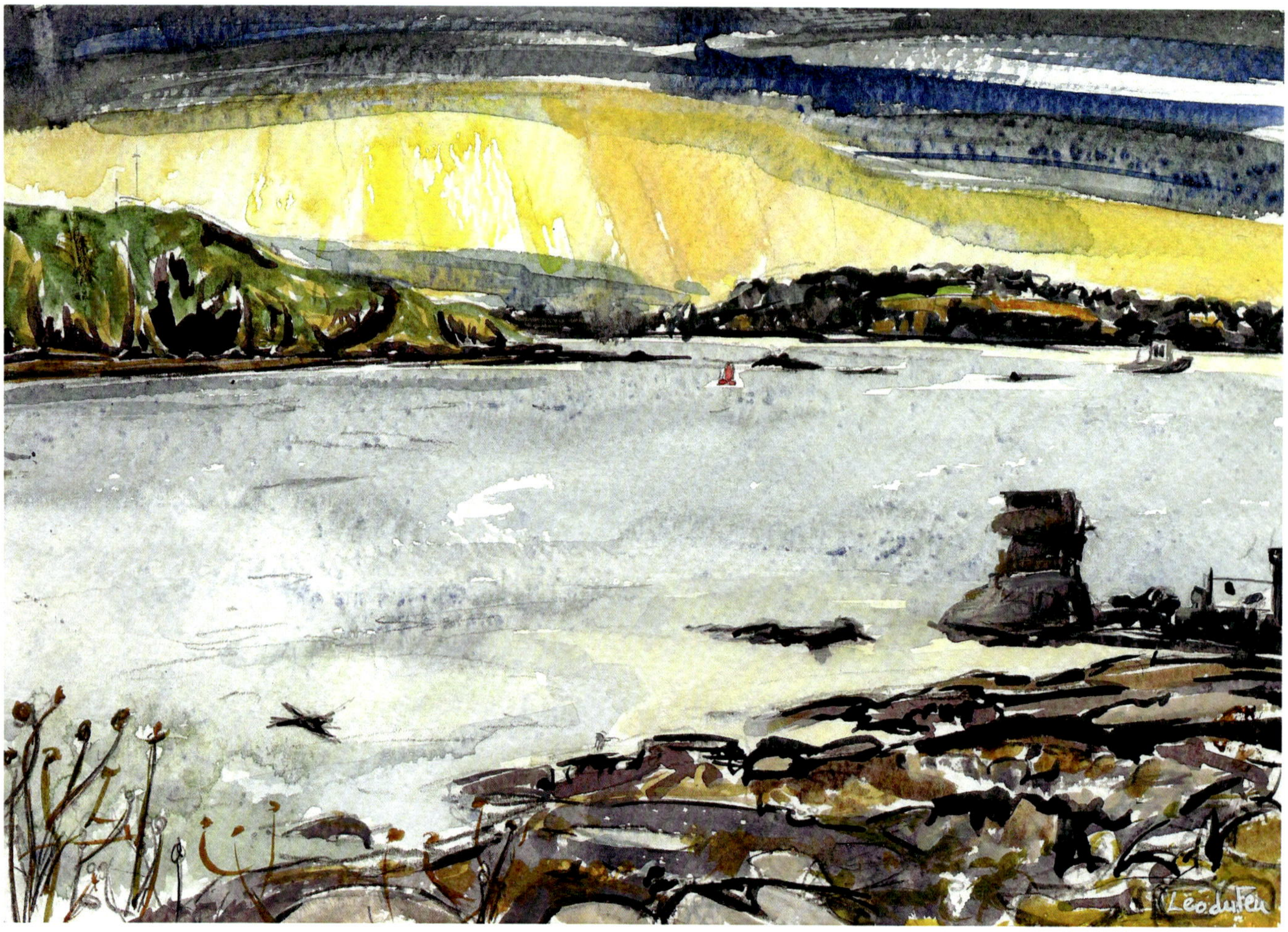

on the Forth
watercolour
14.5 x 21cm

eider studies & curlew
pencil

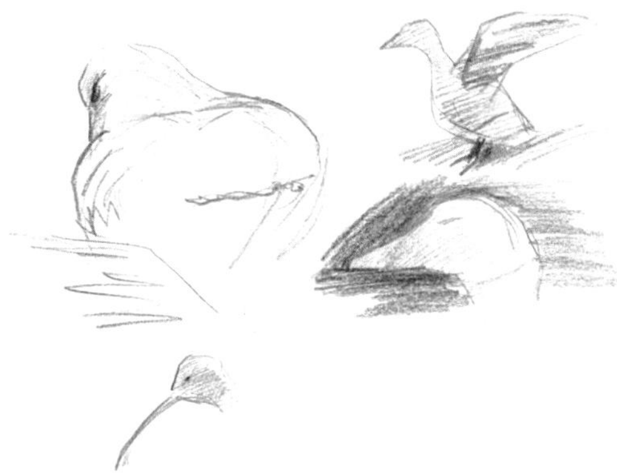

Montrose

My mum has a static caravan in Montrose. We've both found masses of inspiration up there for our art. We discover more and more locations for wildlife and landscape – sweeping sand beaches, rugged rockpool shores, high sea cliffs, woodland and farmland, river estuary, St Cyrus National Nature Reserve, and the Scottish Wildlife Trust's (SWT) brilliant Montrose Basin Reserve and visitor centre.

Outside the caravan are well-grassed dunes, a few orange-berried bushes of buckthorn thrive in sheltered spots between these and the caravans. Then there's the beach, the sea, and Scurdie Ness Lighthouse across the mouth of the River South Esk. There are nearly always seals floating contentedly in the water; dolphins and porpoises can often be seen where river joins sea.

eider studies
pencil in sketchbook
13.5 x 41cm

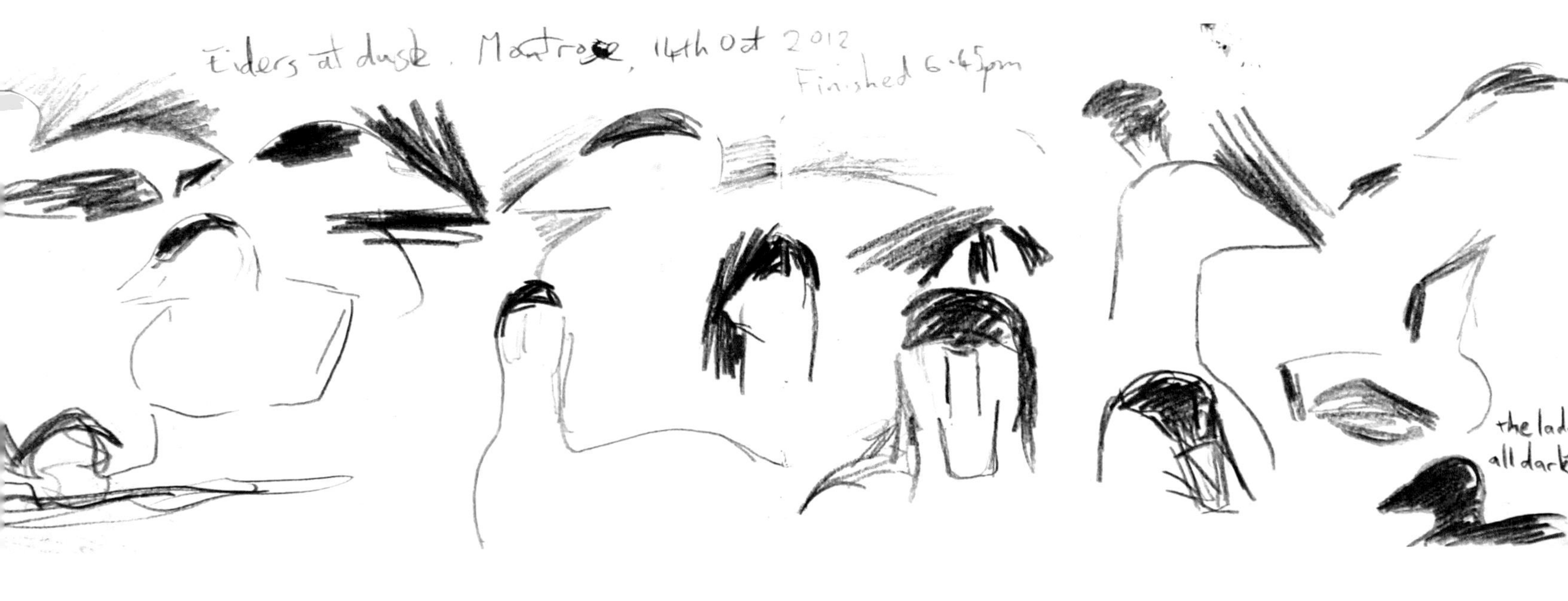

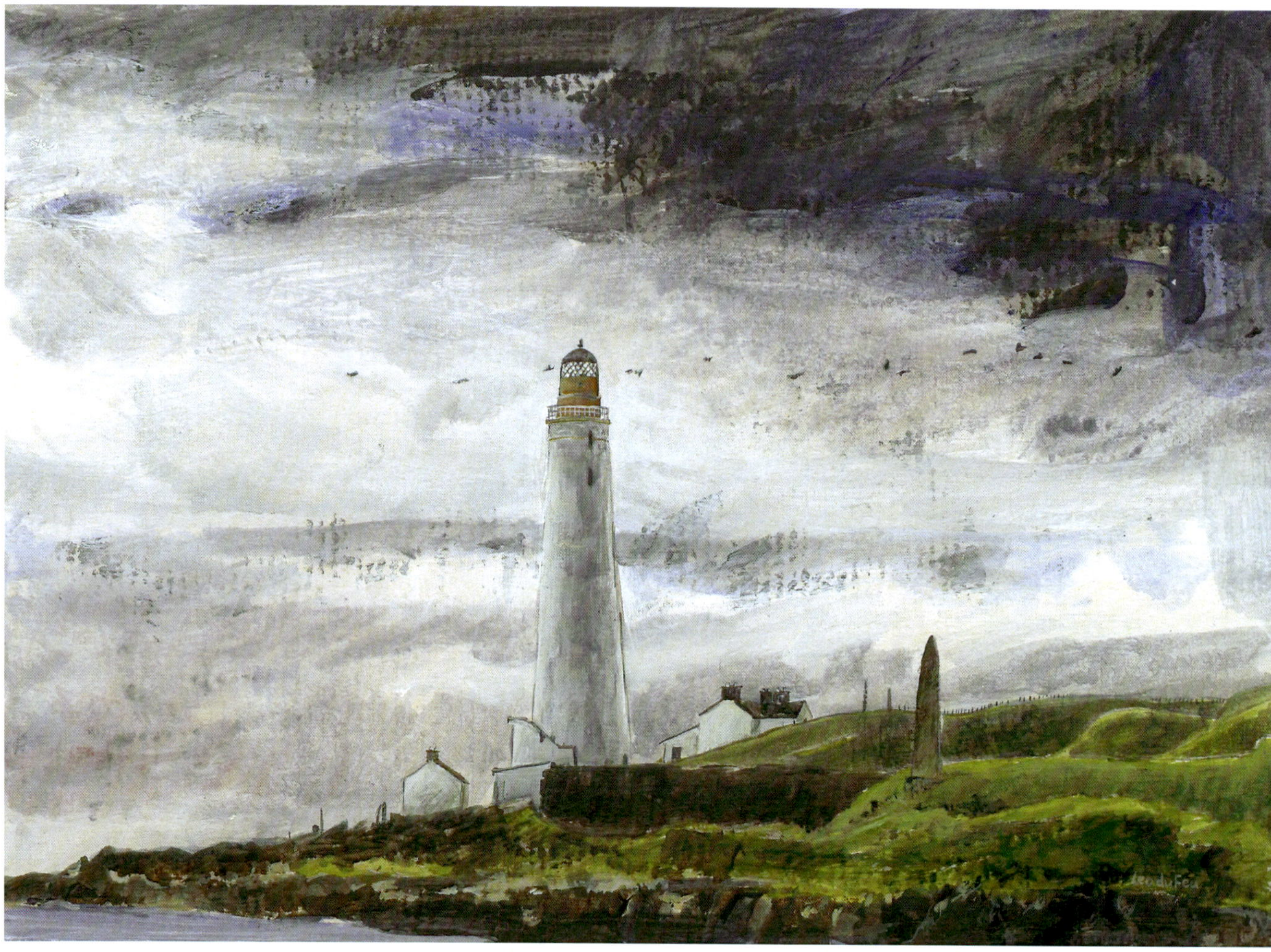

Scurdie Ness, Montrose
acrylic
15 x 21cm

In the mornings before late breakfast I go to the water and draw gulls, shags, cormorants, mergansers, guillemots, razorbills, countless eiders. Ringed plovers can sometimes be seen, but they're so camouflaged among patches of pebbles on the shore. The more obvious redshanks, oystercatchers and curlews are alongside, probing muddy sand with long slender beaks. In spring and summer the creaky cries of terns fill the air: four types – common, arctic, sandwich, and little.

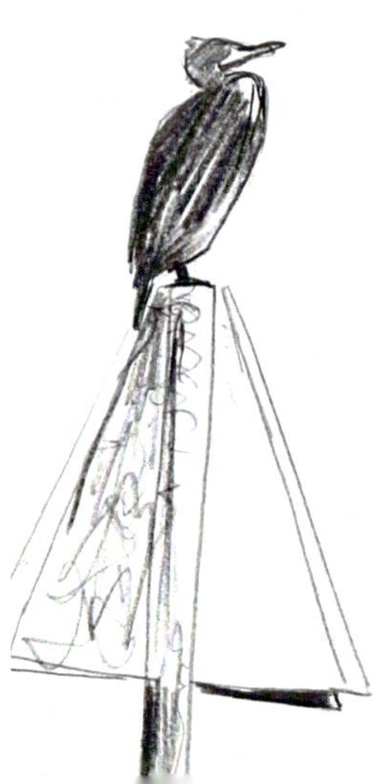

cormorant
pencil

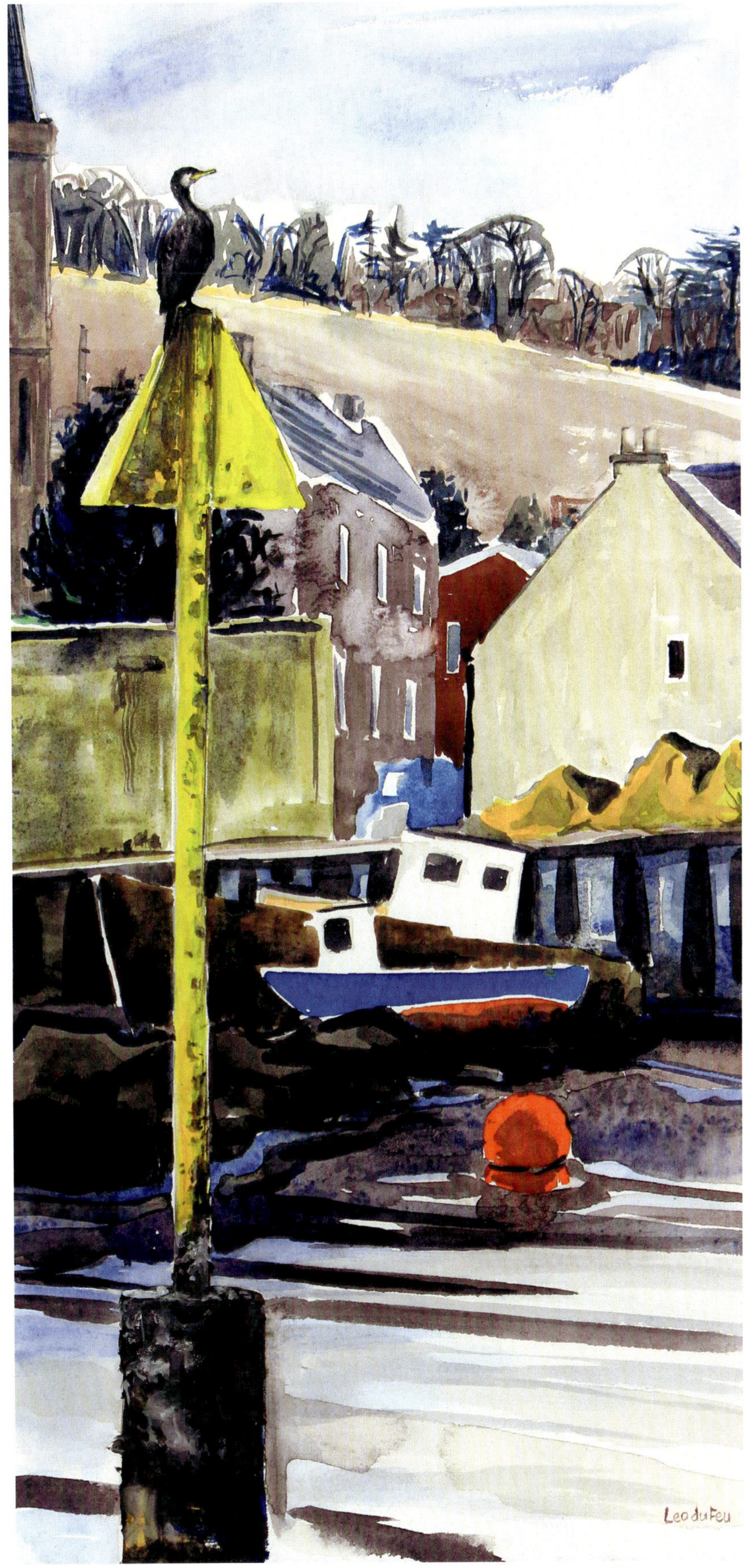

cormorant & Ferryden village, Montrose
watercolour
35.5 x 17cm

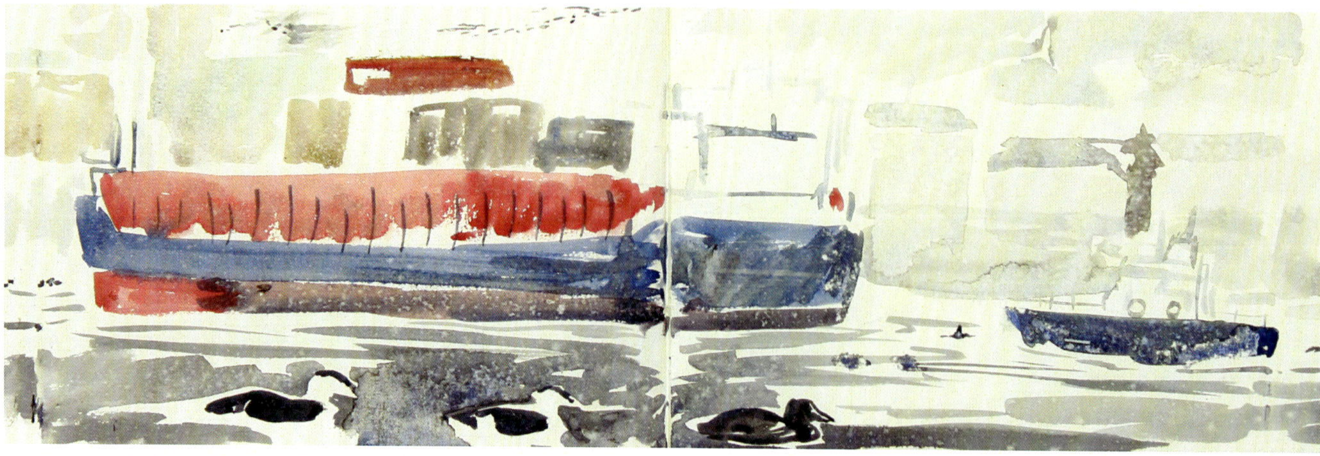

I sketch these soft and smooth shapes of nature and look across river to the angular boxes and lines of Ferryden village and the boats anchored there: the always fascinating (but often disheartening) contrast of man-made versus nature.

eiders & boats, Montrose
watercolour in sketchbook
13.5 x 41cm

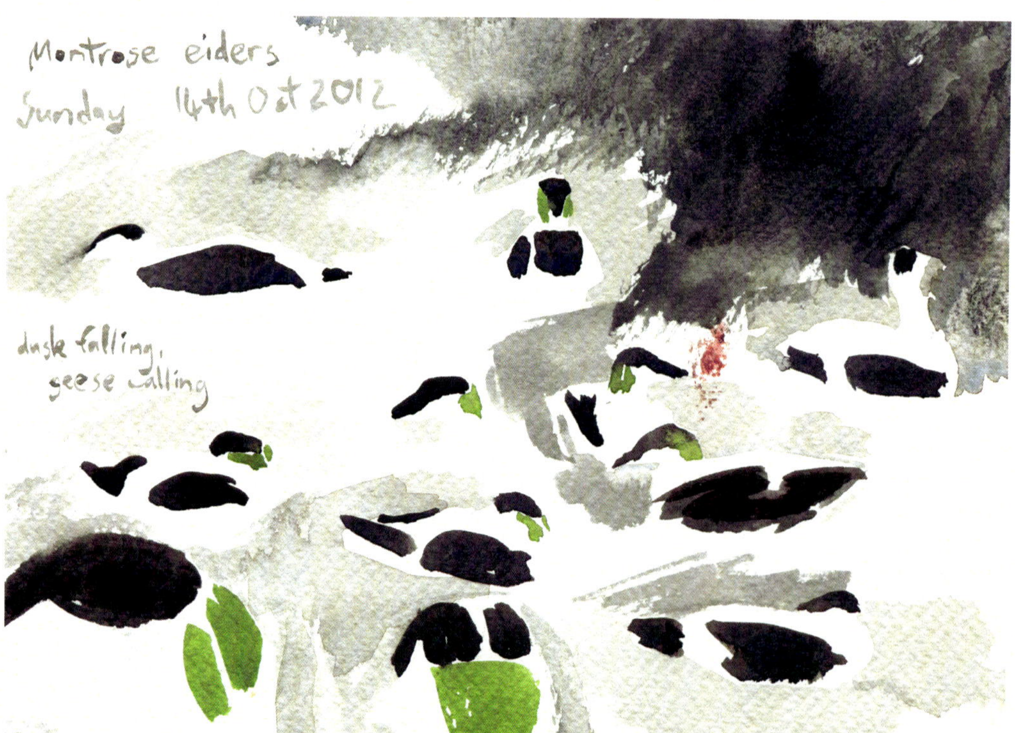

eider studies
watercolour
13.5 x 19cm

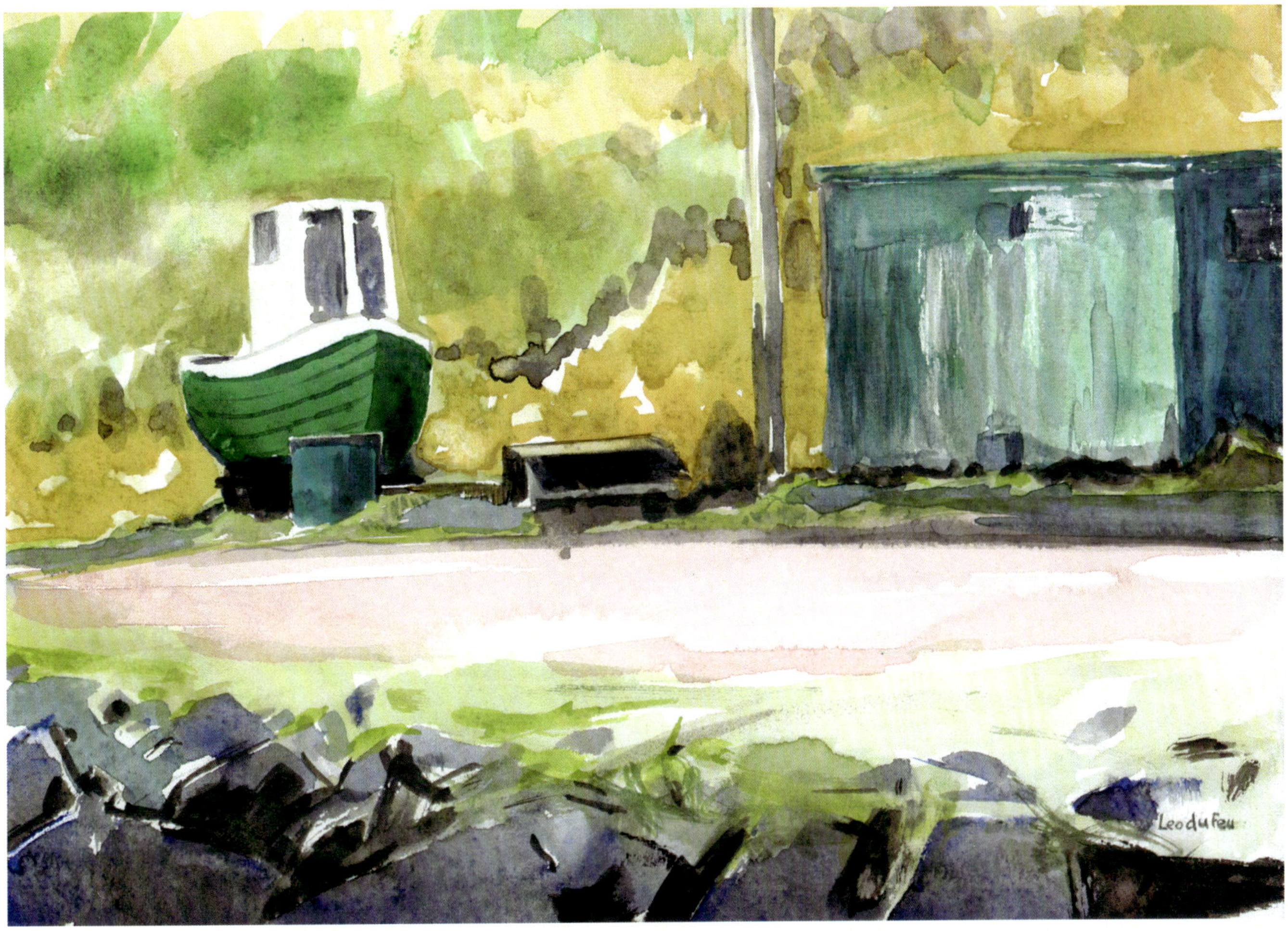

green boat by Ferryden
watercolour
14.5 x 20.5cm

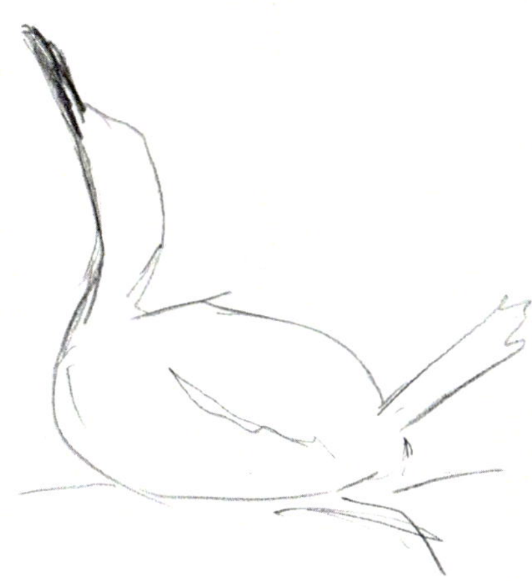

On one visit we spent a full day painting at a stone-walled graveyard on the cliffs south of Montrose. Wrapped well against threatening weather I worked firstly on a view of the whole scene and then focused on a single iron-fenced headstone. A pipit perched momentarily on the grave and brought my paintings their detail and their titles.

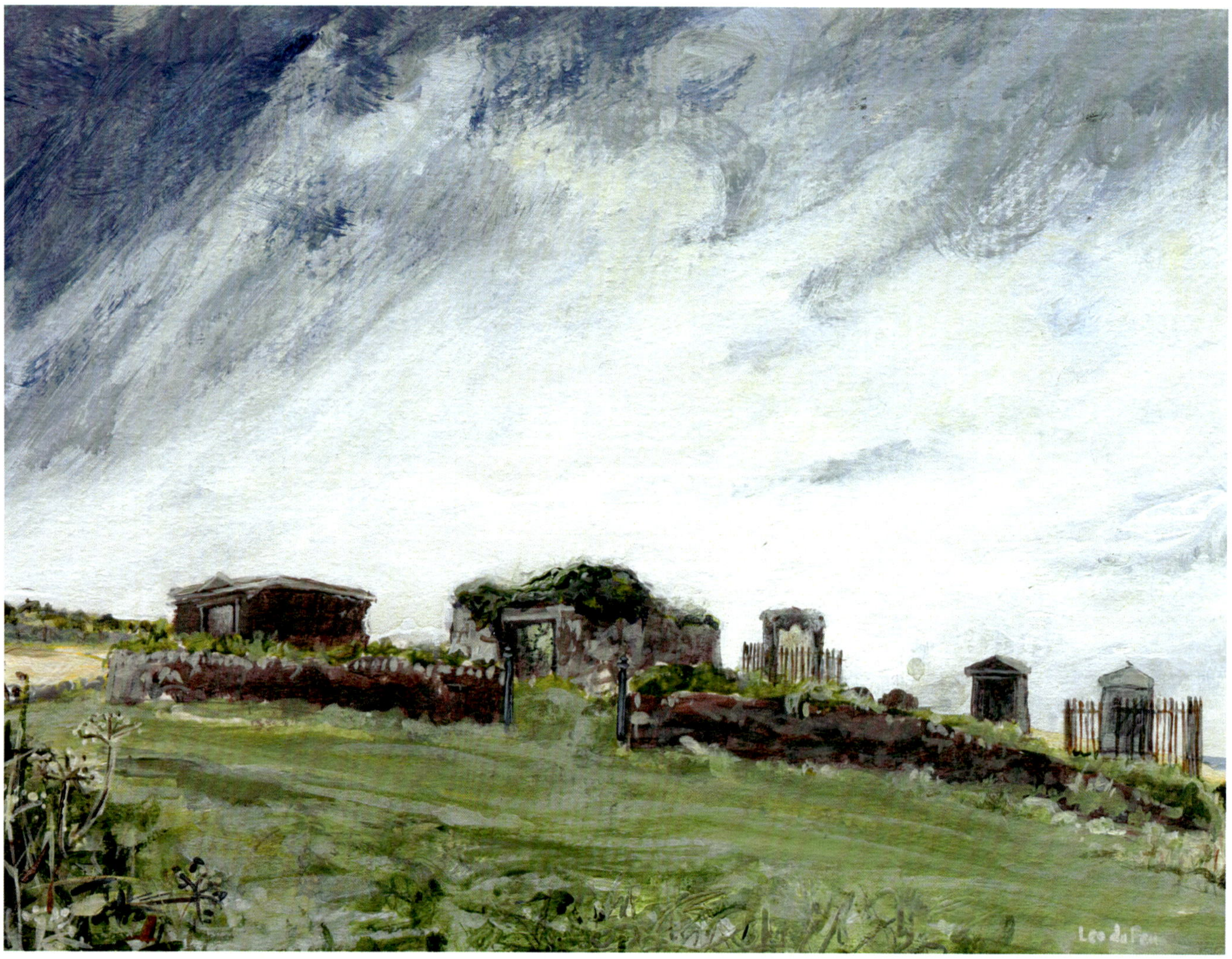

pipit on watch – 1
acrylic
15 x 21cm

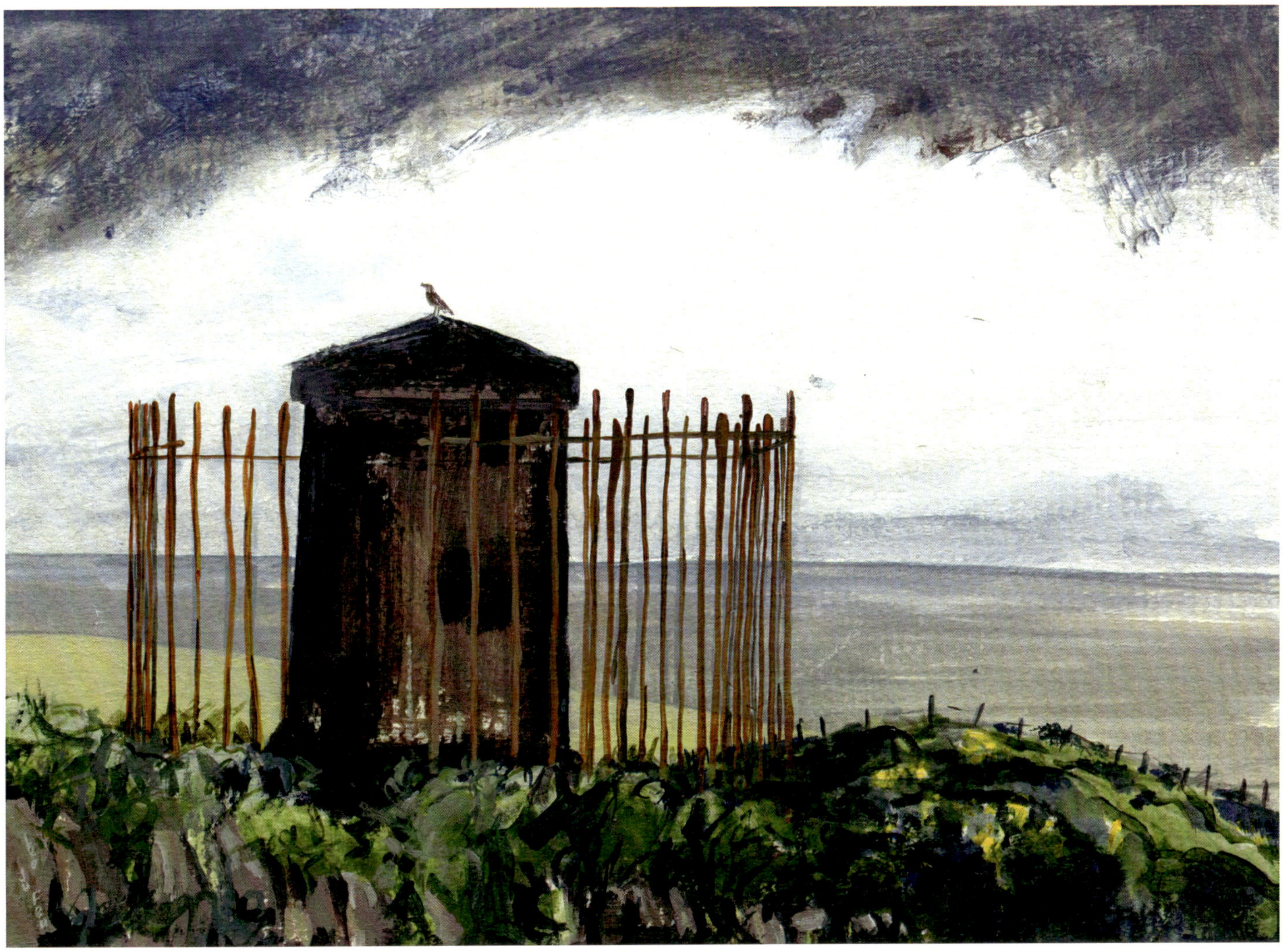

pipit on watch – 2
acrylic
15 x 21cm

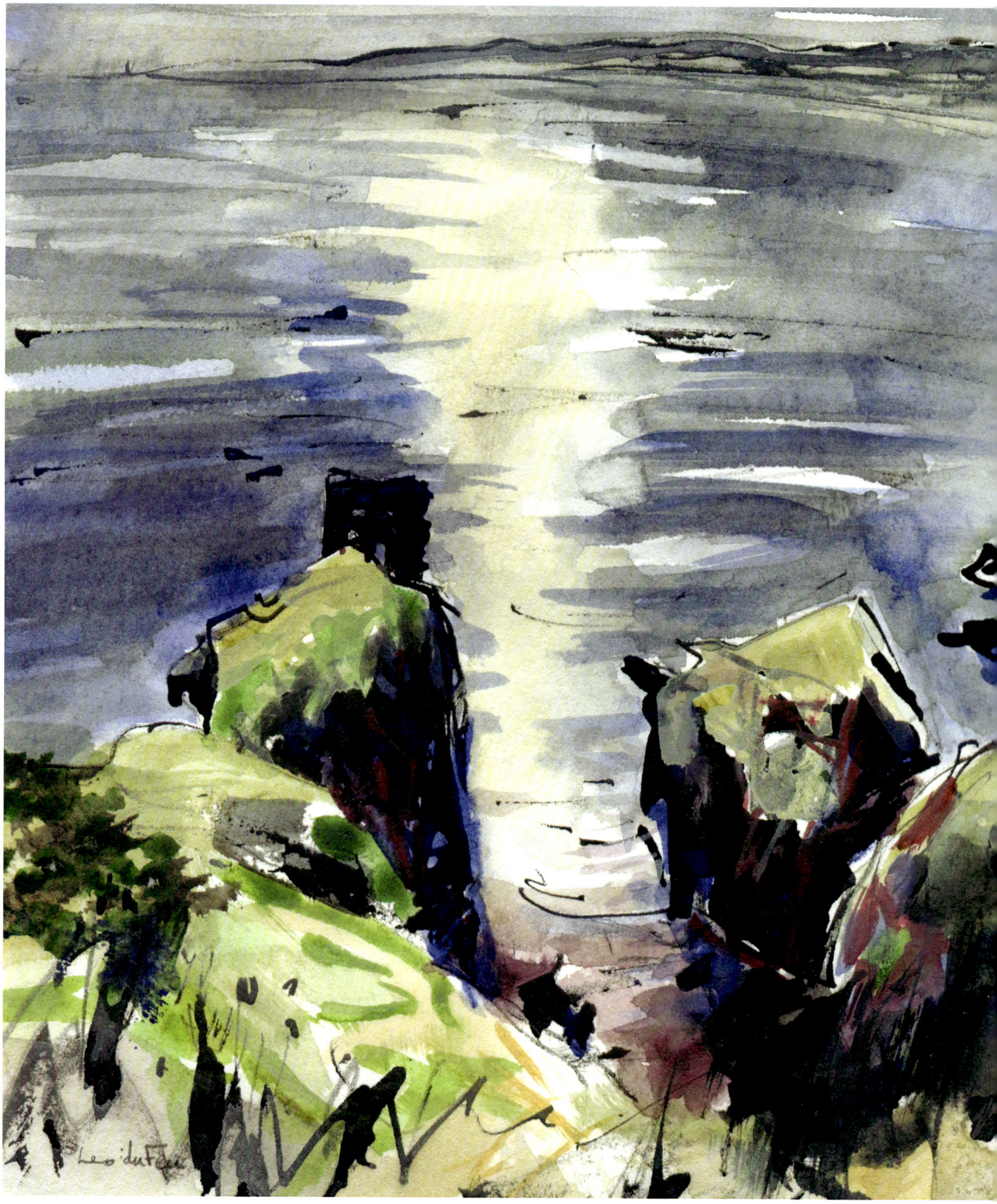

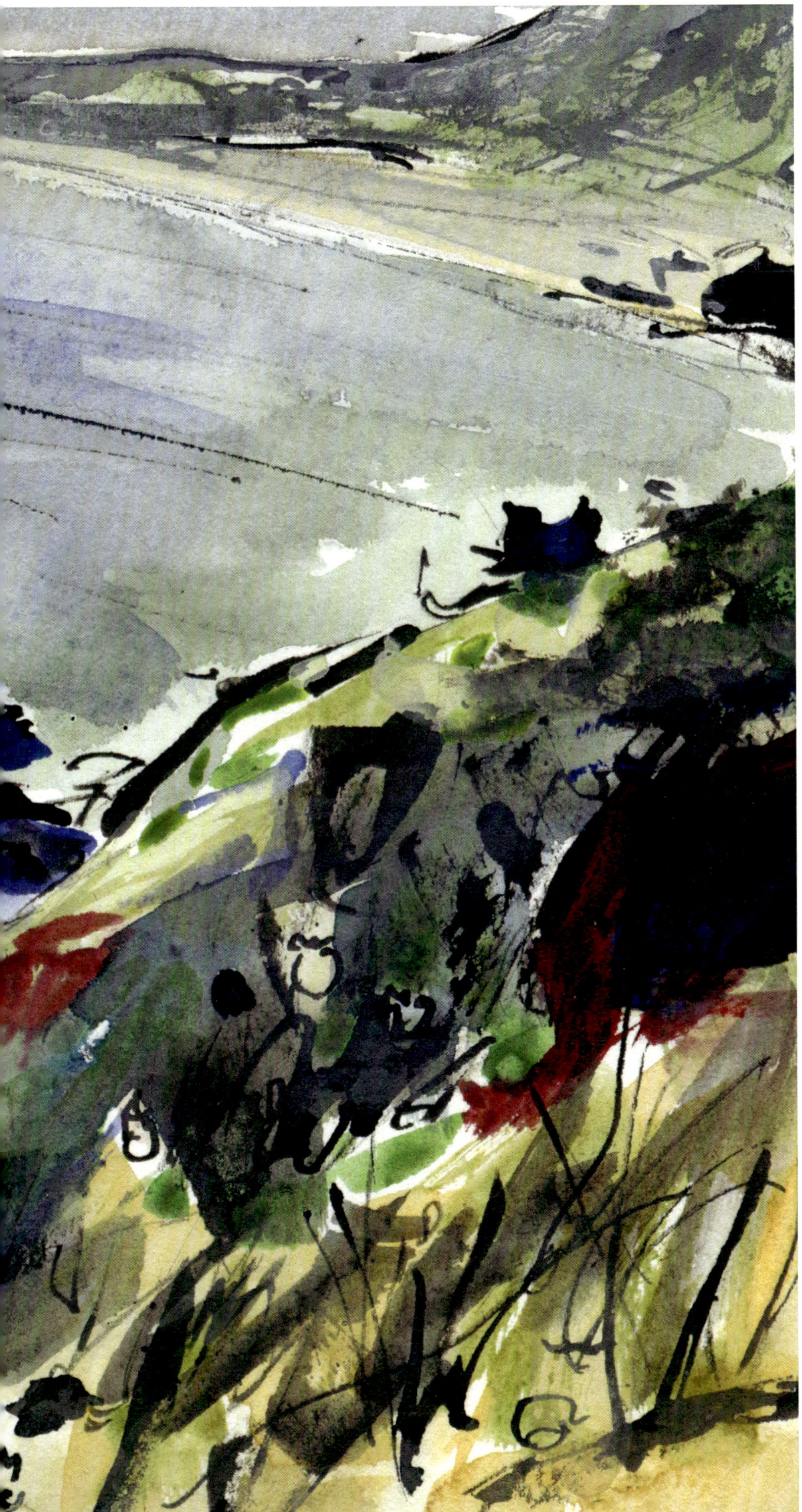

St Cyrus
ink & watercolour
14.5 x 20.5cm

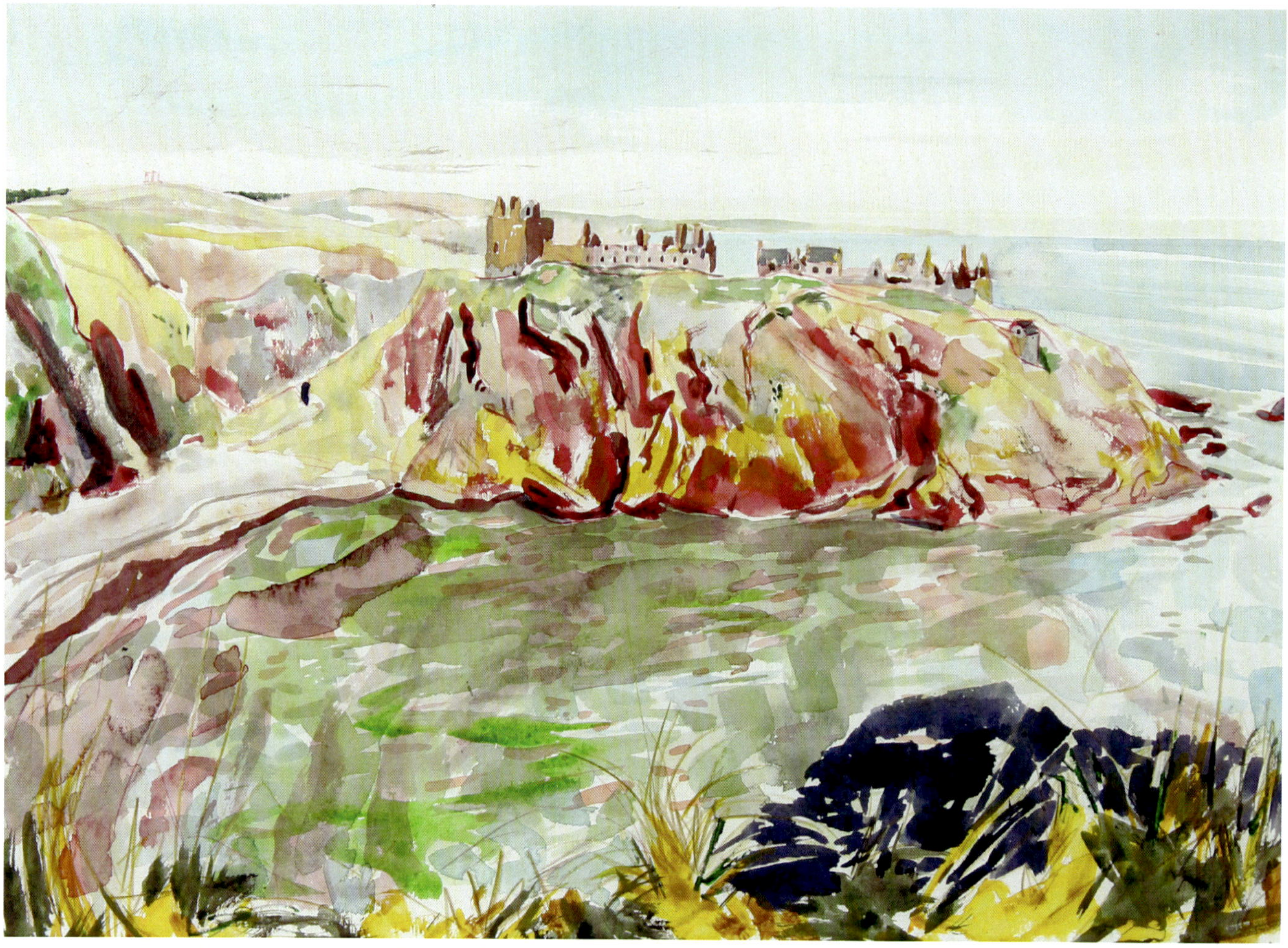

Dunnottar Castle
watercolour
25 x 35.5cm

Aberdeenshire Coast

The coastline of Aberdeenshire is very special to me. I've known the Peterhead to Cruden Bay stretch my whole life; we had regular childhood holidays there to visit grandparents and cousins in Peterhead. The Aberdeen to Newburgh section I discovered when Jennifer was studying in Aberdeen. When we stay with our friends Michelle and Steve in Pitmedden, I always try to find time to go to the coast to sketch.

STONEHAVEN TO DUNNOTTAR CASTLE

A day trip to Stonehaven can be easily managed from anywhere along the Edinburgh–Aberdeen rail line. One February morning I left Linlithgow at 7am and alighted at Stonehaven station only two and a half hours later, a full day still ahead of me.

A fifteen-minute walk takes you to the town centre where there are cafés and shops, and in a minute more you can be right down on the beach. Along at the harbour you might see eiders, shags and gulls. When the tide is out, redshanks and possibly plovers run amongst small beached boats. There's a great pedestal-mounted block of sandstone with a sundial carved on top, over 300 years old – dated 1710.

Two or three miles south along the cliff-top path is Dunnottar Castle. It's a majestic conglomeration of ruins, perched on an almost-island of cliff that juts out from the main body of the coast. There are all the birds you'd expect, and if you're lucky you might see a peregrine falcon. In summer on the water and nesting on the ledges are guillemots, razorbills, kittiwakes and some puffins. A few miles south the RSPB's Fowlsheugh Reserve is home to even larger colonies of seabirds.

ABERDEEN HARBOUR

Beyond Torry on the southern side of the River Dee is the best place I know to see dolphins and porpoises, and great too for watching seabirds and boats. I've sat here painting and been entertained by the regular passage of seabirds and ships in and out of Aberdeen harbour. Eider ducks sit in the sun on concrete sea walls; shags and cormorants spread their wings to dry; waders probe the shore and small birds flit in the scrub. Take note in particular of multiple coloured rings on the legs of pipits; the Grampian Ringing Group is engaged in an ongoing study of breeding ecology and dispersal of rock pipits in the area and would be delighted to be sent your sightings.

Once painting was over and dusk was falling I found a narrow pebble beach and stood elevated on a large rock as the tide momentarily marooned me, then released, marooned, then released.

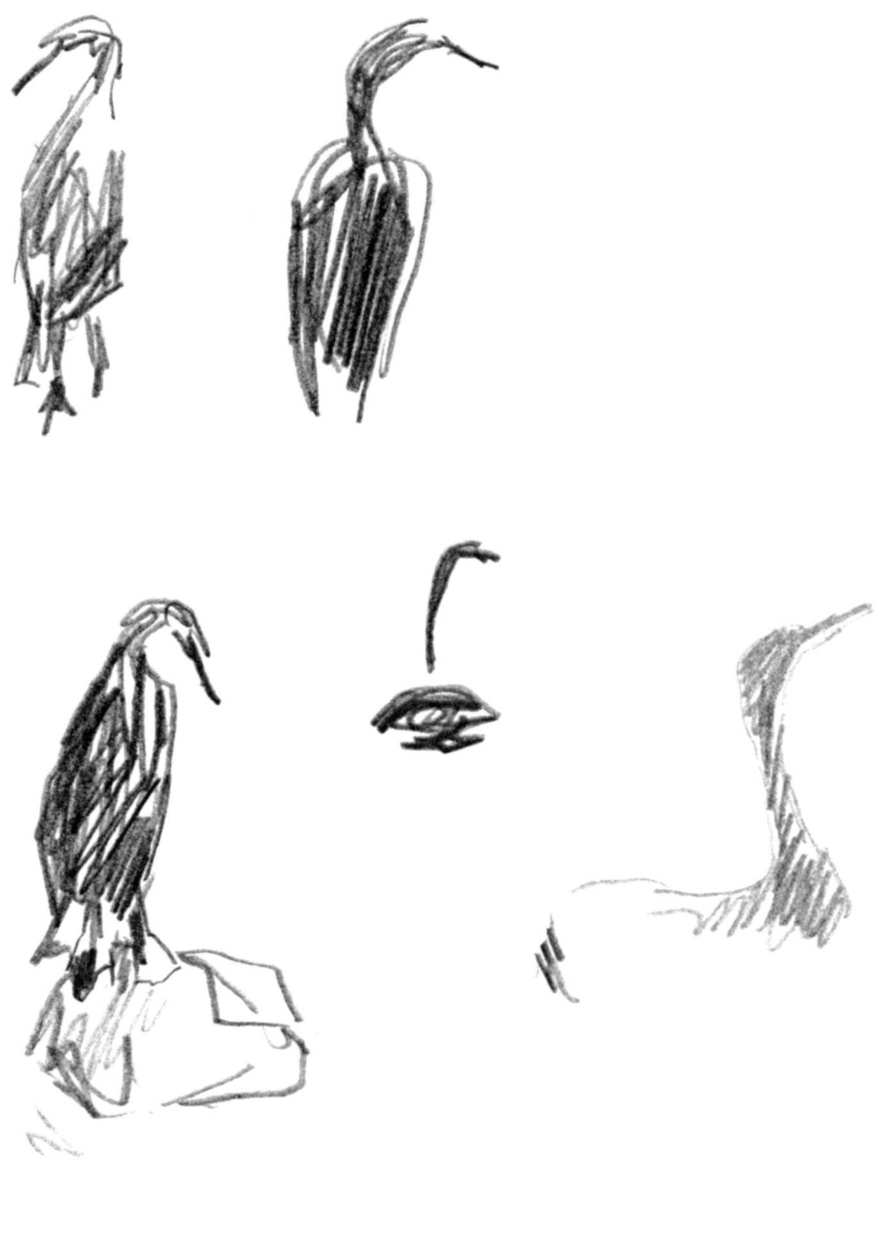

shag studies
pencil

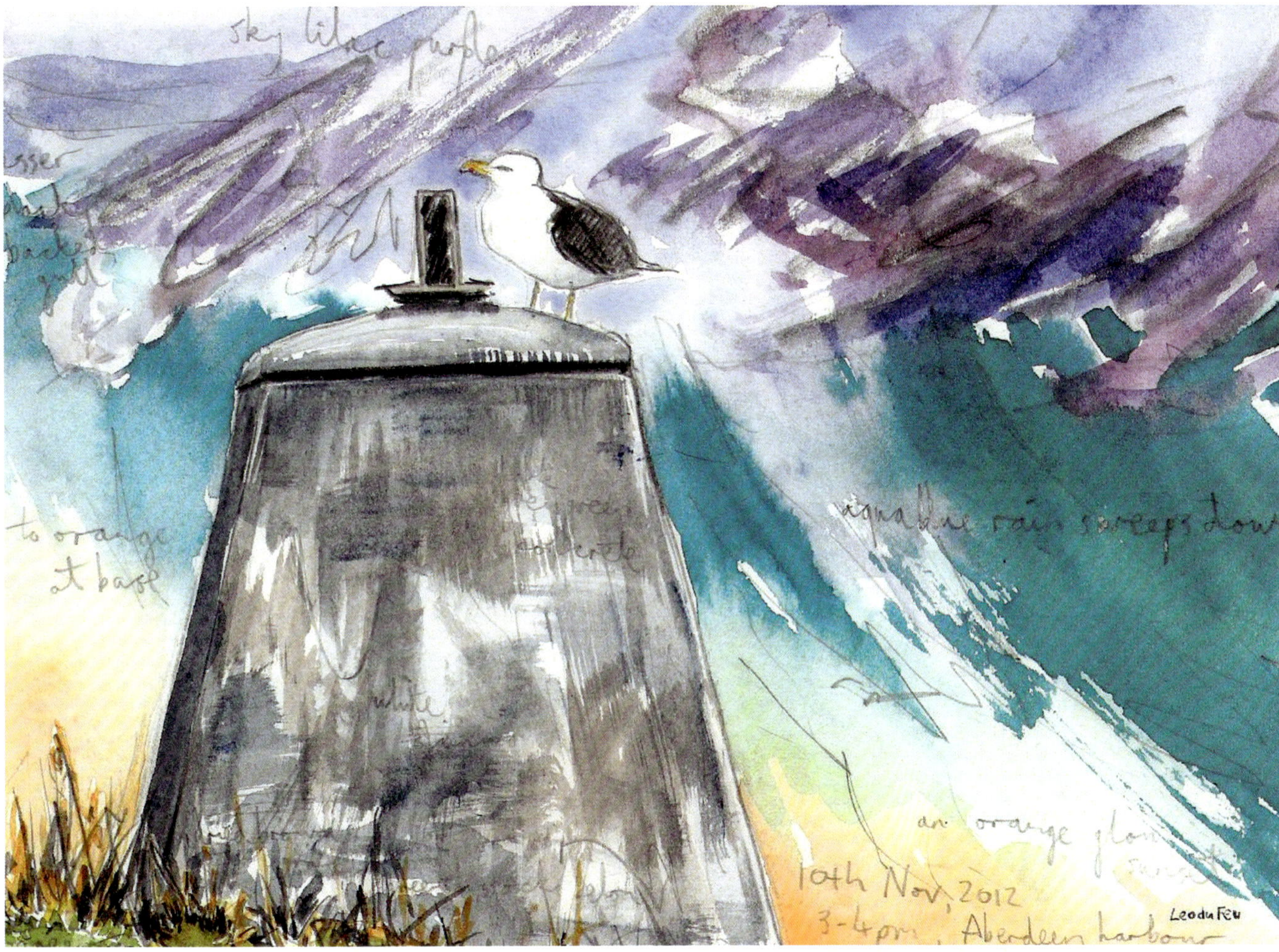

lesser black-backed gull,
Aberdeen Harbour
pencil & watercolour
12.5 x 17.5cm

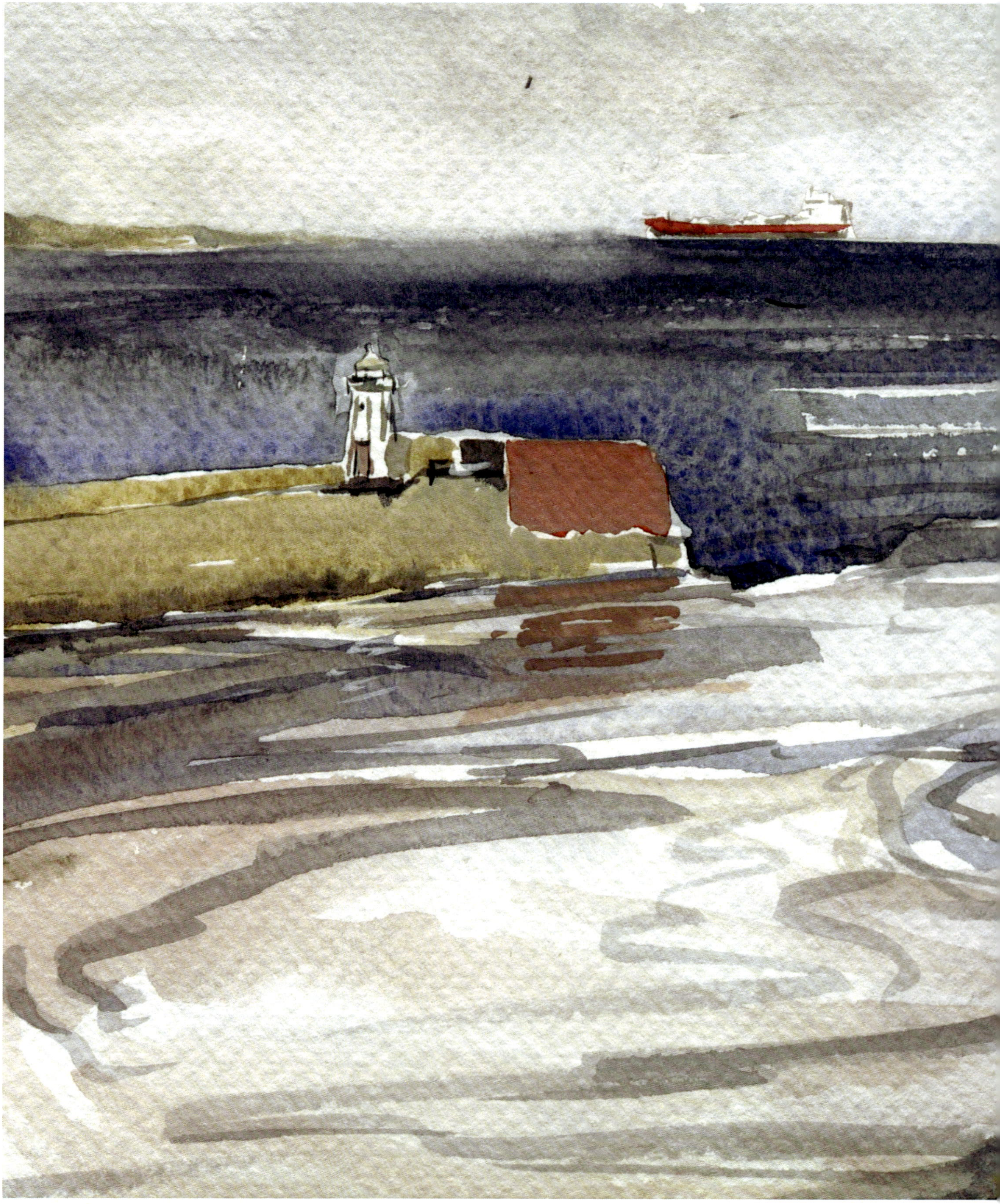

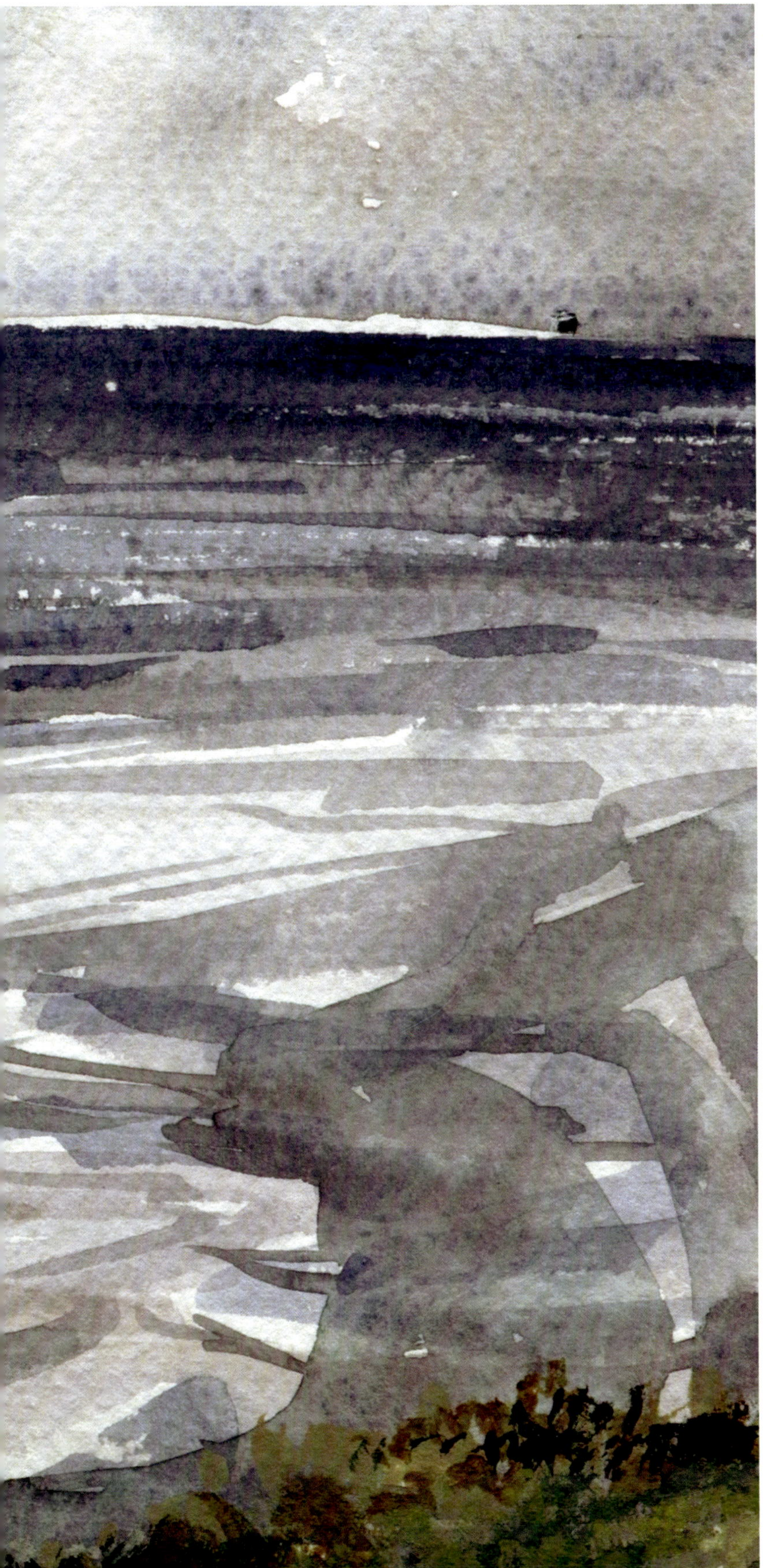

leaving Aberdeen
watercolour
13.5 x 19cm

NEWBURGH ESTUARY

The Forvie National Nature Reserve at Newburgh is home to countless waders and wildfowl that feed on the invertebrate-rich mudflats of the River Ythan estuary. Eider ducks and terns are the star species here: 4,000–5,000 eiders in summer make their strange cooings and murmurings and 1,500 pairs nest on the dunes. Among terns, the sandwich is most numerous at Forvie, with 1,000 spring-summer breeding pairs. There are also Arctic, common and little terns, all breeding but in much smaller numbers. Outwith tern nesting season you can walk across the dunes from river to sea; in the very depths where you can neither see nor hear the waves you feel you might be on another planet. A colony of hundreds of seals socialises on the sand at the mouth of the river.

On a circular walk from nearby Collieston village to Forvie we stopped for lunch on the cliffs. Jennifer and Michelle chatted whilst I made a landscape panorama and studies of a small colony of fulmars. Watercolour was added later.

below: Forvie sands, Jennifer sitting
pencil & watercolour in sketchbook
14.5 x 41cm

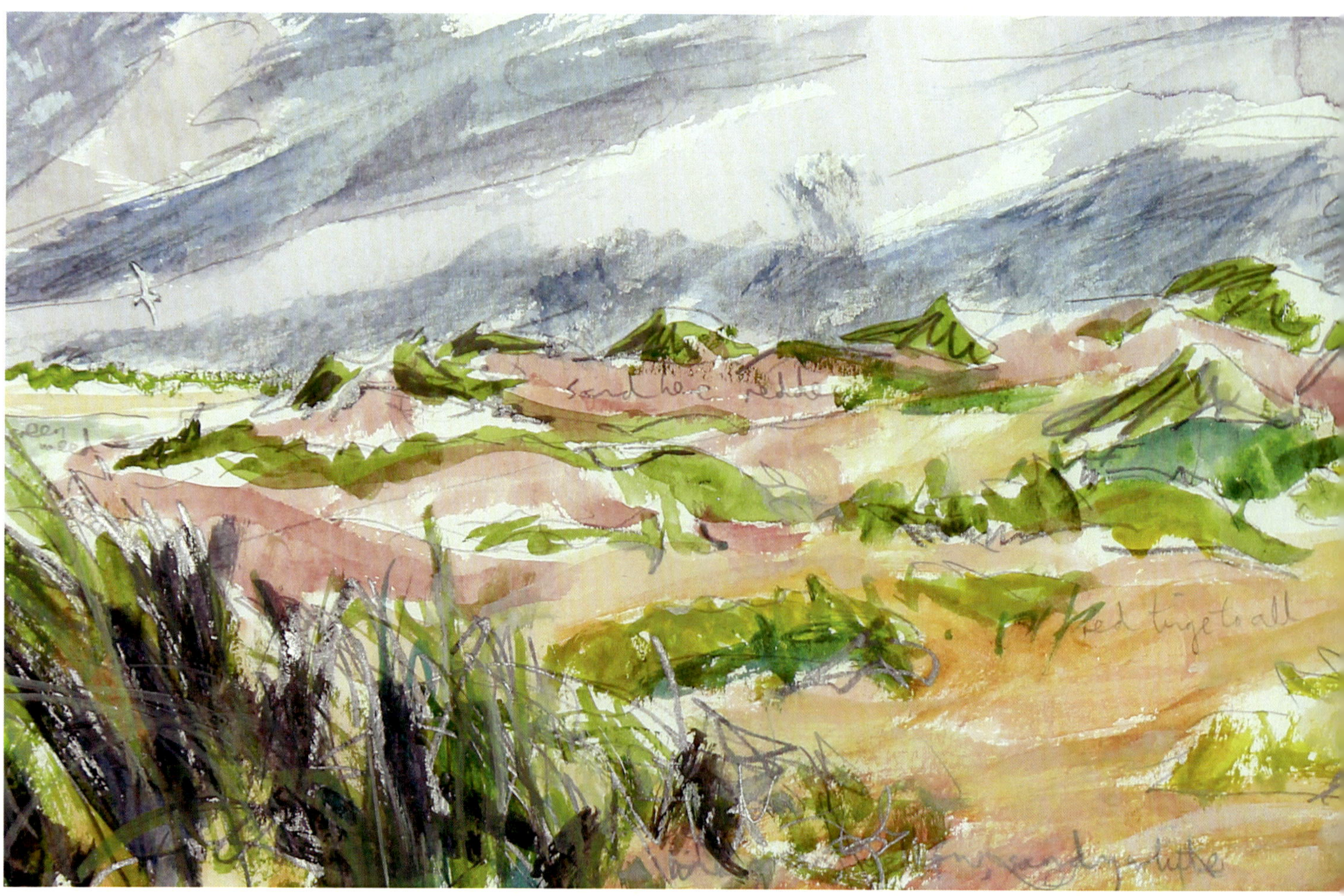

fulmar studies, near Collieston
pencil
14.5 x 20.5cm

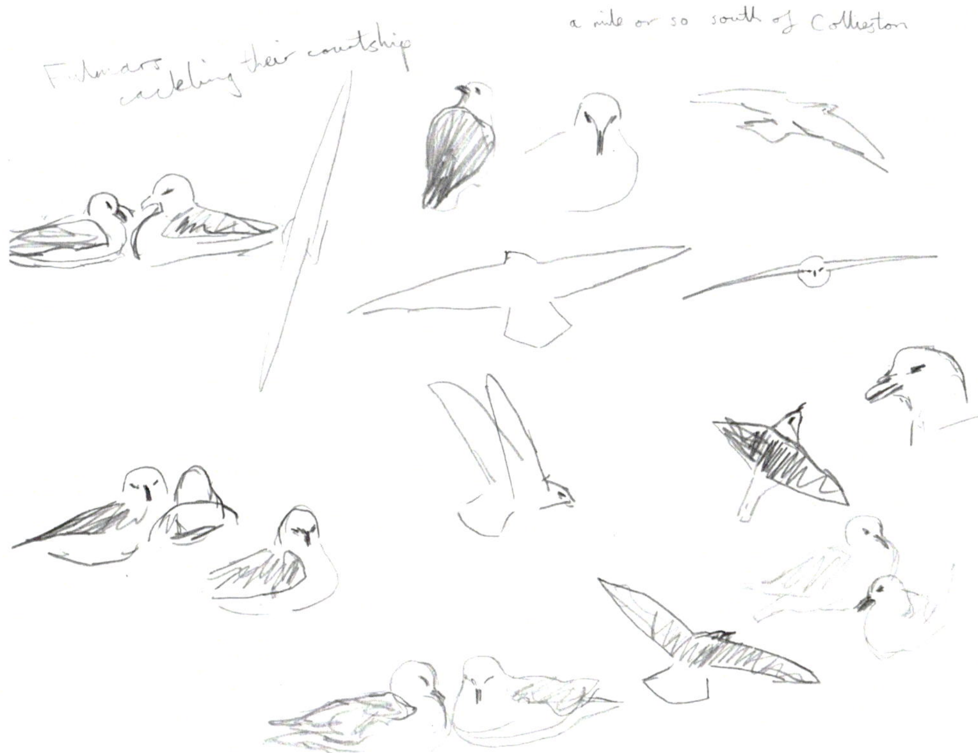

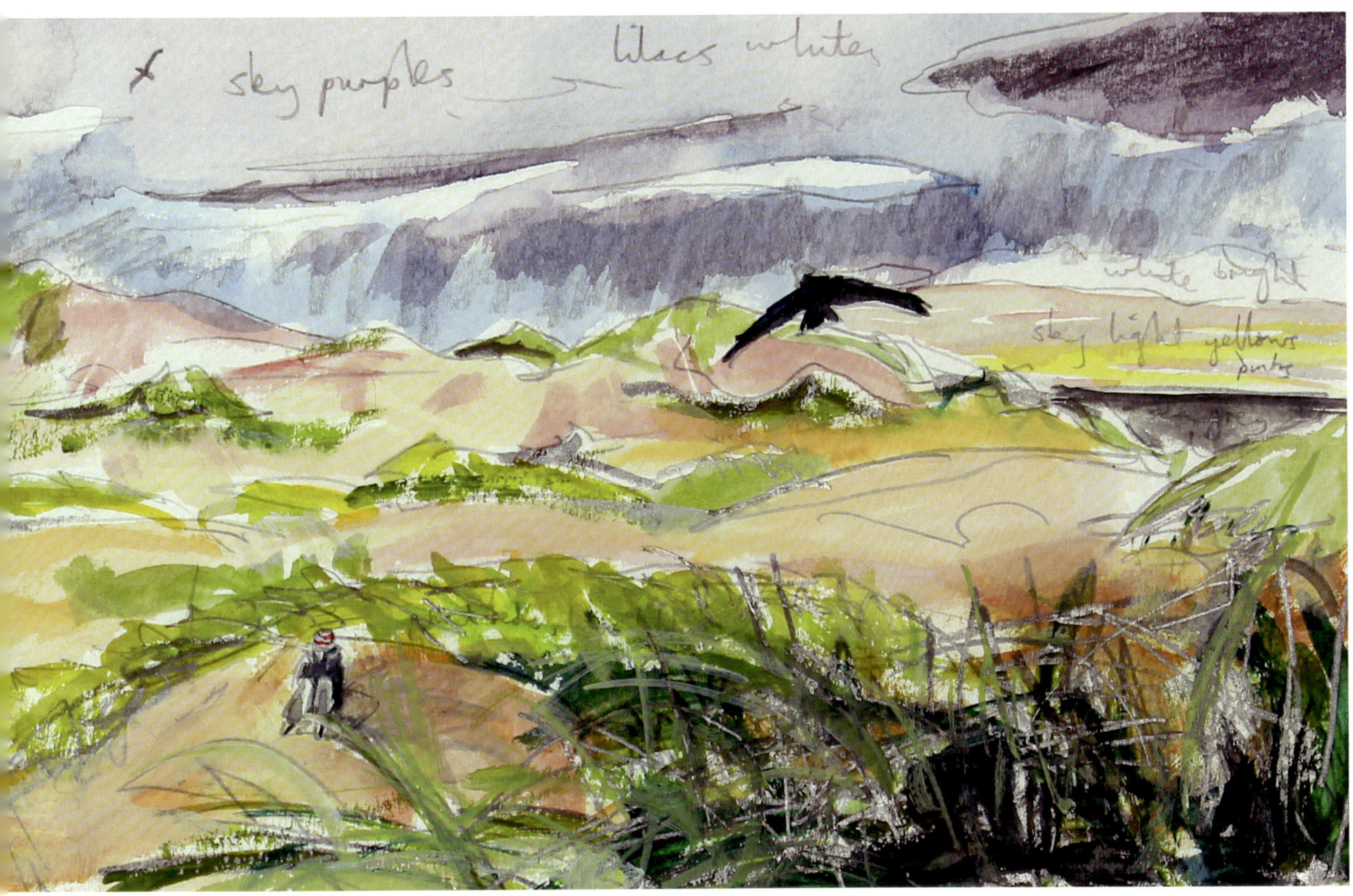

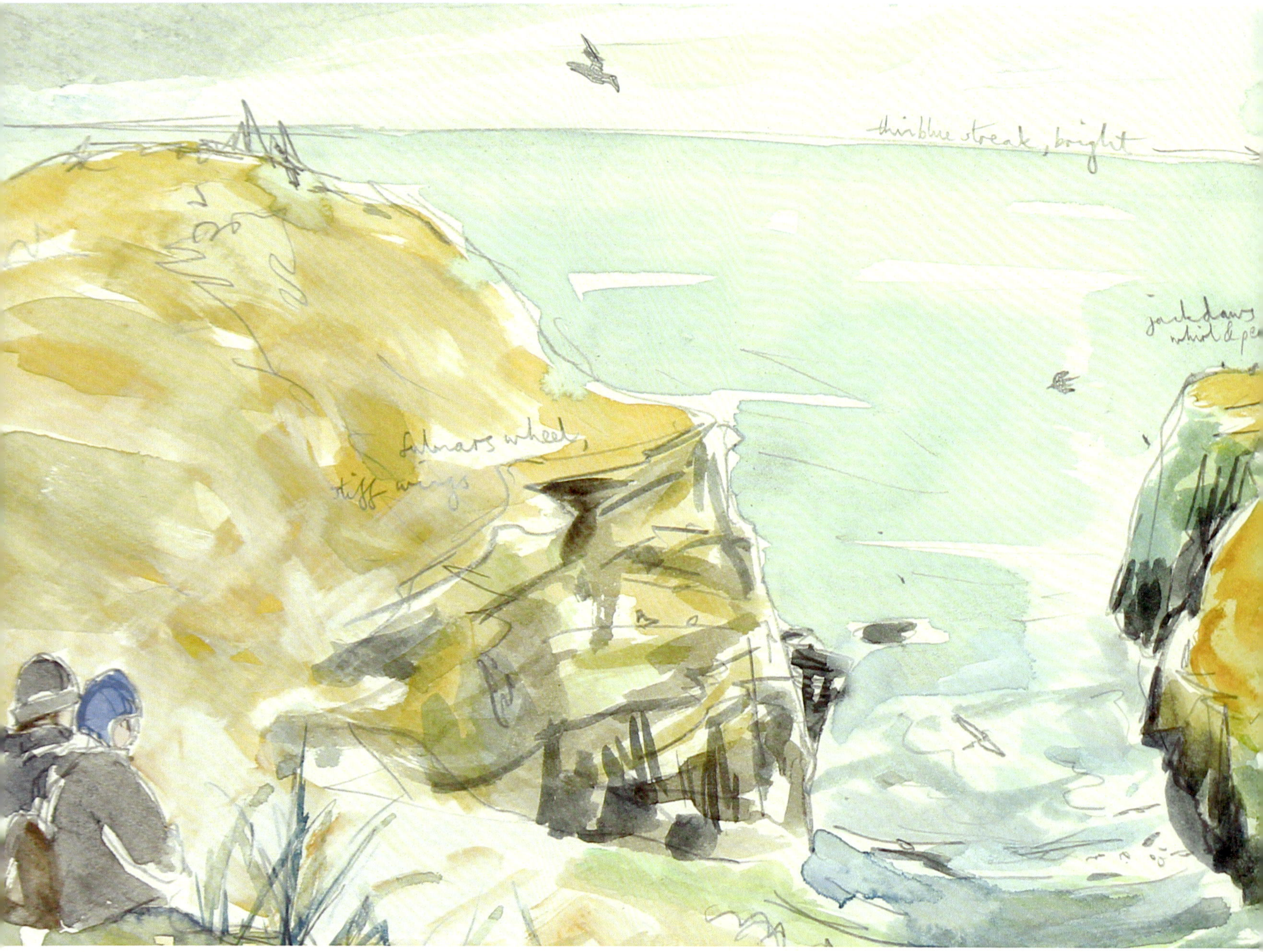
thin blue streak, bright
fulmars wheel,
stiff wings
jackdaws

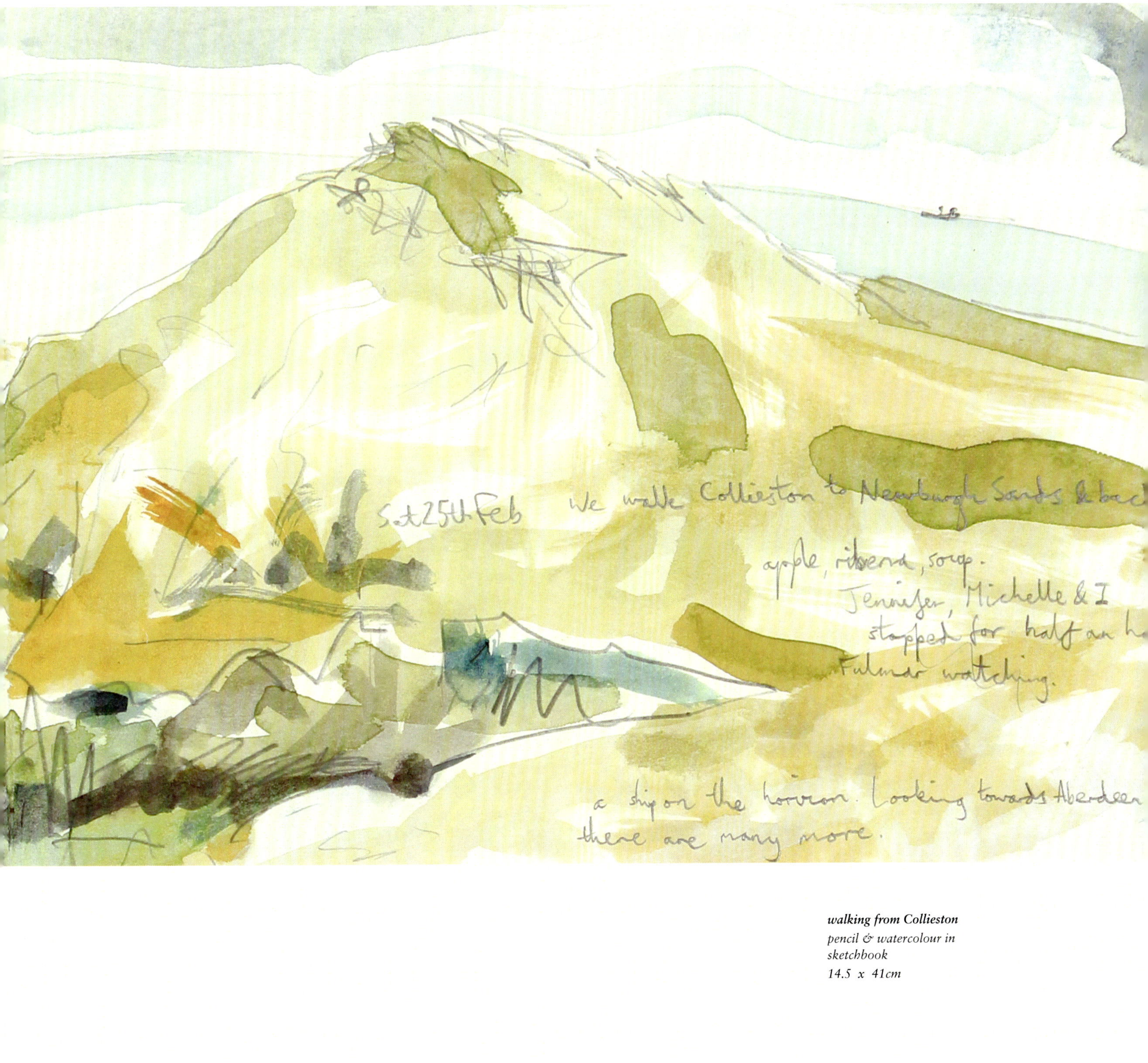

walking from Collieston
pencil & watercolour in sketchbook
14.5 x 41cm

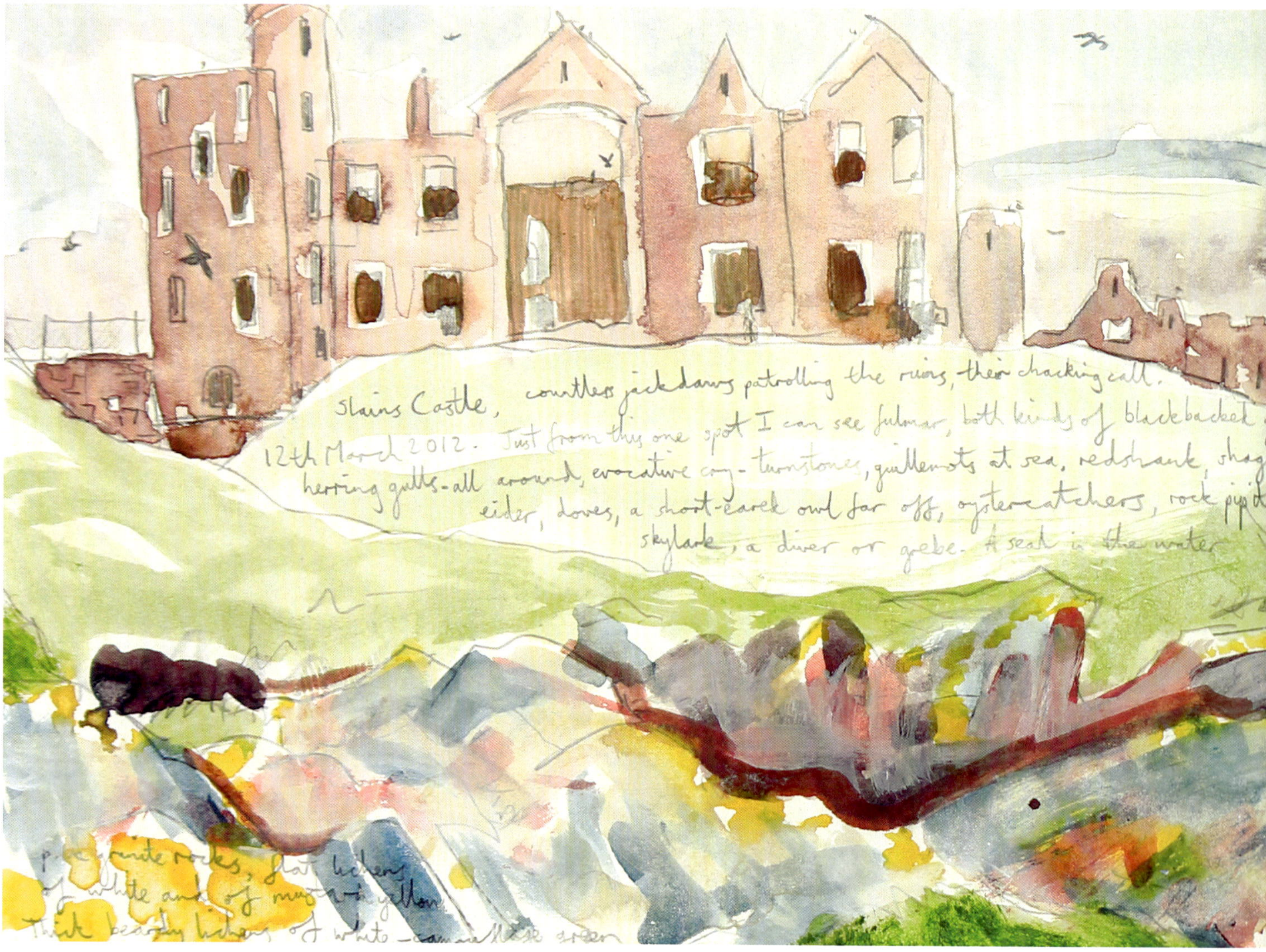

SLAINS CASTLE & BULLERS OF BUCHAN

Slains Castle and the Bullers of Buchan lie between Cruden Bay and Peterhead. The stately cliff-edge ruins of Slains Castle inspired Bram Stoker's writing of Dracula when he stayed in a hotel in Cruden Bay in the 1890s.

This watercolour sketch and large acrylic of Slains Castle are an example of one of those happy occasions when I end up really pleased with both initial drawing and finished painting. It doesn't always work like that.

Two kilometres north of Slains Castle is the stretch of cliffs known as the Bullers of Buchan. An absolutely stunning place, but be wary of taking younger children; even adults should be extra-careful to keep a decent footing. Most impressive here is the underwhelmingly named 'tub', where the roof of a sea cave collapsed long ago to leave a cliff-sided seawater-filled cauldron. Waves pour and seabirds fly in and out through a sea arch that would once have been the entrance to the cave.

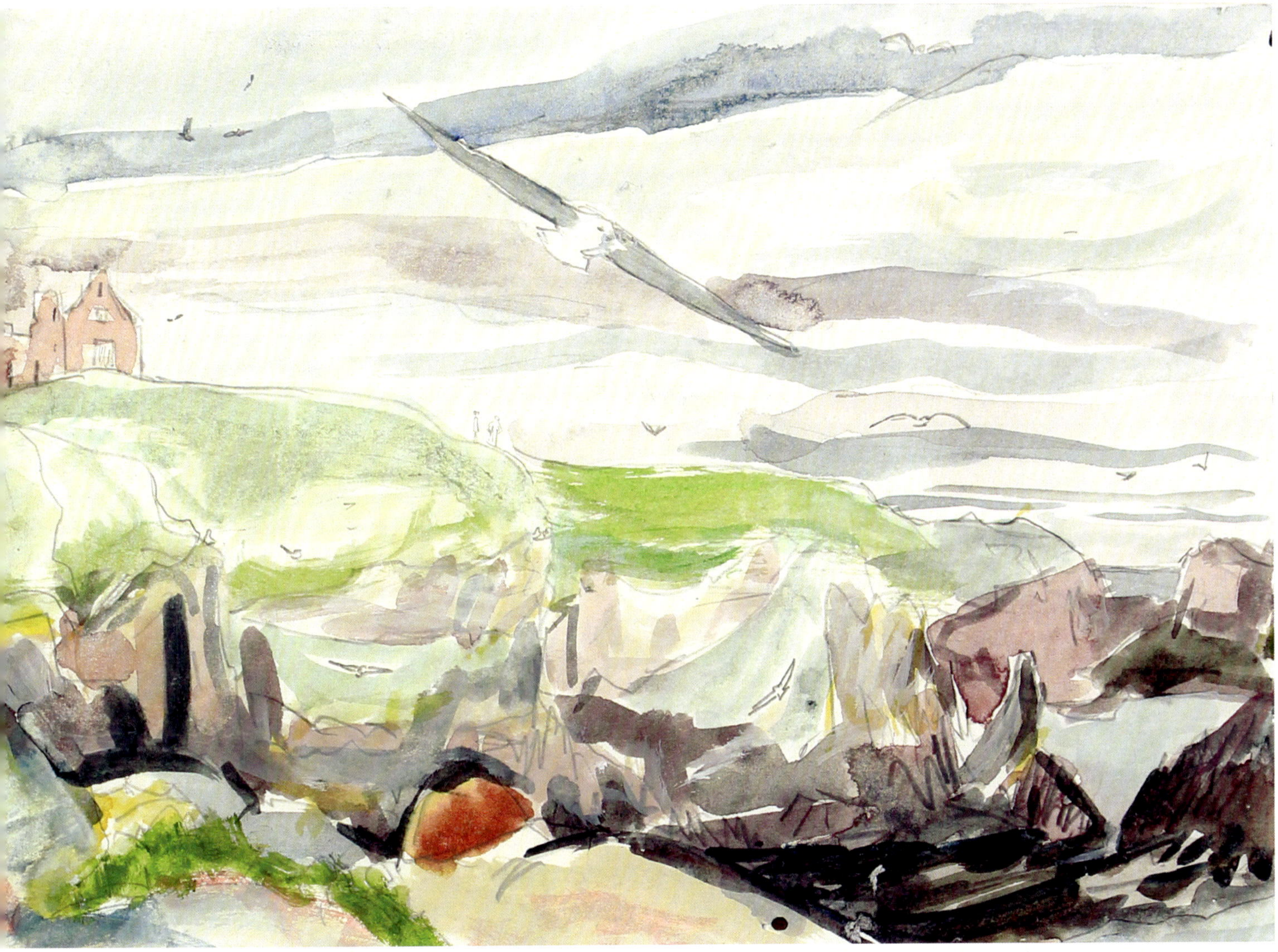

Slains Castle
pencil & watercolour in sketchbook
14.5 x 41cm

My best-ever views of peregrine falcons were around here. A single peregrine perched for many minutes as I watched through binoculars until it flew towards and past me and landed on a ledge beside its mate. I could see in perfect detail their bright yellow legs and eye-rings, and the same primary yellow where beak meets skull before turning through grey-blue to black at its flesh-tearing tip.

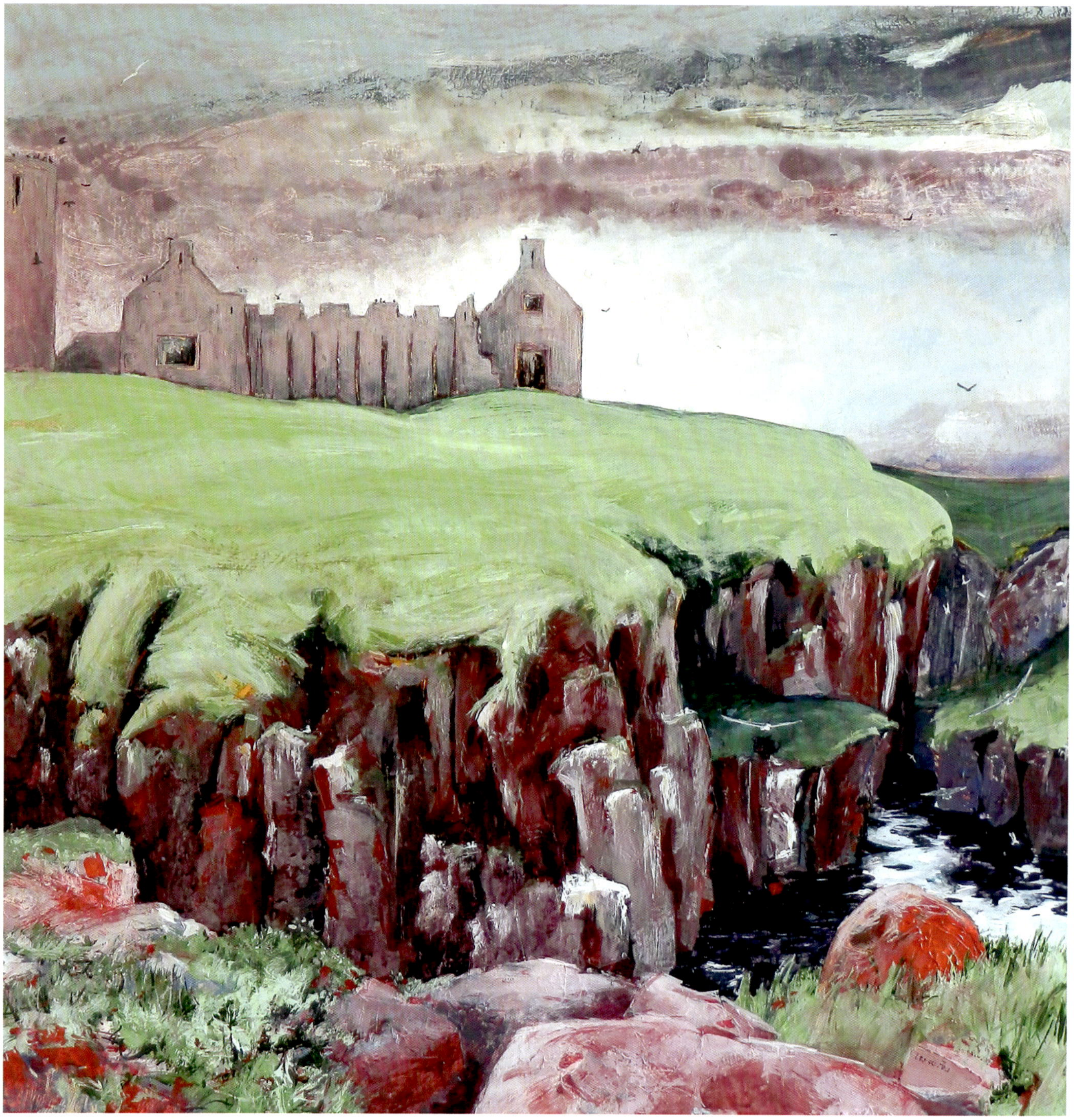

Slains Castle
acrylic
50 x 50cm

short-eared owl,
Asio flammeus,
Slains Castle
acrylic
14.5 x 21cm

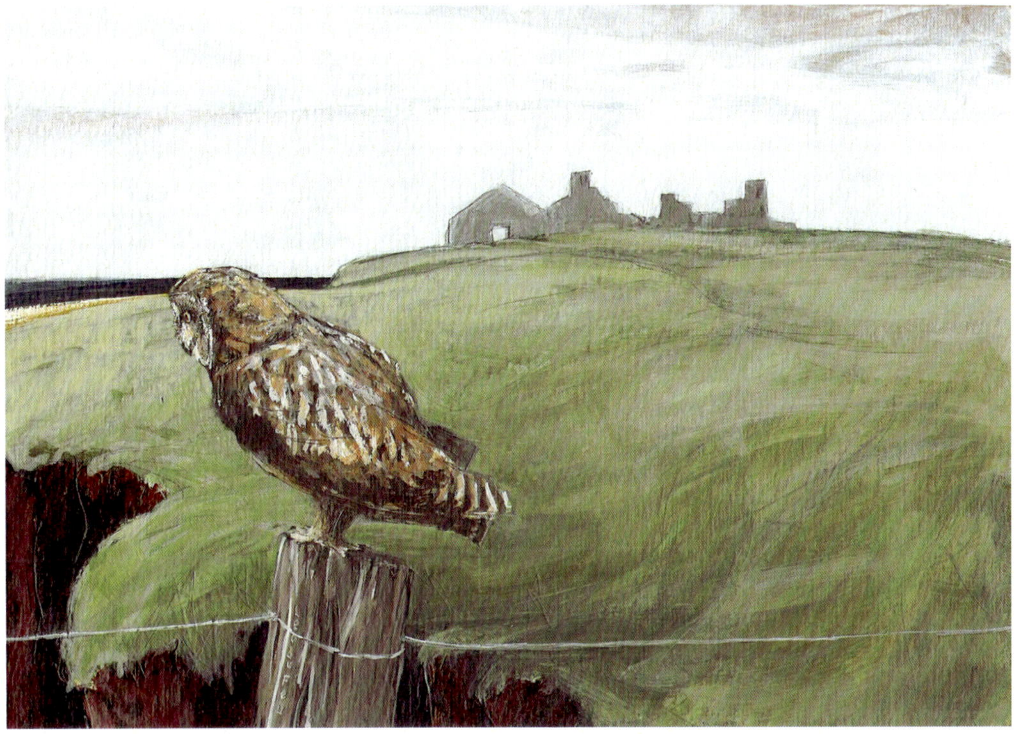

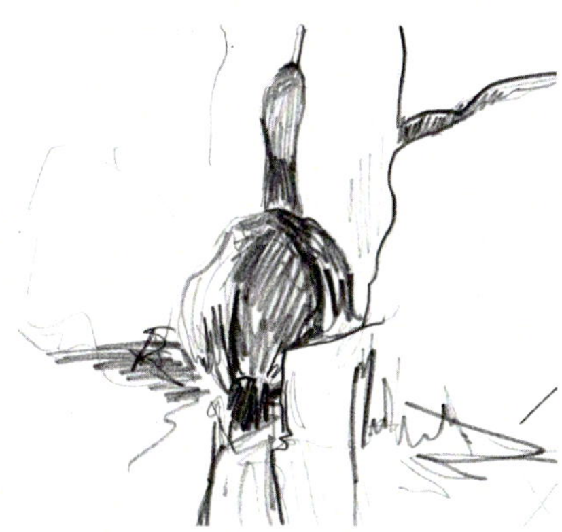

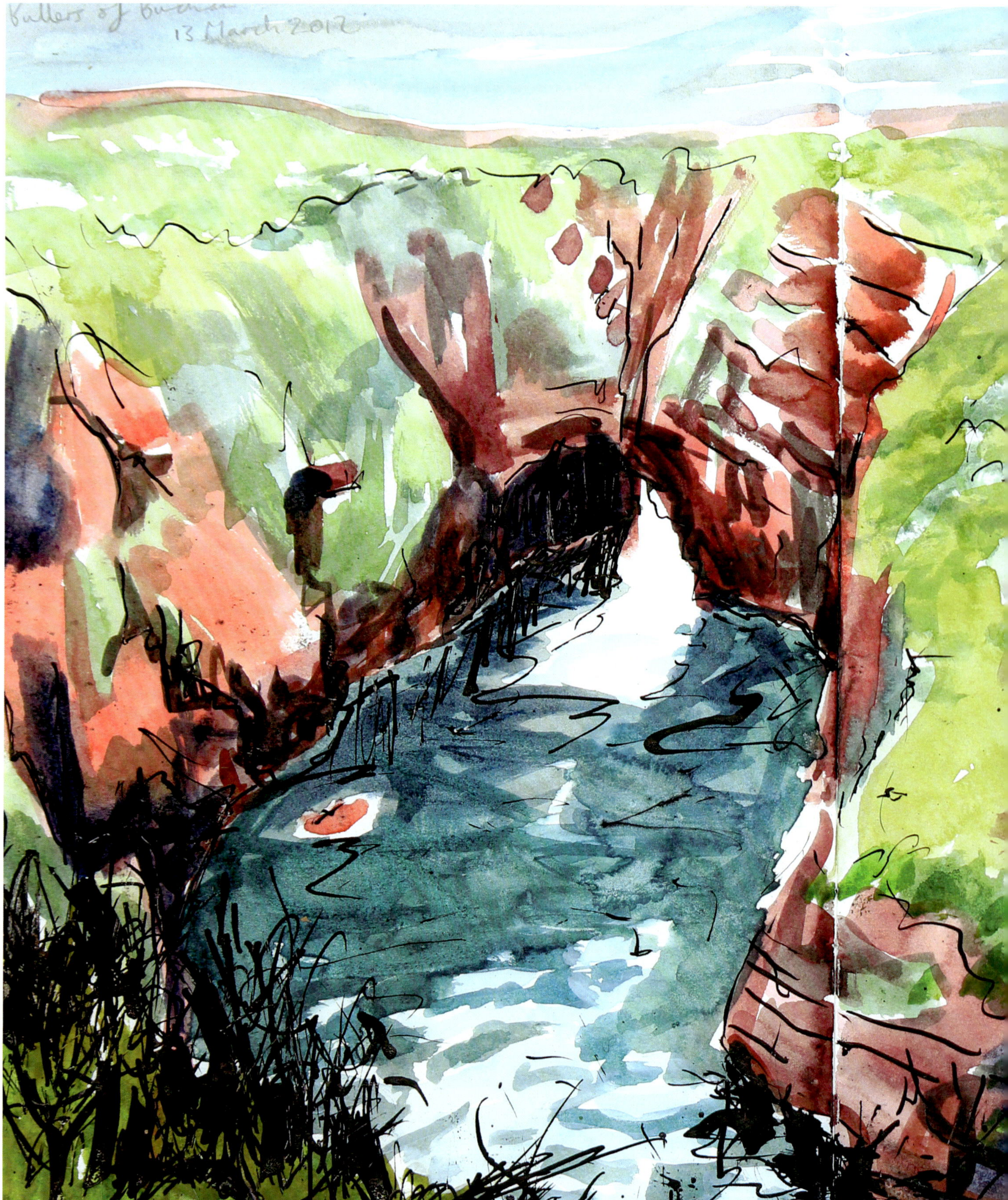
13 March 2012

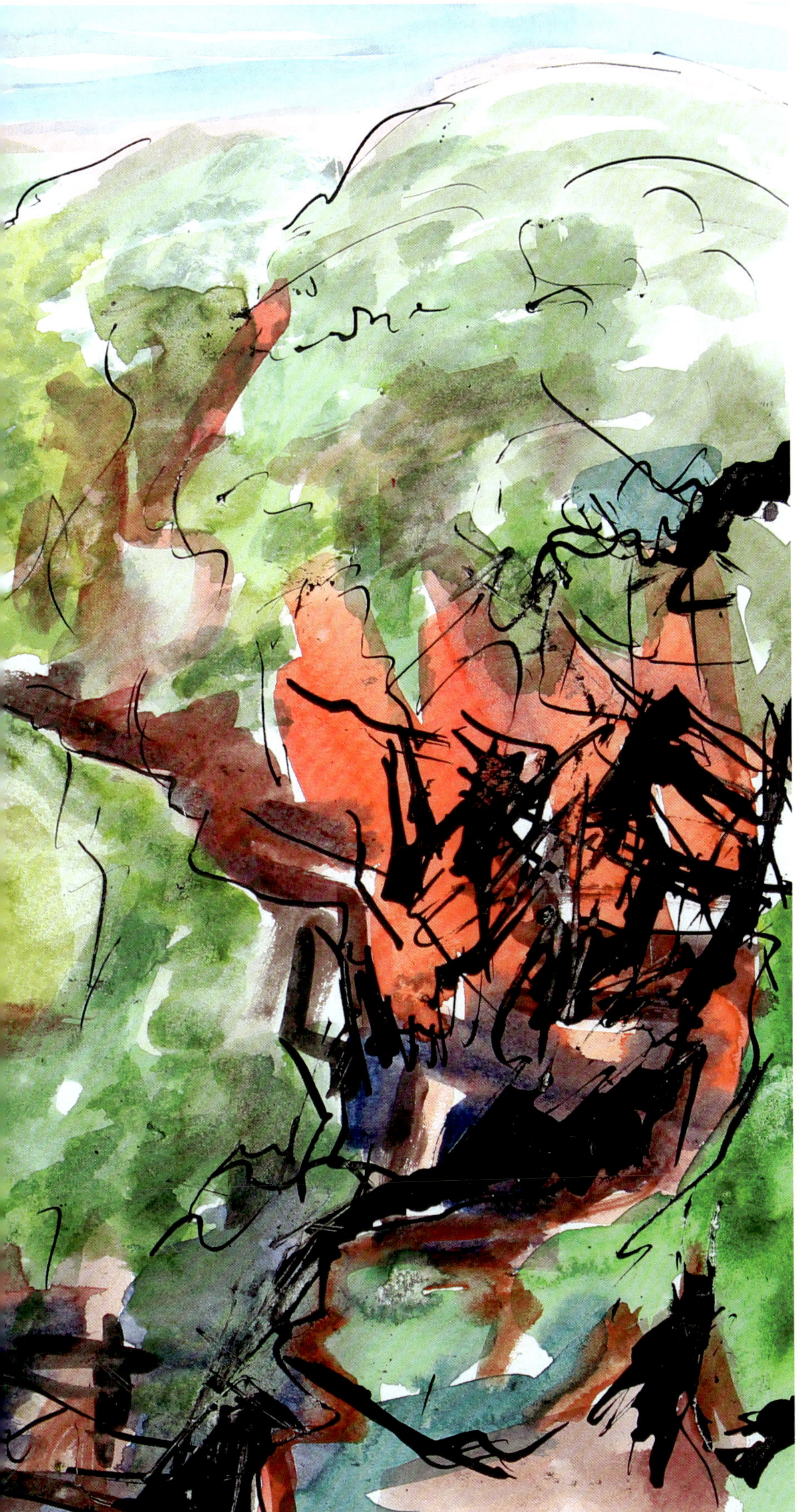

Bullers of Buchan
ink & watercolour in sketchbook
29.5 x 41cm

RATTRAY BEACH

Rattray beach is halfway between Peterhead and Fraserburgh. It has sand dunes like hills and a lighthouse on a stone plinth that stands alone off the shore. Nearby is the RSPB's Loch of Strathbeg reserve, winter roost site for twenty percent of the world's population of pink-footed geese.

I was commissioned to do this diptych painting for Woolmanhill Hospital in Aberdeen. I love placing little details in my works. Hidden in the grasses here are six-spot burnet moths and a variety of shells.

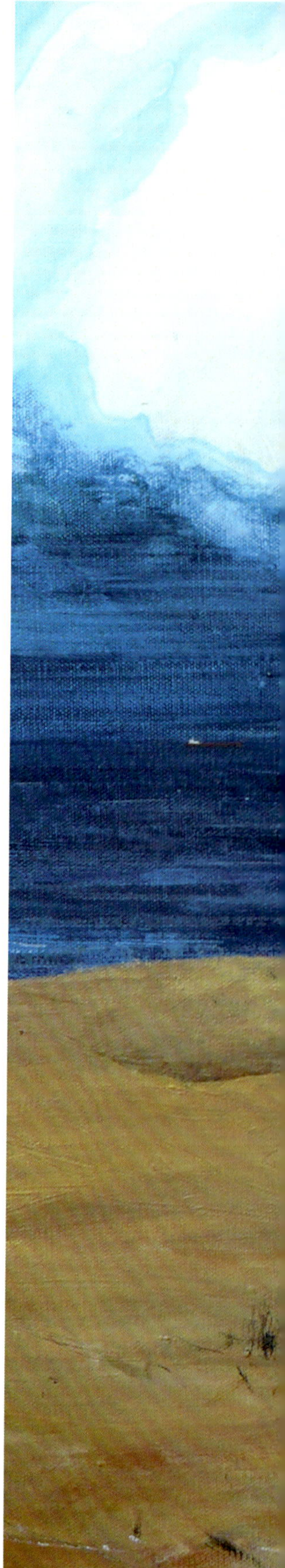

Rattray Head lighthouse (detail)
acrylic

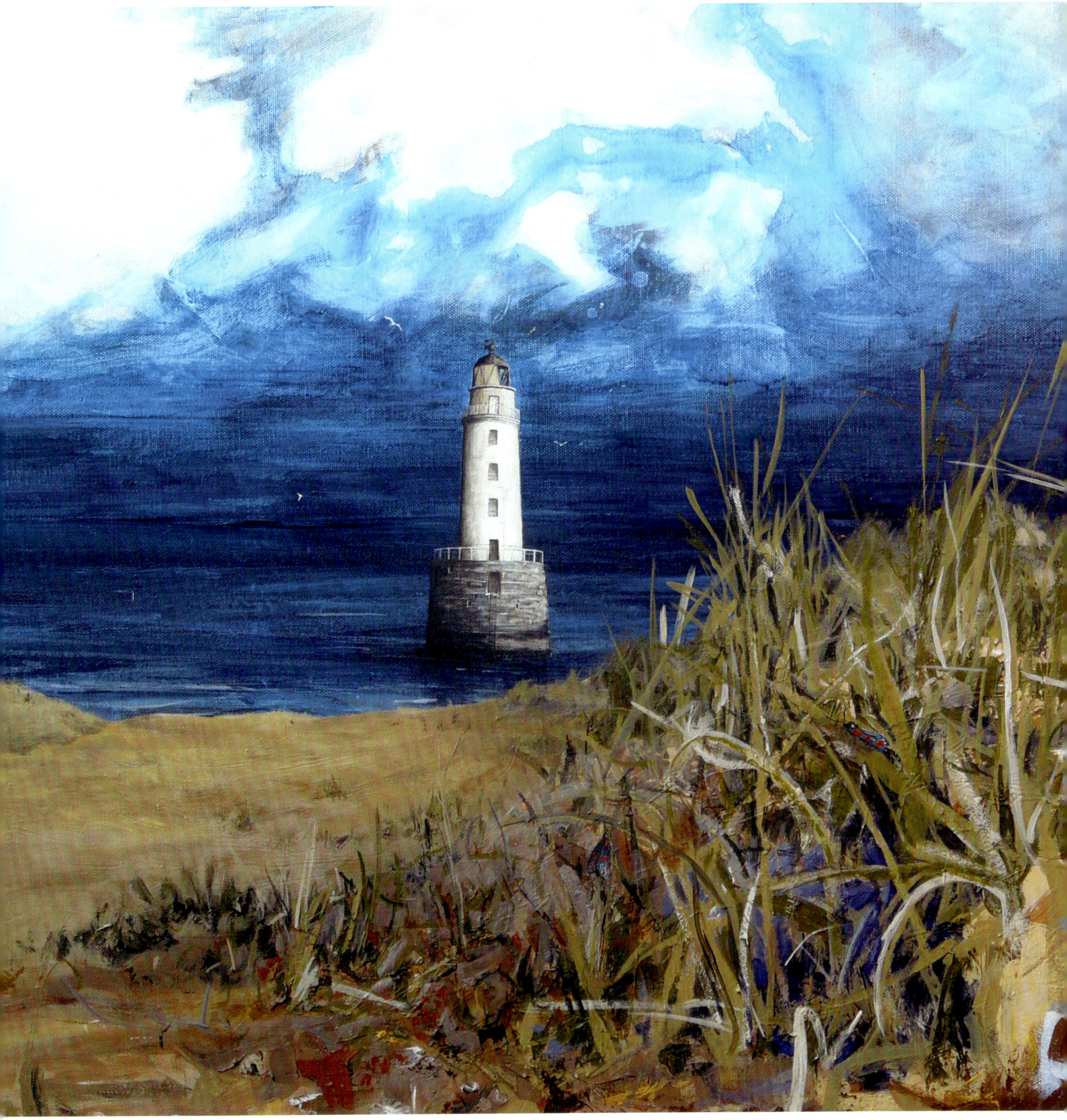

Insch

By train from Aberdeen it takes only half an hour to reach the little village of Insch. Jennifer and I explored old graves around the remaining gable wall and bell-cot of St Drostan's Parish Church before we walked along a country road and up-slope to the hill fort of Dunnideer. The fort is a combination of prehistoric and 13th-century ruins.

A pair of buzzards circled on a thermal above and rainclouds swept across the land. A train trundled clackety-clack through the valley below us. Jennifer read while I sketched the scene.

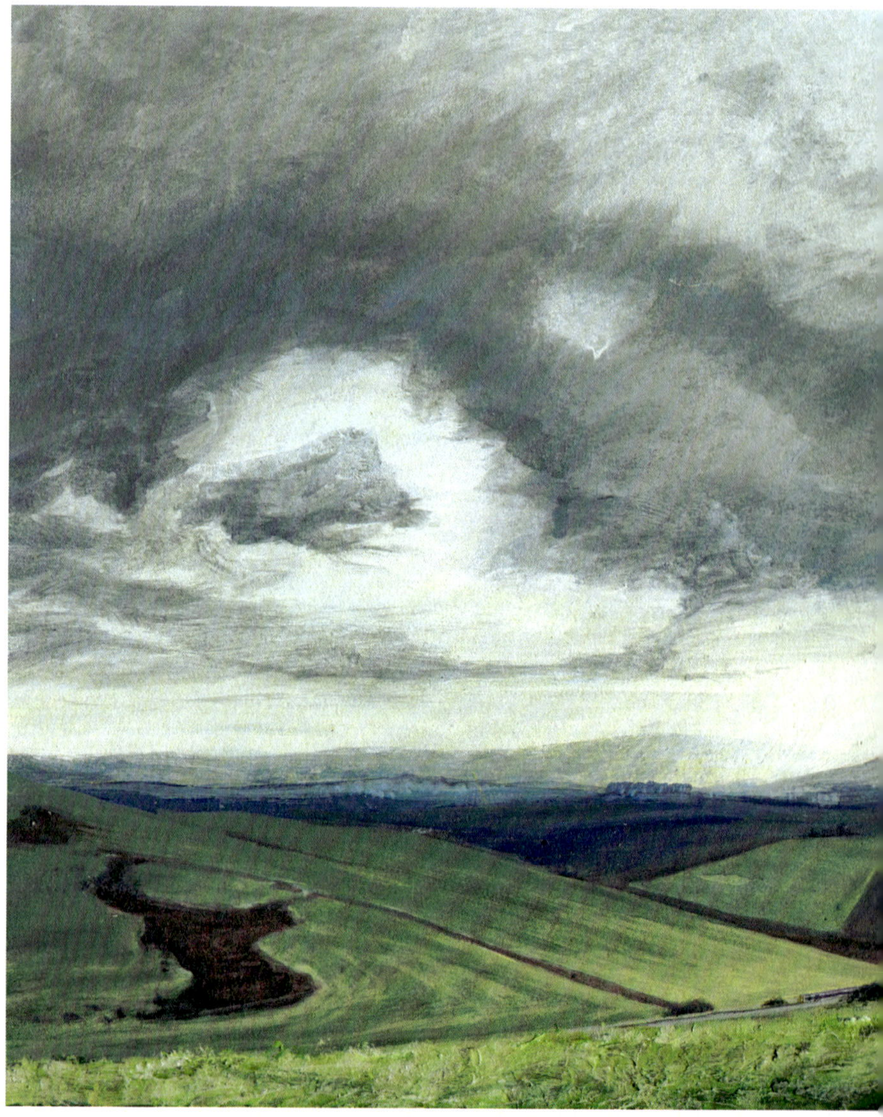

the hill fort of Dunnideer
acrylic
28 x 12.5cm

right: Dunnideer sketch, Jennifer reading
pencil
21 x 28cm

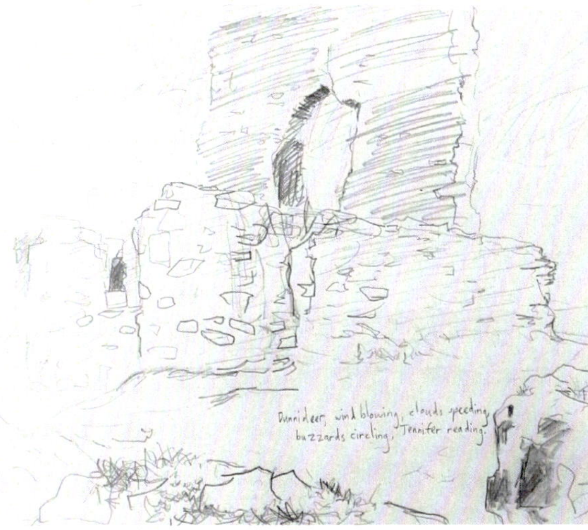

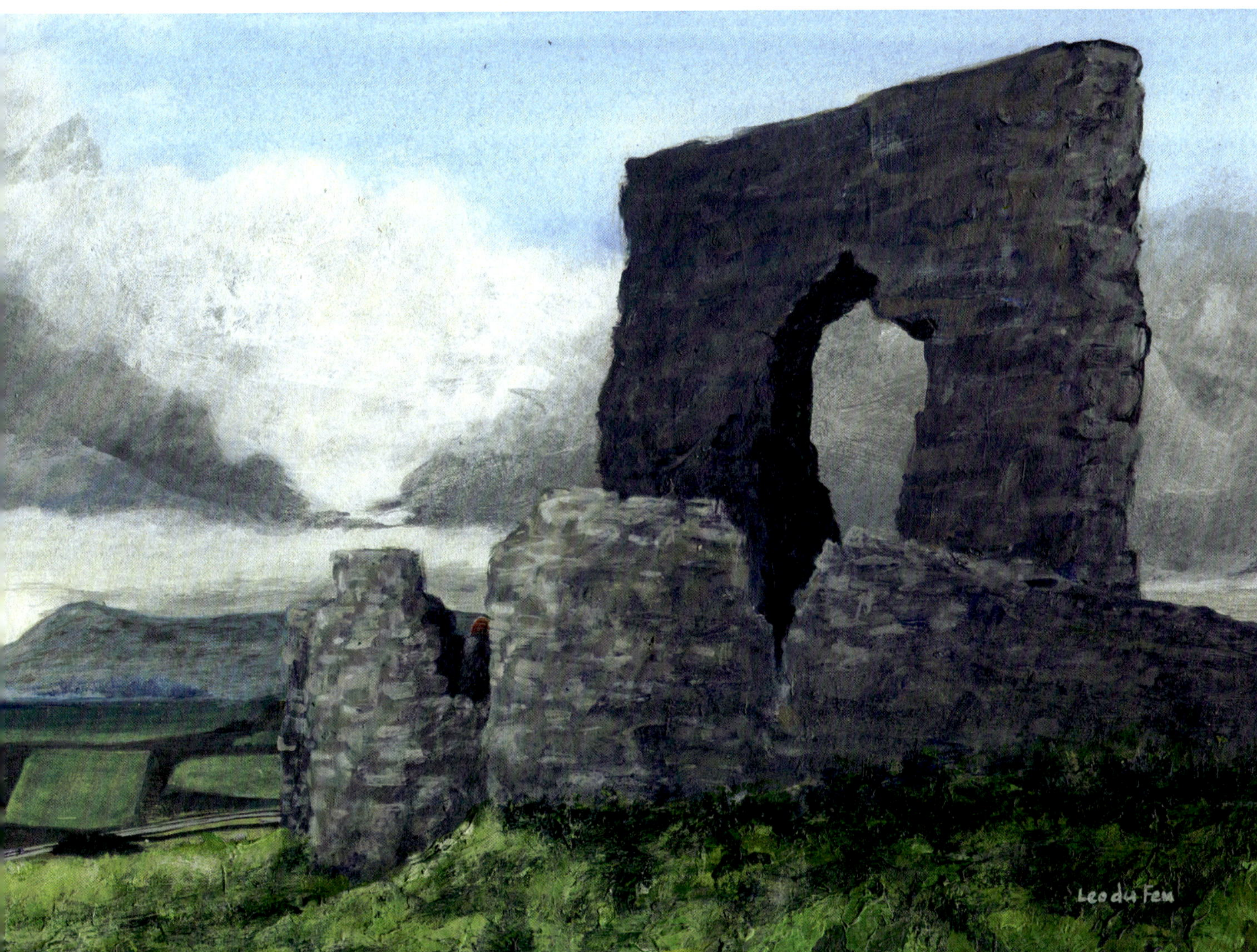

Elgin

My first season of ScotRail collaboration concluded with an exhibition of my railway landscapes in the excellent, independently run Elgin Museum. I got to know parts of Elgin quite well: river walks; an old mill; the sweet smell of baking shortbread that sometimes drifts over the station area of the town. There are several distilleries which for some reason I overlooked, and the grand ruins of Elgin Cathedral where I watched a group of actors rehearsing for an outdoor performance of a Shakespeare play.

In The Wards wildlife wetland a male pheasant would have remained perfectly hidden if it wasn't for the vibrant red fleshy wattles that decorate the cheeks of all males of his species.

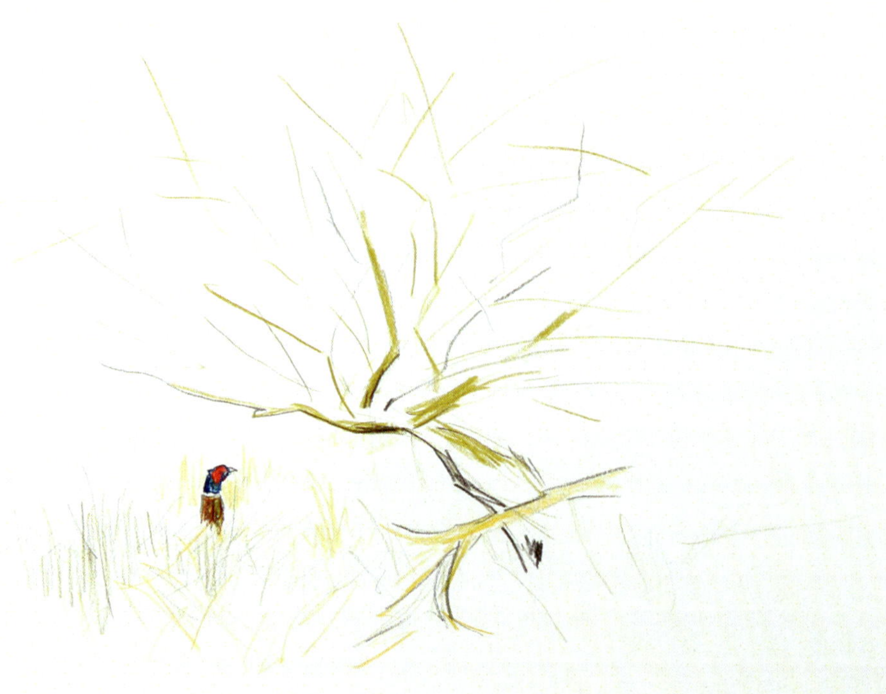

right: Elgin Cathedral
acrylic
14 x 10.5cm

left: pheasant abstract
coloured pencil
21 x 28cm

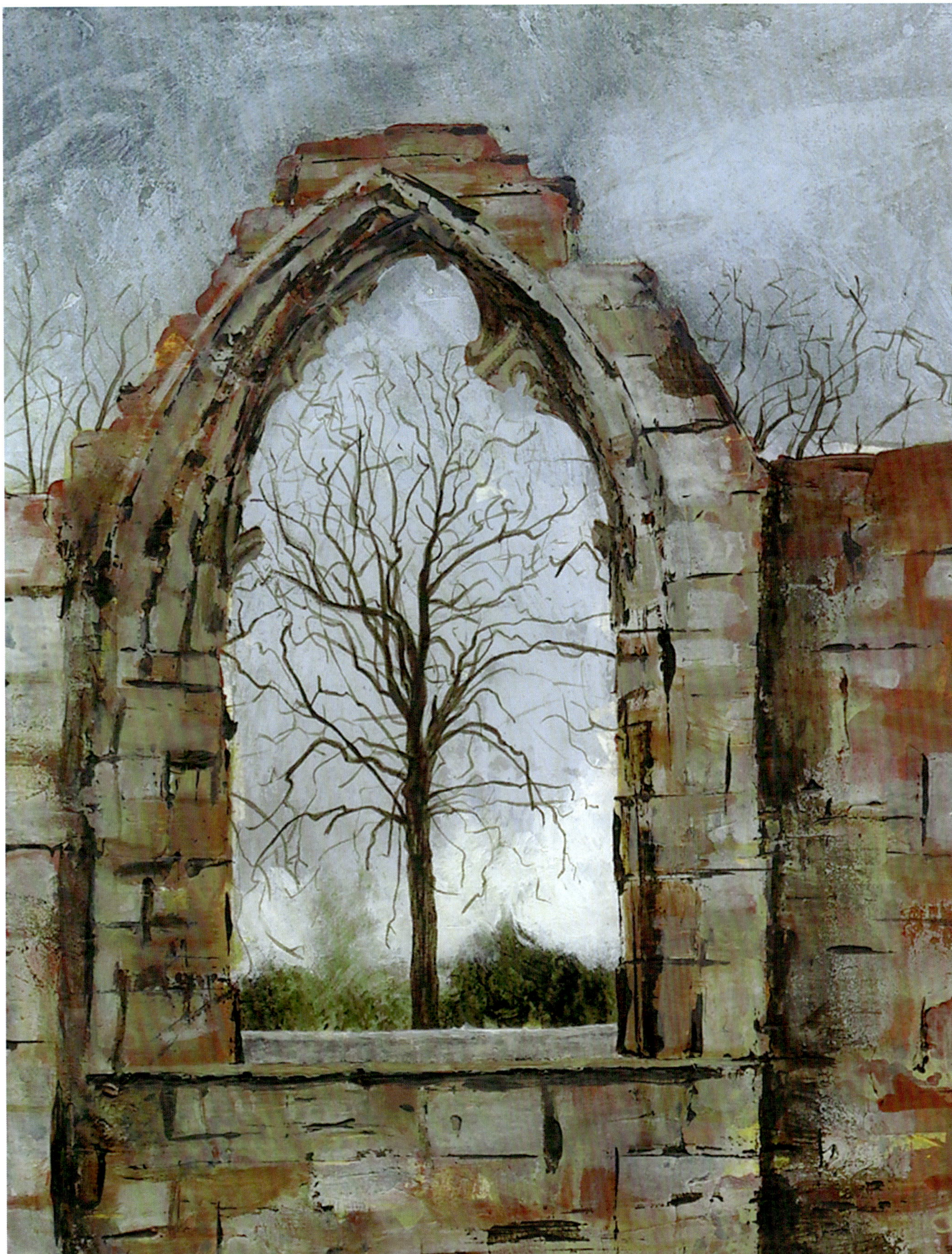

Central Highlands

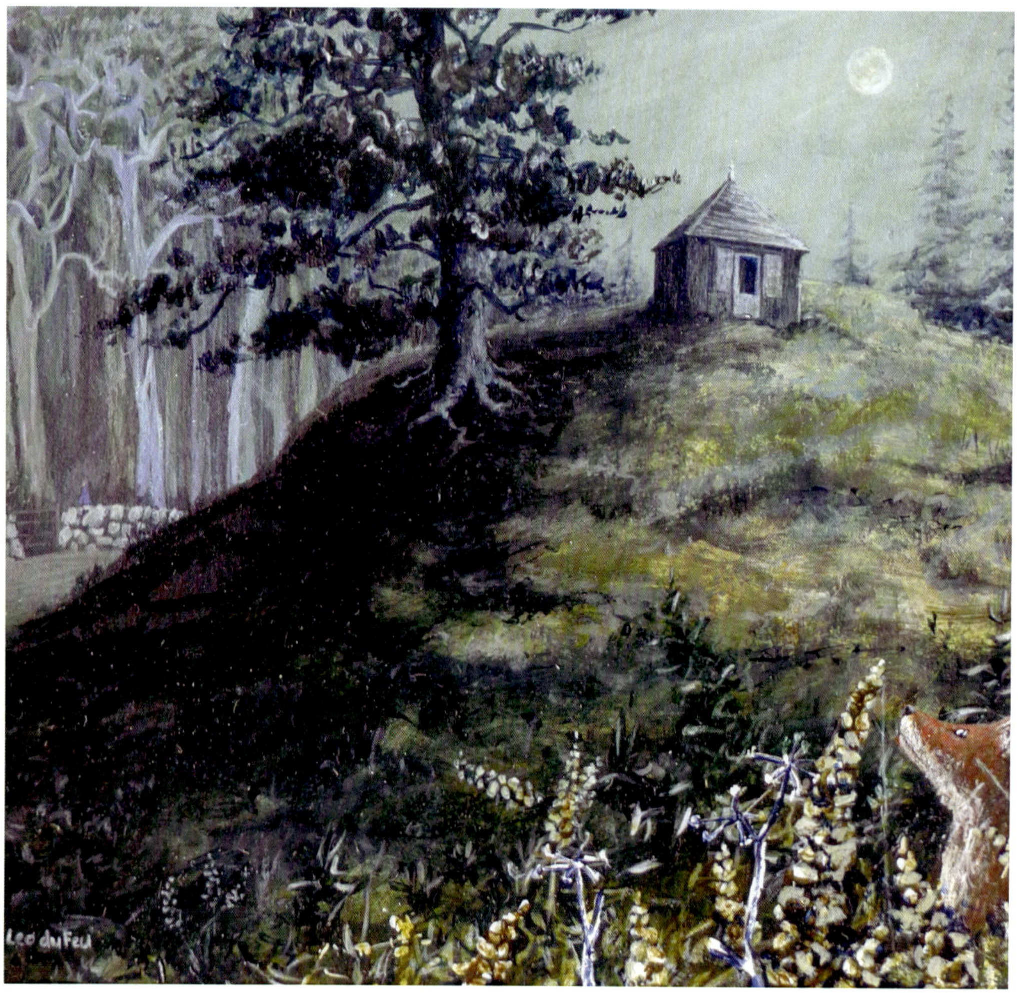

Earthquake House
acrylic
10 x 11cm

Comrie

A quaint Perthshire village, full of character. A collector friend commissioned this painting of Earthquake House; a one-room, slate-roofed building built in the early 1870s to house a seismometer. It still performs its earthquake-measuring function to this day, although with slightly updated equipment.

A circular walk can be made from the centre of Comrie along country lanes to Earthquake House and beyond into grand estate land. Look for red kites as they deftly manoeuvre overhead, twisting deep forked tails. I saw a mixed column of at least 30–40 buzzards and red kites here, circling high over a forest.

Kingussie

Each New Year we go with a big group of friends for a self-catering holiday somewhere in Scotland. Three times now it's been to Kingussie.

Kingussie is a small town in the Cairngorms National Park. It's one rail stop south of Aviemore and has good local shops, instant access to lots of walks and a really friendly celebration on New Year's Eve. You're almost guaranteed to see red squirrels if you go out and look; I spot them when I walk in the early mornings before others are up. The best places seem to be peanut feeders in gardens on the northern slope of the town.

My favourite spots around here are Ruthven Barracks and Insh Marshes RSPB reserve, a mile and two miles south of the town respectively. The reserve is expansive and you probably need a telescope to get detailed views of individual birds but just with binoculars and my bare eyes I've watched waders, gulls, geese and ducks. Buzzards and corvids and wintering small birds are about as you walk along the wooded footpaths.

At the start I said 'holiday', although for me there's usually not much difference between that and 'sketching trip'. I'm nearly always armed with sketchbook and binoculars – I hate to find inspiration but be in a situation where I can't get it down on paper.

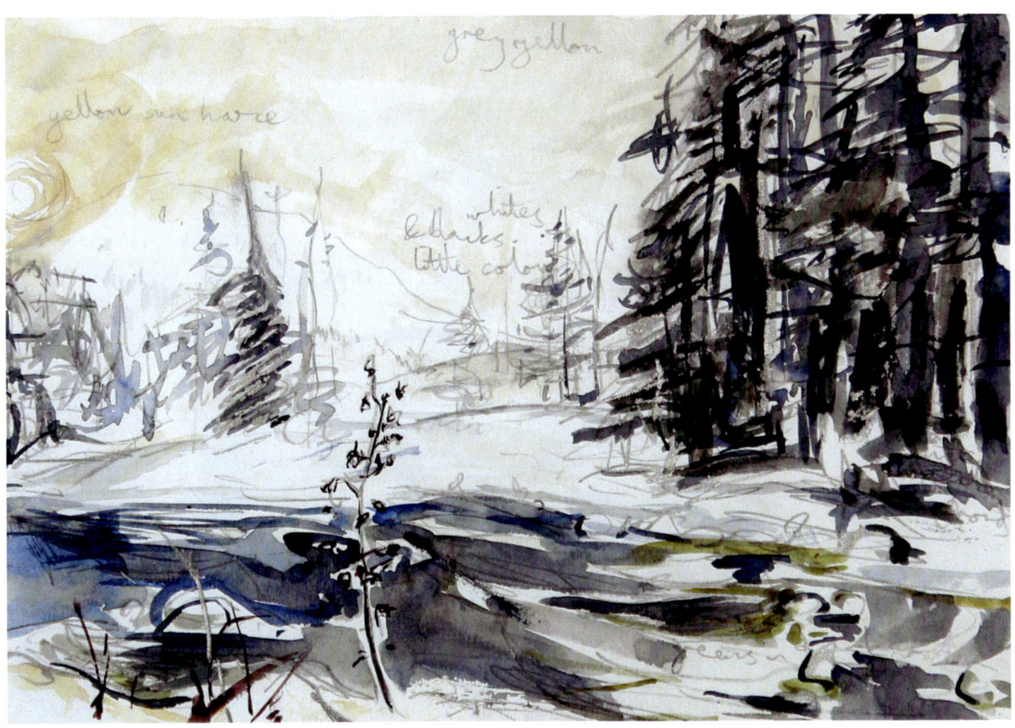

Gynack Burn, snow & sun
pencil & watercolour
19 x 28.5cm

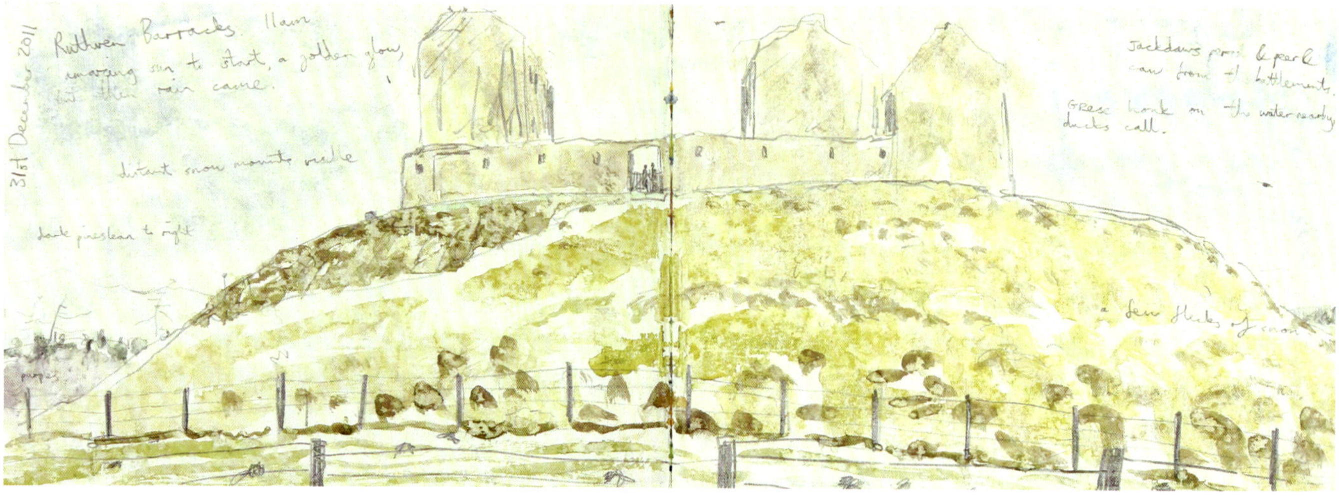
31st December 2011
Ruthven Barracks 11am
amazing sun to start, a golden glow,
but then rain came.
distant snow mounts visible
Jackdaws
a few flecks of snow

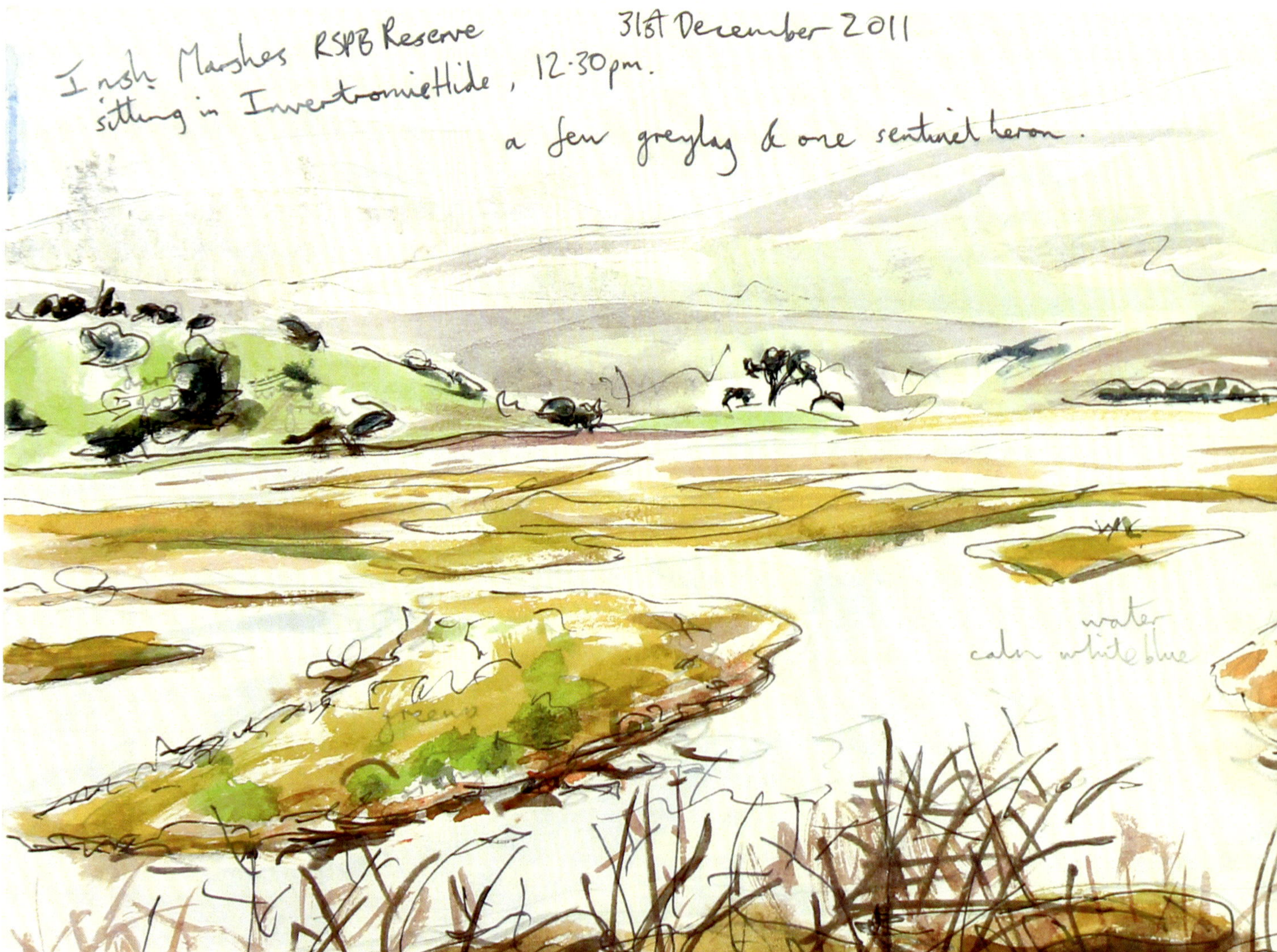
Insh Marshes RSPB Reserve
31st December 2011
sitting in Invertromie Hide, 12:30pm.
a few greylag & one sentinel heron.
water
calm white blue

left: Ruthven Barracks
pencil & watercolour in sketchbook
14.5 x 41cm

below: Insh Marshes RSPB reserve from Invertromie Hide
pen & watercolour in sketchbook
14.5 x 41cm

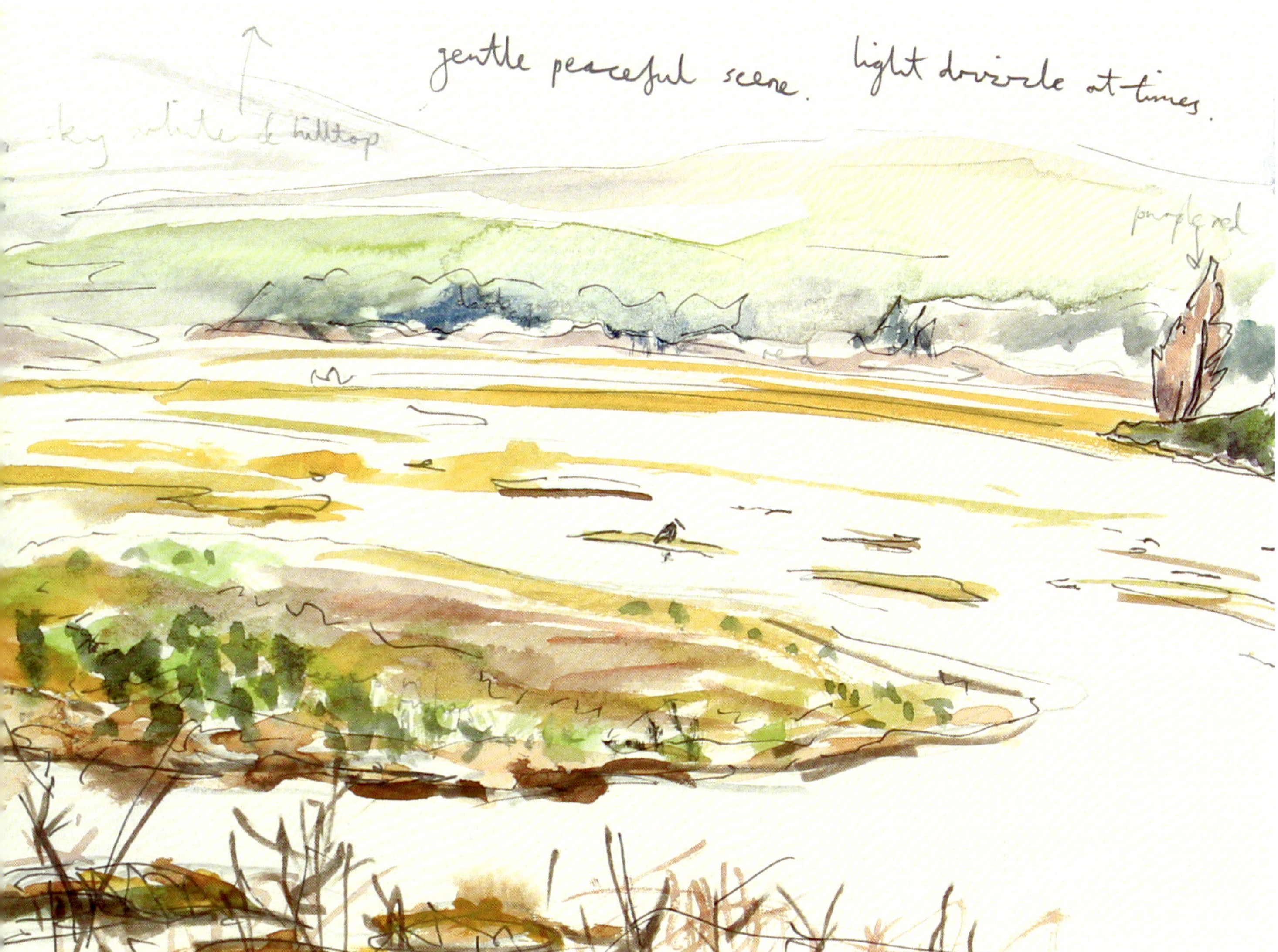

Balvenie Castle

After a night camping below Ben Rinnes near Dufftown, Jennifer and I visited Balvenie Castle. We hadn't slept well: thick tufts of heather underneath and a wind that thrummed on our guy ropes the whole night through. Before bed we'd cooked pasta on an old gas stove and sat looking across the darkened valley; pinpricks of light here and there showed us distant cottages. In the morning we awoke to the strange bubblings and gurglings of grouse on the heathery slopes above.

I was impressed by the mysterious atmosphere of Balvenie Castle and made a ten-minute pencil sketch from which I later created an acrylic painting. An element of fantasy and fairy tale is suggested by a figure in the castle gateway and by dark corvids flocking in the mists above. In the foreground, two crows converse croakily.

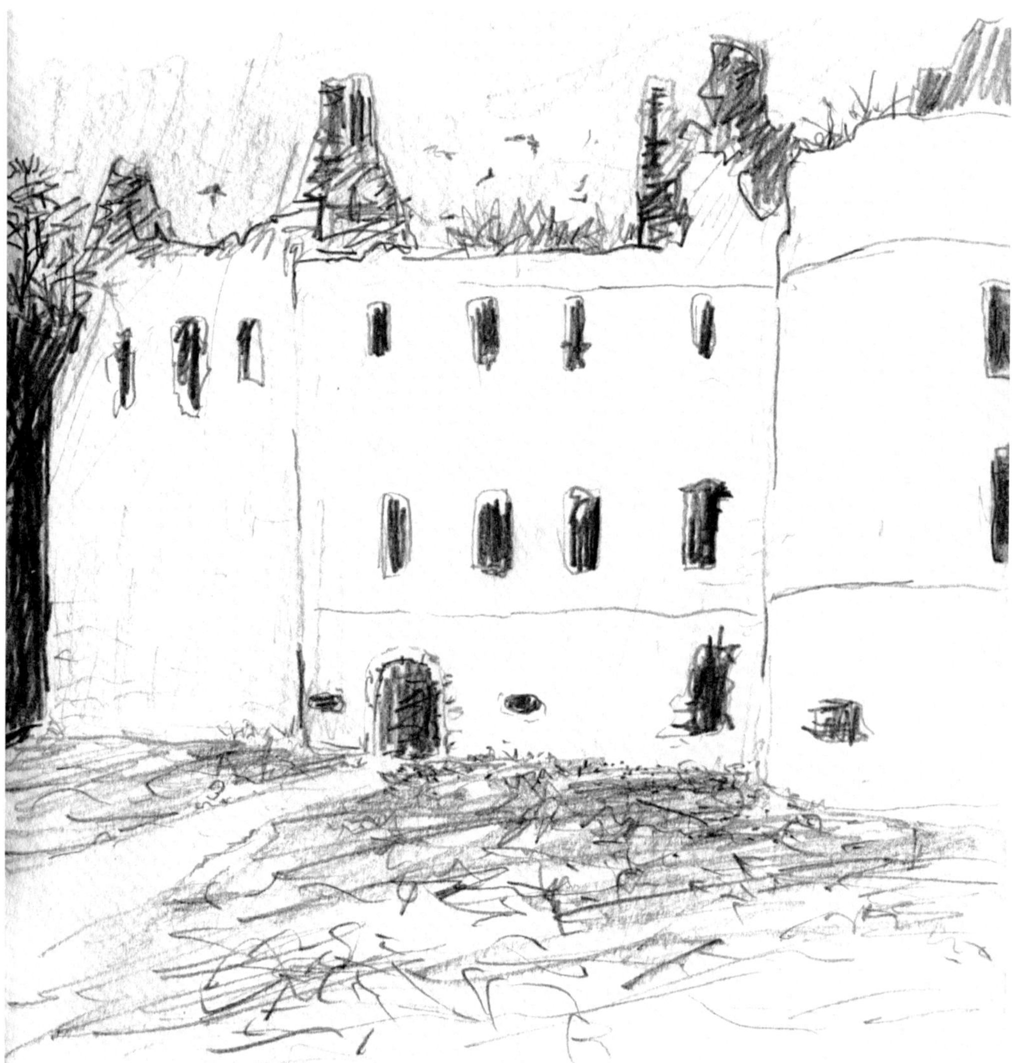

Balvenie Castle
pencil
14 x 13.5cm

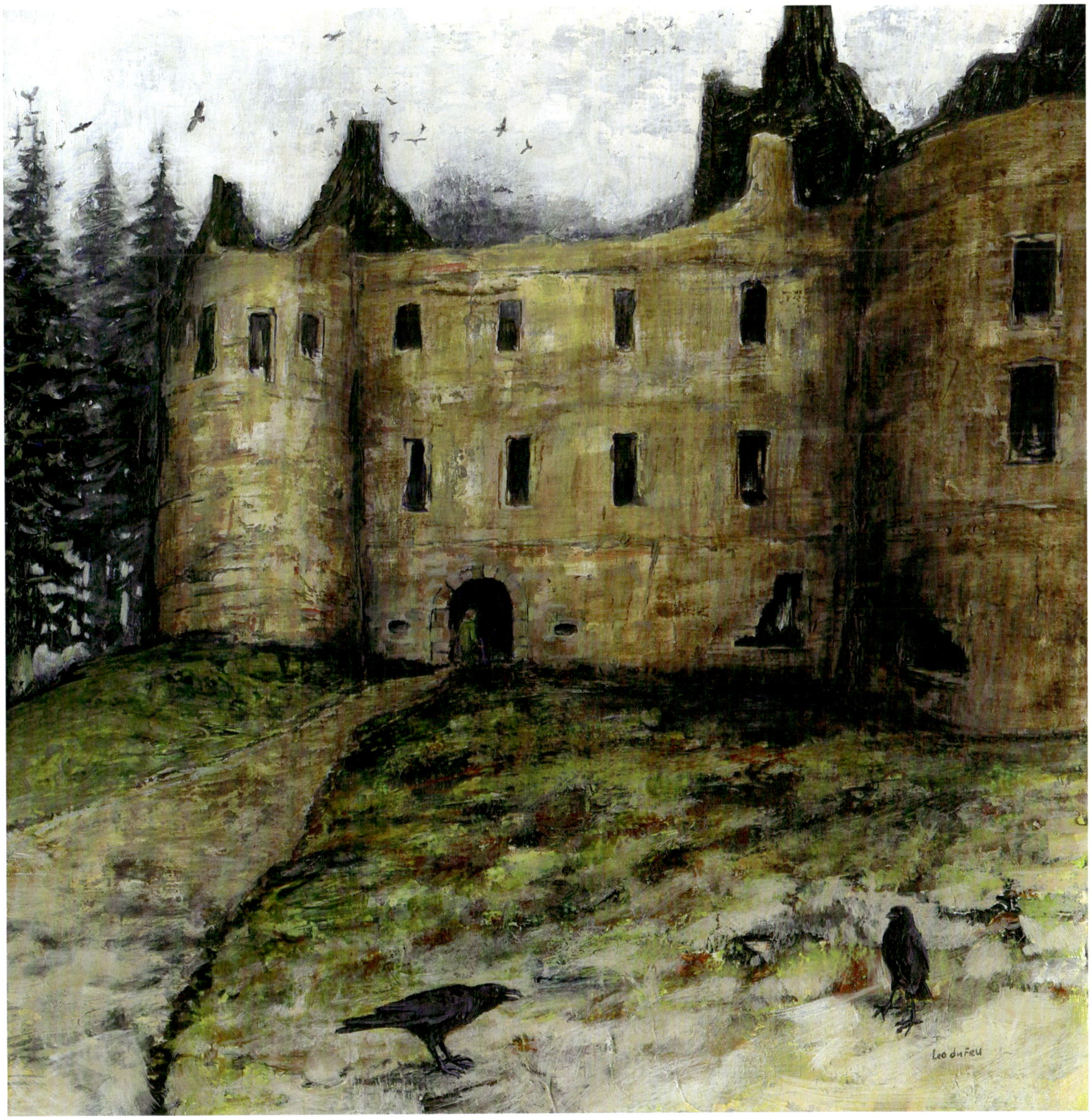

at the castle gate
acrylic
19 x 19cm

Nairn

Towards the Inverness end of the Aberdeen-Inverness railway line is Nairn. I spent three really productive work days travelling to this seaside town from Aberdeen and setting up in the shelter of a well-weathered whitewashed beacon at the harbour entrance.

Across the waters of the Moray Firth I saw high cliffs and farmland beyond. Details such as a lighthouse or a distant ship appeared when I scanned with my binoculars. Two boats were much closer, anchored a few miles out; big red hulking oil tankers that seemed to call out to be included in my sketches. Gannets dived or bobbed on the waves and far off a yellow buoy played island to a succession of shags, cormorants and gulls. Sometimes razorbills or guillemots or a seal would swim to within only a few metres of the sea wall upon which I sat. This area is famous for sightings of dolphins, porpoises, and whales – although I didn't see any.

A beach of white sand stretches east from the town and leads eventually to Culbin Forest; a vast expanse of trees that grow from the dunes, and a must for every 'places-to-explore' list. In late summer and autumn all imaginable colours of fungi grow among the trees. In the heart of Culbin a 65 foot viewing tower built on a 99 foot sand dune gives you views for miles around, high above the forest canopy.

right: gannet, Moray Firth
watercolour & acrylic
20.5 x 14.5cm

below: gannets diving, Moray Firth
pencil
13.5 x 20.5cm

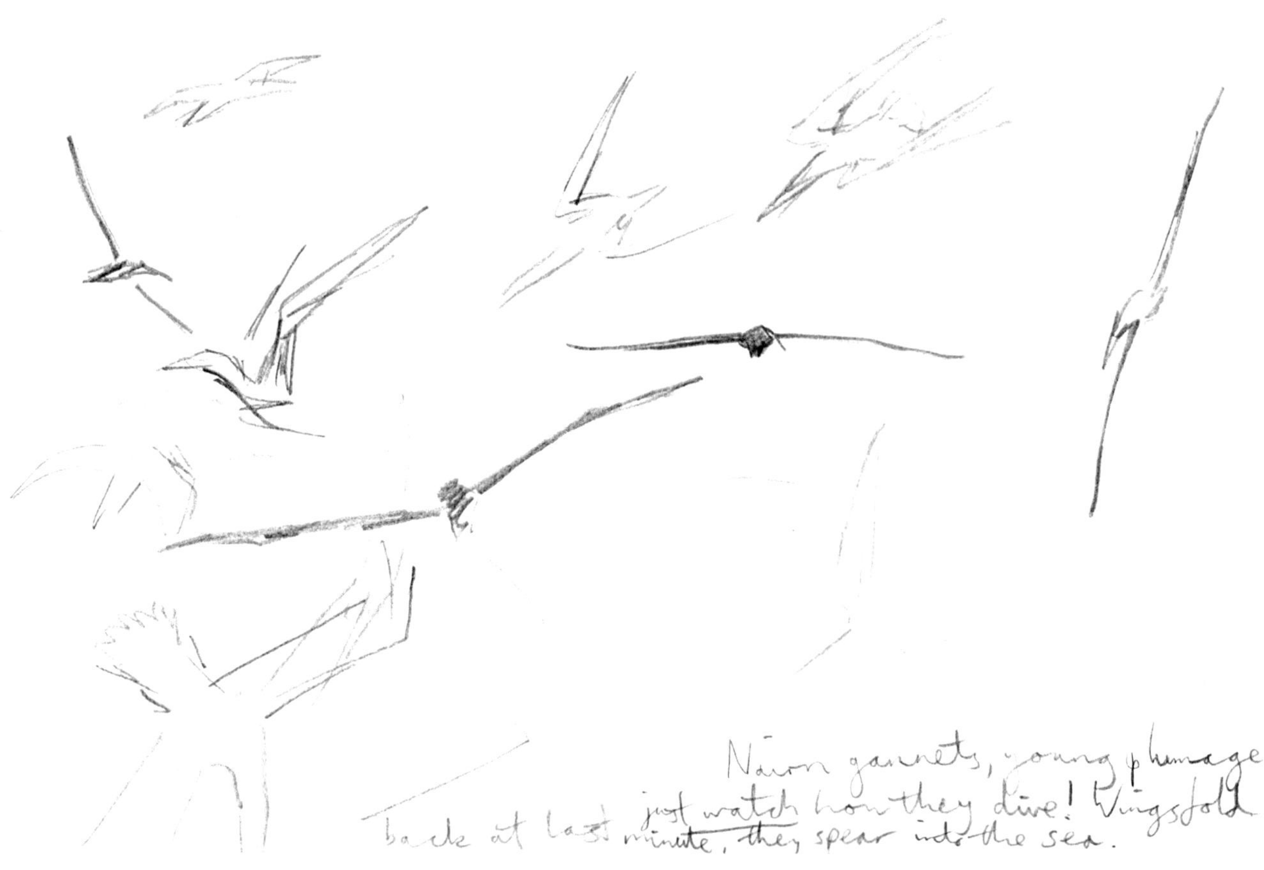

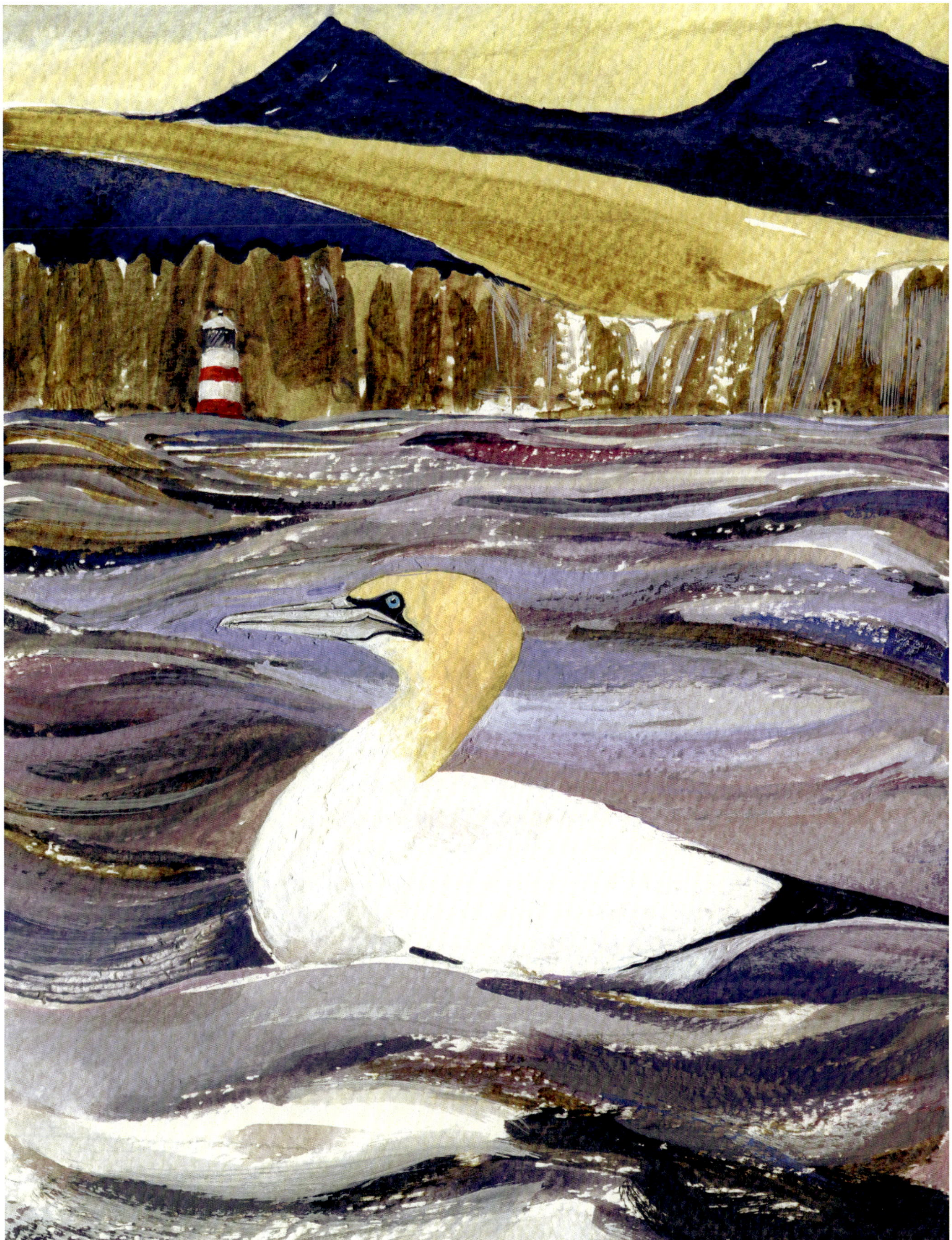

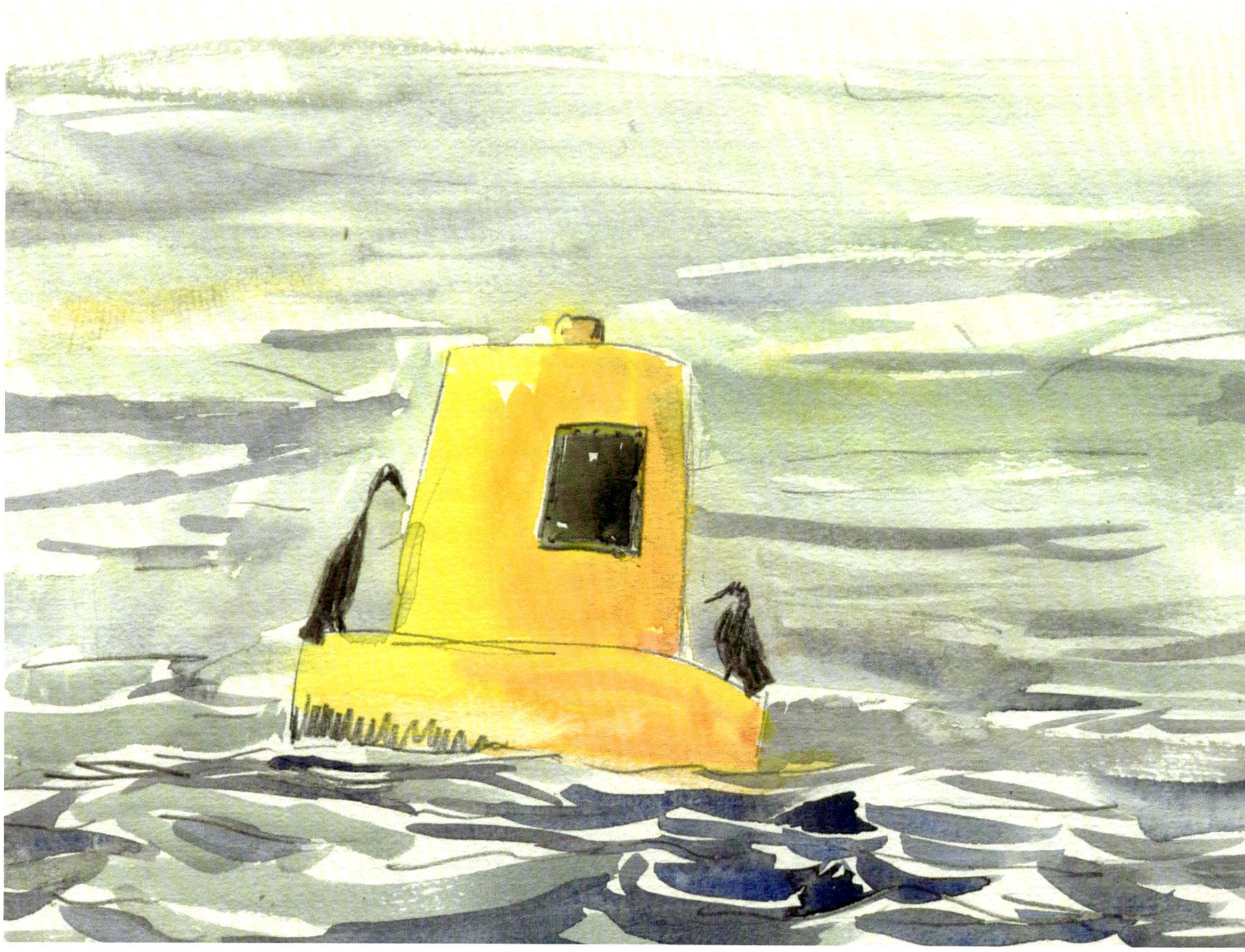

resting seabirds
pencil & watercolour
13.5 x 20.5cm

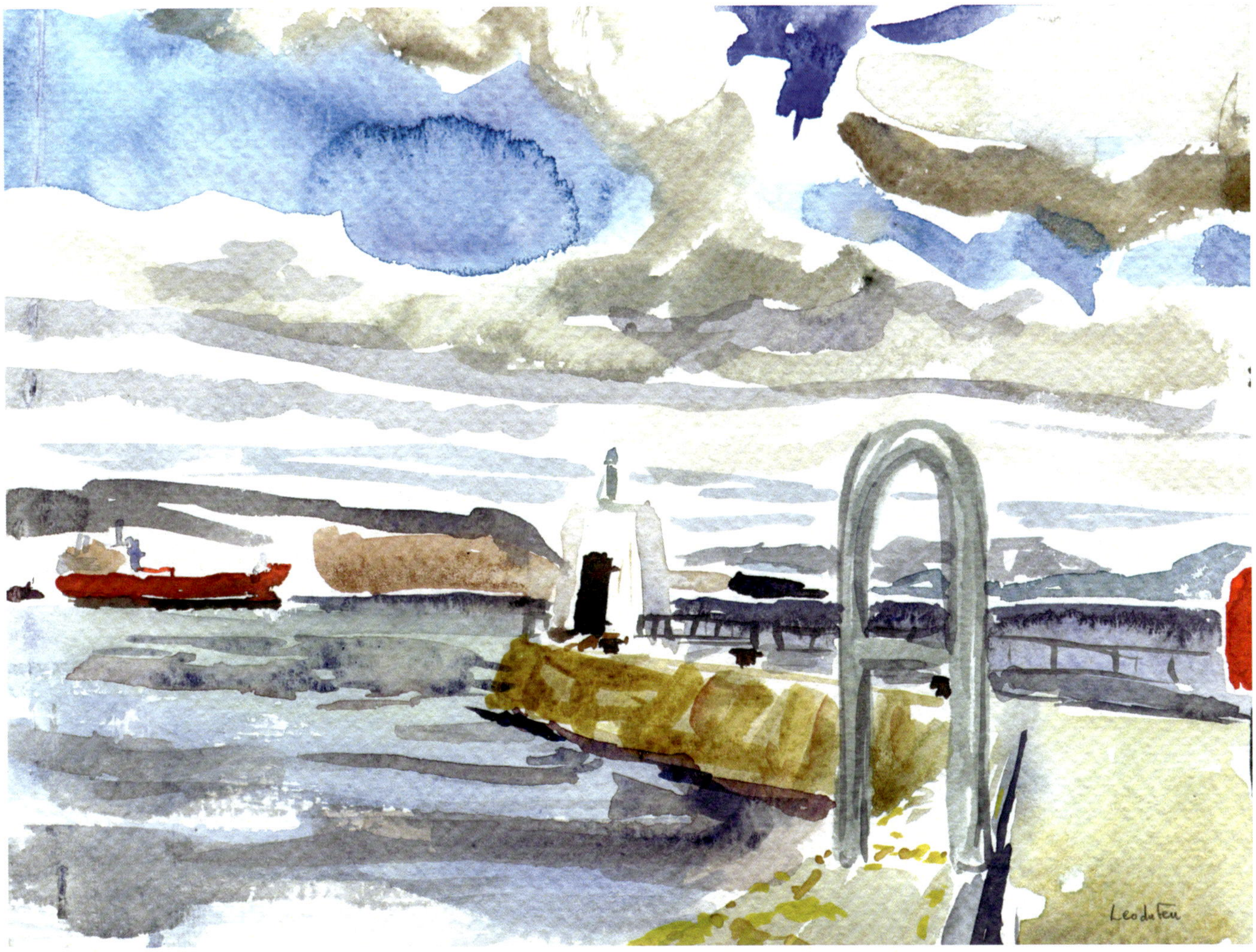

the pier at Nairn
watercolour
13.5 x 19cm

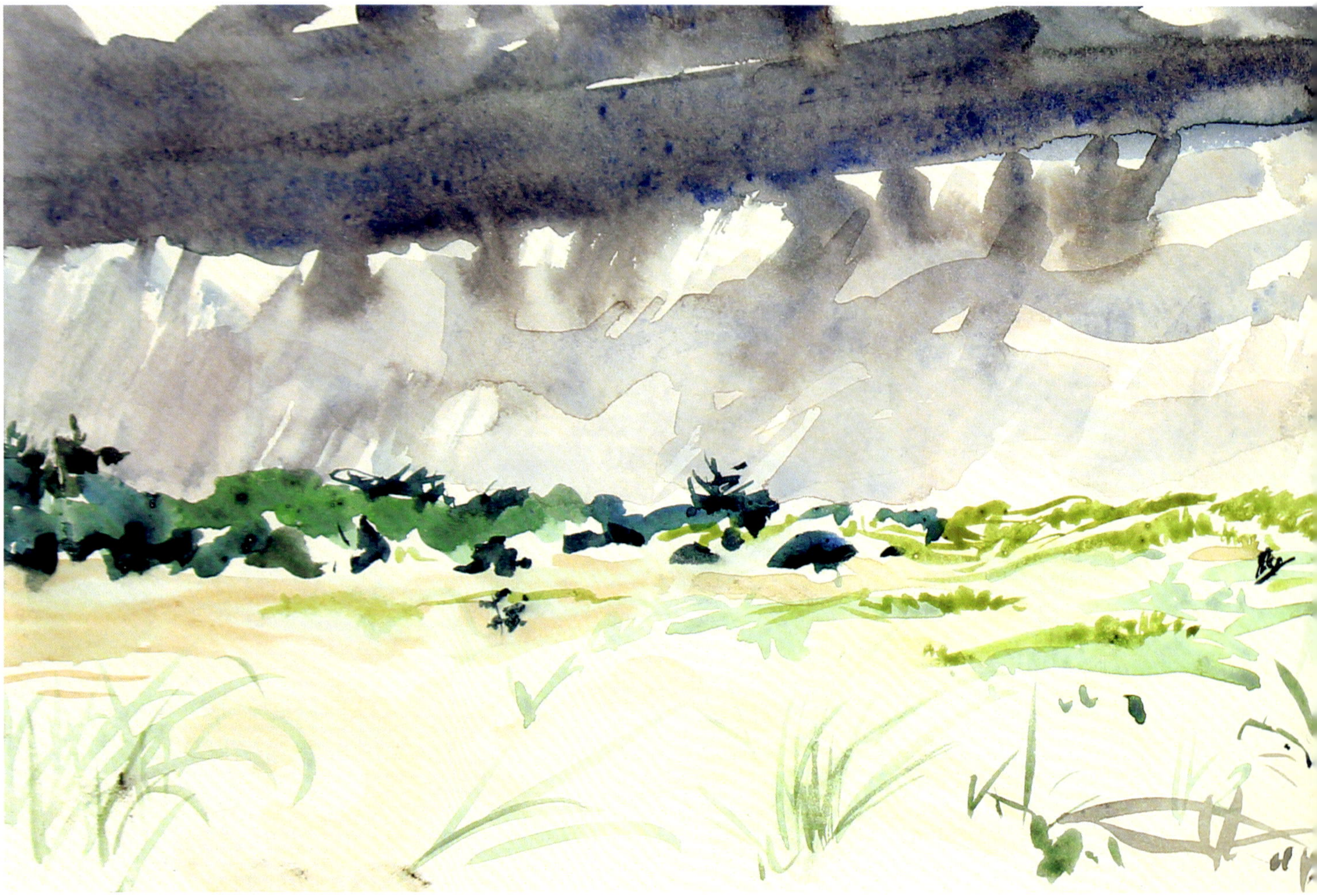

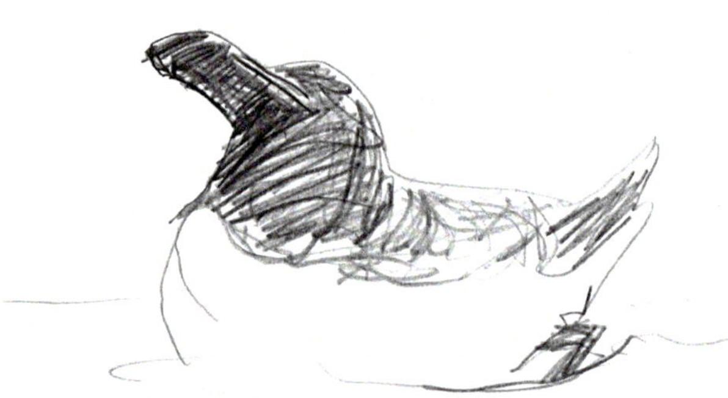

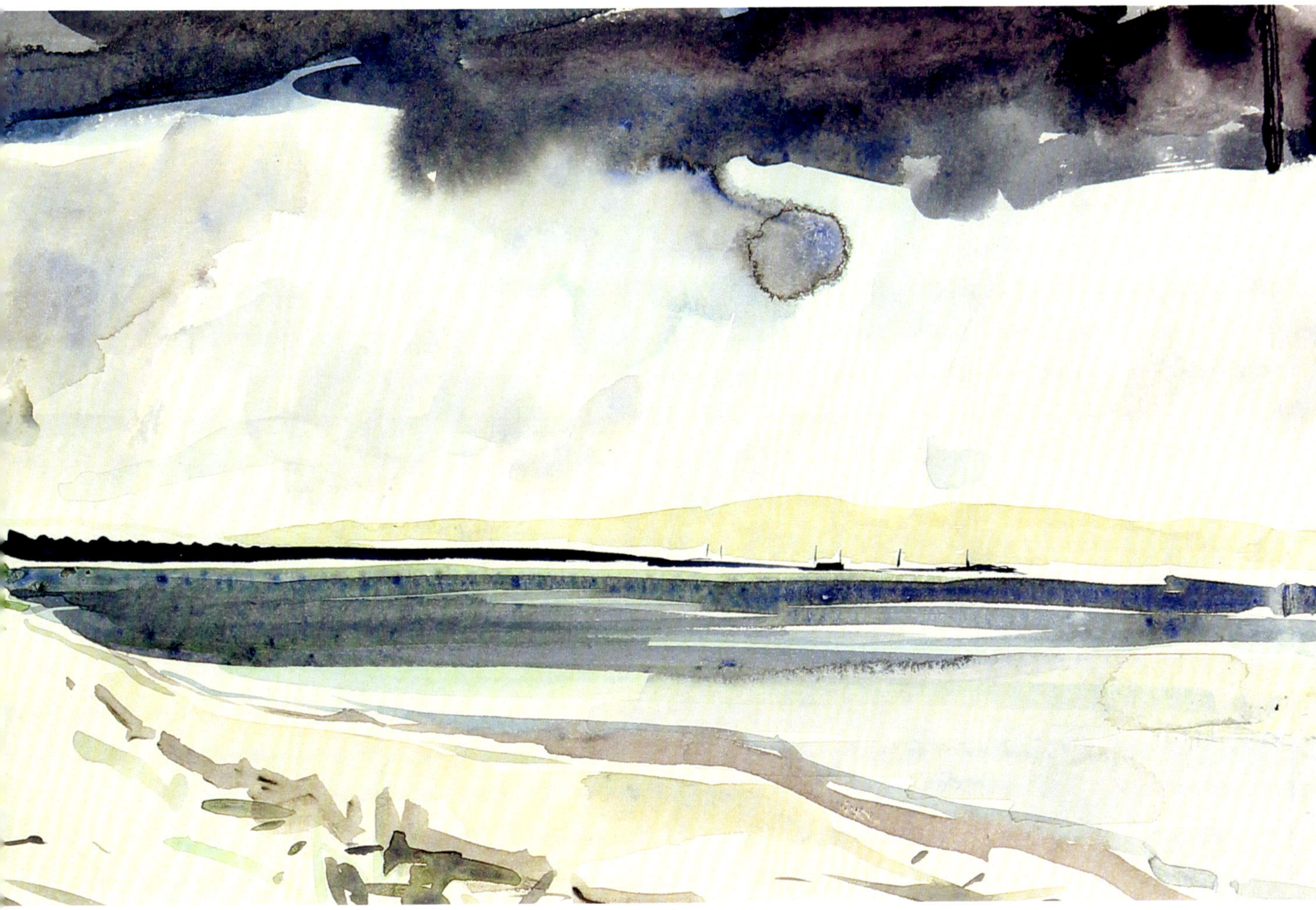

the beach at Culbin
watercolour in sketchbook
13.5x41cm

West Highlands

Loch Lomond

Probably one of the best known Scottish landmarks, thanks in no small part to it having such 'bonnie banks', so here it is. The West Highland Line from Glasgow to Oban, Fort William, and eventually Mallaig, runs the length of the loch. This view is from the same level of elevation as the line. A path guides you from behind Arrochar & Tarbet station through the woods alongside the railway.

I've also painted down on the shore, only metres from the road but hidden. A strong wind was blowing, churning the waters of the loch and numbing my fingers.

below, left: Loch Lomond from the rails
acrylic
9 x 9cm

below, right: Loch Lomond woodland
ink & watercolour
25x35cm

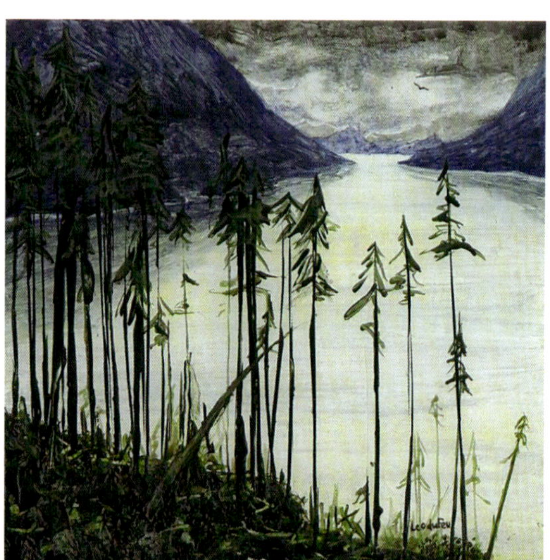

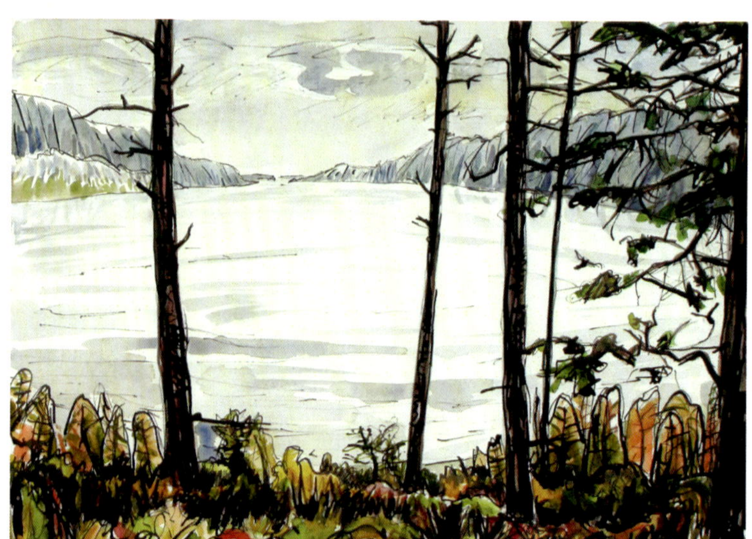

Bridge of Orchy to Tyndrum

A really nice walk can be done between these two station villages on the northbound fork of the West Highland Line. There are options to extend up into hills and valleys north and east of the route but the direct walk is 10–11km and follows the well-surfaced and pedestrianised Old Military Road. A lot of the time you're beside the railway. You get spectacular views of the famous 'horseshoe curve' where the rails sweep in a half loop around the inner slopes of three great hills. Two viaducts carry the track across the wide expanses between each.

In trees at Bridge of Orchy I saw coal tits, great tits, siskins and the orange-red and mustardy green of male and female crossbills. Below the horseshoe curve I sketched by a stream as a dipper chittered its song from a triangle of rock. Five or six goldcrests were in the branches above, squeaking their high-pitched calls. A great spotted woodpecker drummed nearby and right beside me a treecreeper climbed, searching bark for insects. Treecreepers always climb up a trunk, never down. They fly to the base of the next tree and begin their climb again. Often they spiral around the tree as they climb.

I passed a sign on a rusty old gate that read, 'please close gate'. There was no fence on either side, just this gate with its black-on-white lettering.

As I approached Tyndrum at dusk I saw a man in a stream, panning for Highland gold. It does exist here.

approaching the horseshoe curve
ink & watercolour
25 x 35cm

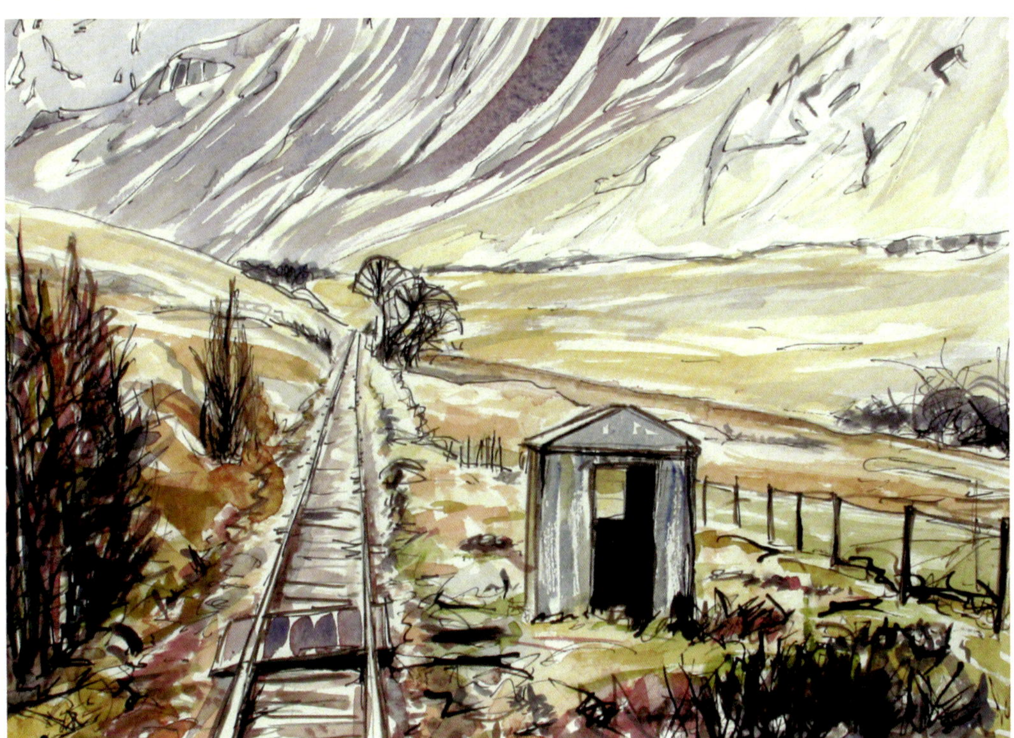

Rannoch Moor

Travelling between Glasgow and Fort William by train you pass over Rannoch Moor. You can alight at Rannoch station, one stop south of Corrour, one north of Bridge of Orchy. Rannoch Moor is wild and remote, a place to go only if you're well prepared to spend the night if caught by unexpected and fast-changing weather. This painting sums up my impressions of the place – two walkers taking shelter in the shadow of a ruin. People used to *live* here.

I have a strong picture in my mind of a scene that I didn't actually witness: my mum and a friend during their Edinburgh College of Art days, rucksacks on their backs as they trudge in wellies across the snow-covered moorland, strong night shadows cast by a clear bright moon.

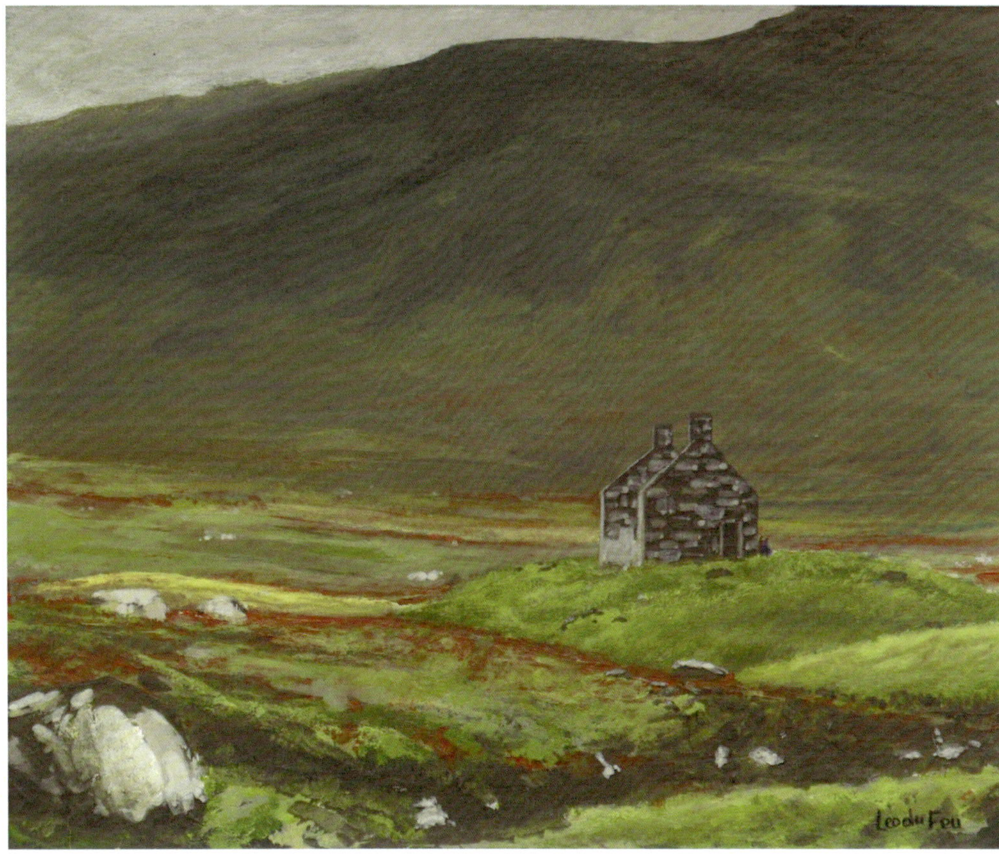

a place to shelter
acrylic
14 x 18cm

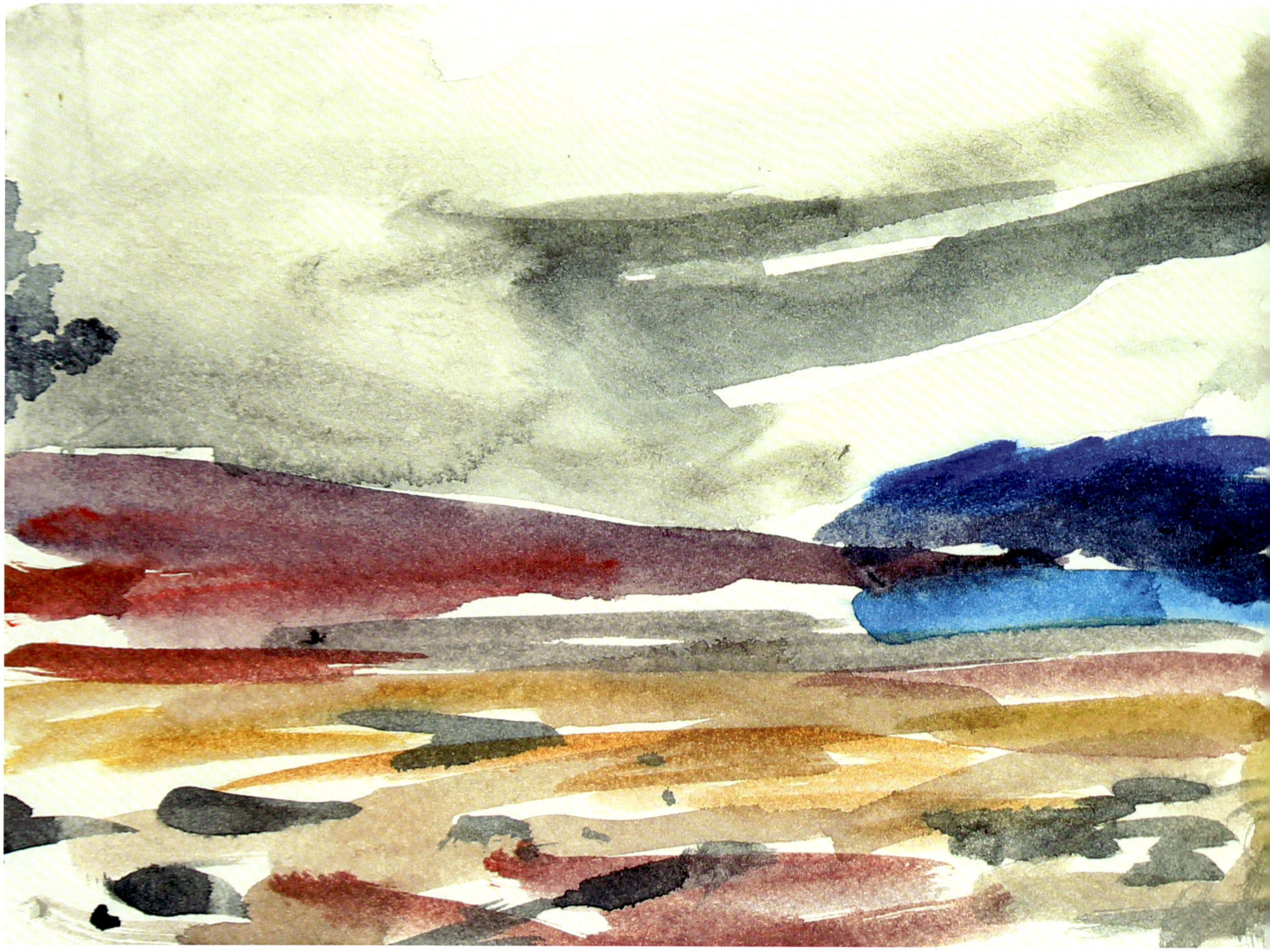

Loch Ossian

I spent a few days here thanks to sponsorship from the Scottish Youth Hostels Association (SYHA). Friends Kittie and Paul were with me but Jennifer was taking part in a research trip, experiencing life on the choppy seas around Scotland.

Loch Ossian is one of the most remote hostels in the country, reached only by walking in from the hills or by train to Corrour station then a mile walk to the loch. It's an eco-hostel; you take all your supplies in with you and you remove all rubbish at the end. It has reed bed filtration and its own mini wind turbine. There are no showers but that doesn't seem to matter when you're in such wonderful surroundings.

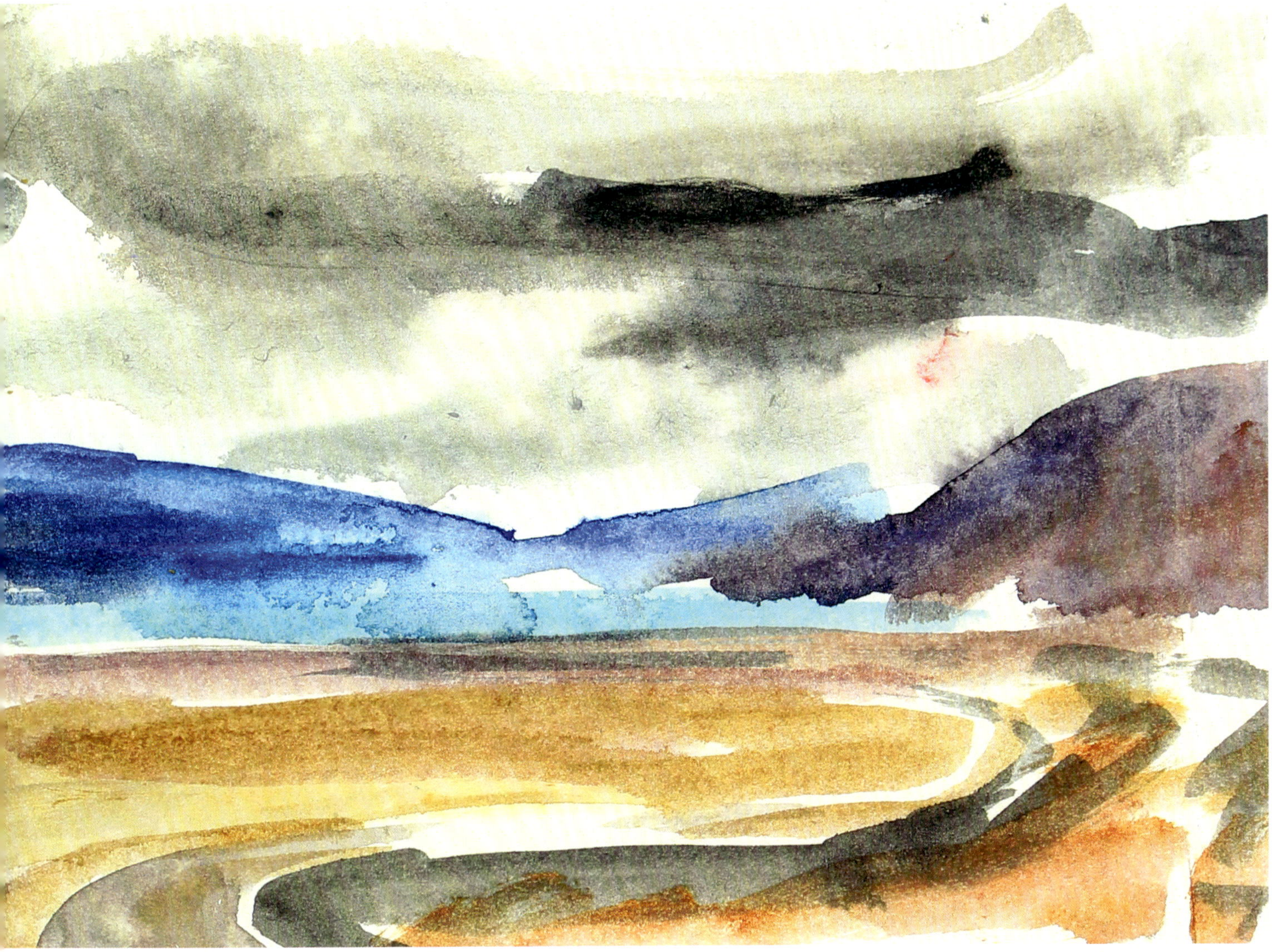

at a ruin by the River Ossian
watercolour in sketchbook
14.5 x 41cm

Stepping out of the hostel you're immediately out there, in the wild, on the shore of a misty highland loch. I saw my first golden eagle soar over a valley here and realised that possible golden eagles in the past were definitely just buzzards; a golden eagle is so much bigger, its wingspan is over two metres, nearly seven feet. It shows.

On Loch Ossian itself was a black-throated diver. Once, already flying fairly high above the water, it began an upwards clockwise curve, circling higher and higher until no more than a white-black cross shimmering against the summer sky. Another time we watched it on the water and could distinctly make out its highly contrasting lines and streaks of pure white and pure black; its black dagger beak, its light charcoal head.

Loch Awe

Loch Awe is only 40 minutes by train from Oban, or two and a half hours from Glasgow. From the station you can get really quickly up into the hills.

I spent my first half hour on a little disused jetty below the station. A raven was in a ragged pine above as I sketched the ruins of Kilchurn Castle and its mountainous backdrop. Across the loch flew ones and twos of honking geese and one solitary cormorant. Chaffinches, tits, house sparrows and goldcrests were in the trees as I walked south-west along the village road. After a kilometre is St Conan's Kirk, a fascinating amalgamation of architecture, only completed in 1930 and eccentrically adorned with all sorts of carvings and gargoyles. Try to make time to look around inside.

Immediately beyond the church is a small barriered road on the right that leads to Cruachan Dam. I loved it up there; a man-made loch lurking darkly in a half-bowl of green hills. In a full day and wearing the right clothing you can continue beyond the dam to the summit of Ben Cruachan.

Cruachan Dam
watercolour & acrylic in sketchbook
14.5 x 41cm

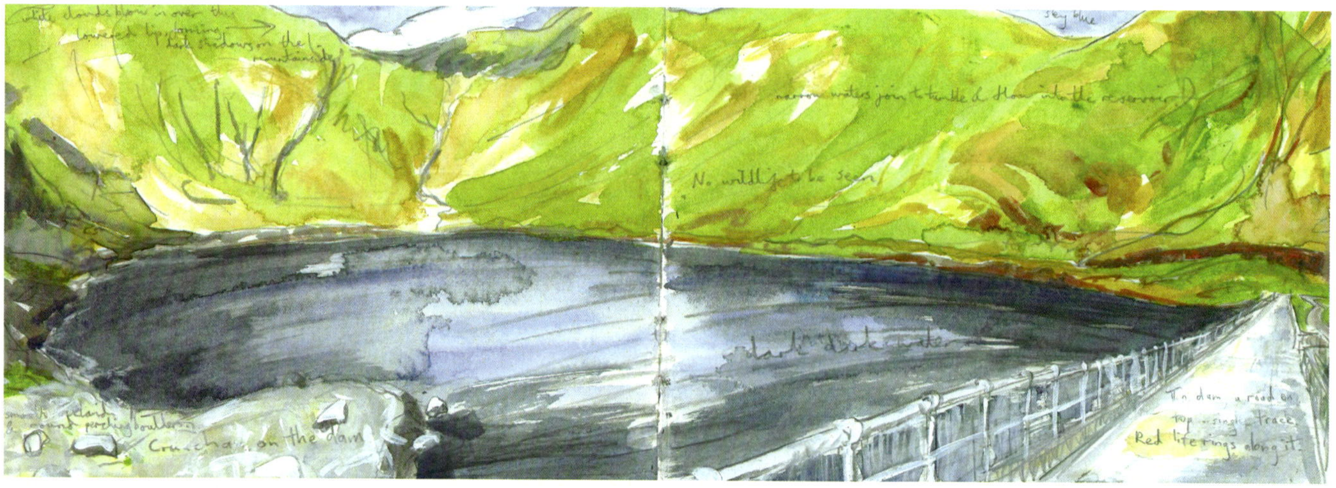

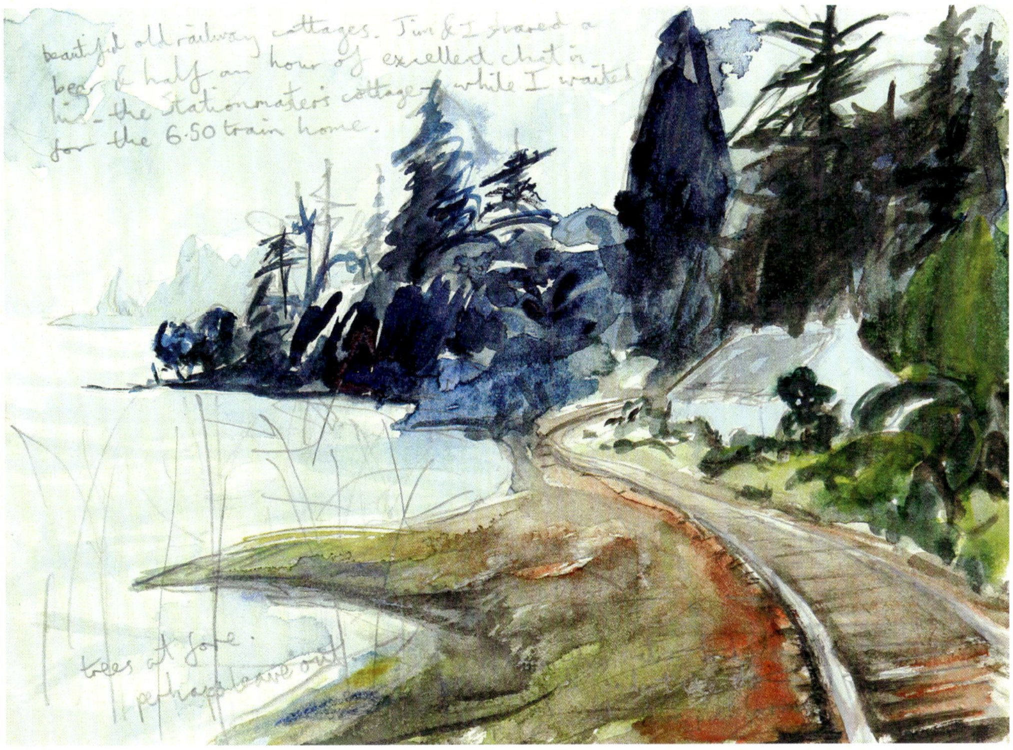

old station buildings, Loch Awe
watercolour in sketchbook
14.5 x 20.5cm

Back at the station I stood on the footbridge and drew the curve of the rails as they sweep towards a row of old railway cottages. Half an hour earlier I shared a beer and conversation there with resident Jim. Jim cares for several local stations under ScotRail's Adopt A Station scheme. Station adopters do all sorts; weeding, planting, general tidying. Across the country people have opened station bookshops, hostels, cafés, galleries and more.

Ardnamurchan

The Ardnamurchan peninsula on Scotland's west coast has it all – sea and sky, beaches and cliffs, moorland and woodland and mountains. I holidayed here with my brother Roan, and Kittie and Paul, back when I was just beginning to get more interested in birds.

I loved Mingary Castle that sits silent and deserted a little way from Kilchoan village; thrift and lichens (and midgies!) on the shore. On the day of climbing Ben Hiant we found a dry-stone enclosure housing ancient graves down by the sea. Up on the slopes we got close to a herd of 30–40 deer and back in the valley we spotted something else: three of us decided golden eagle, one decided buzzard ...

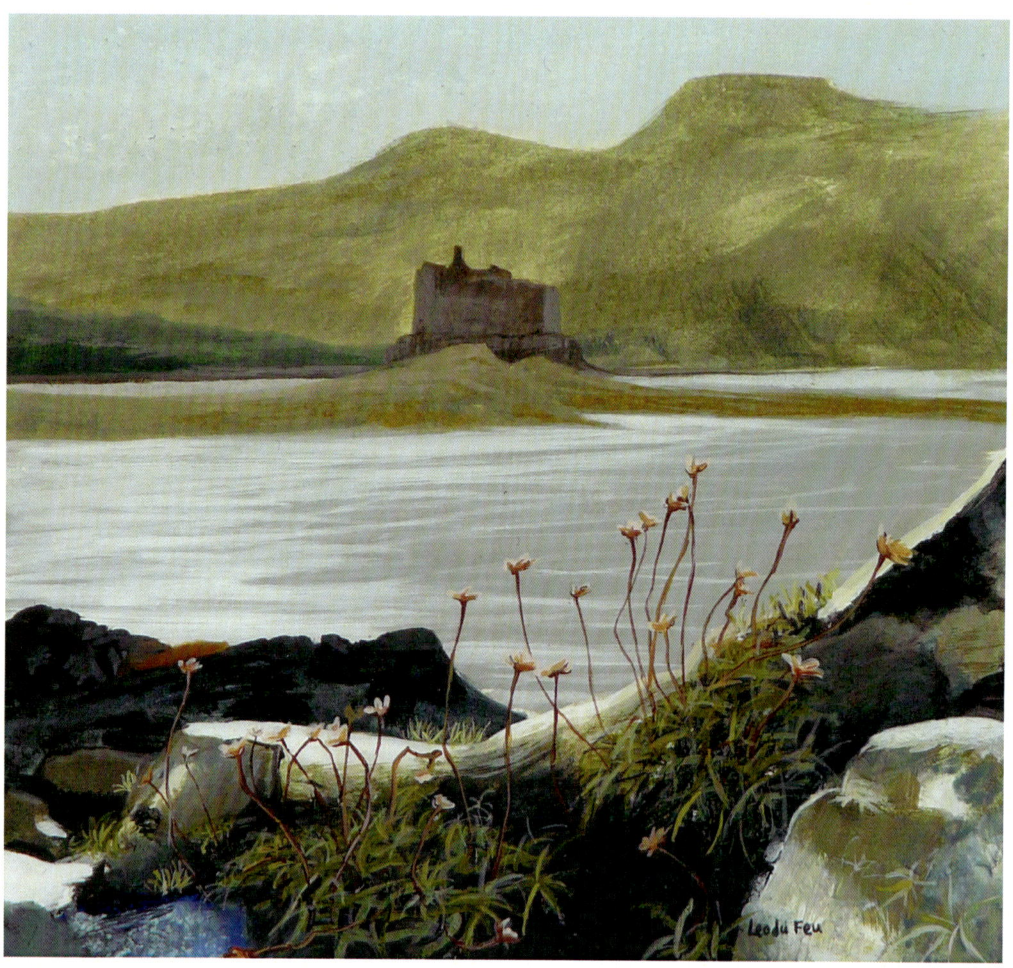

Mingary Castle, wind-blown thrift
acrylic
10 x 11cm

overgrown graves below
Torr na Moine
coloured pencil
26 x 29cm

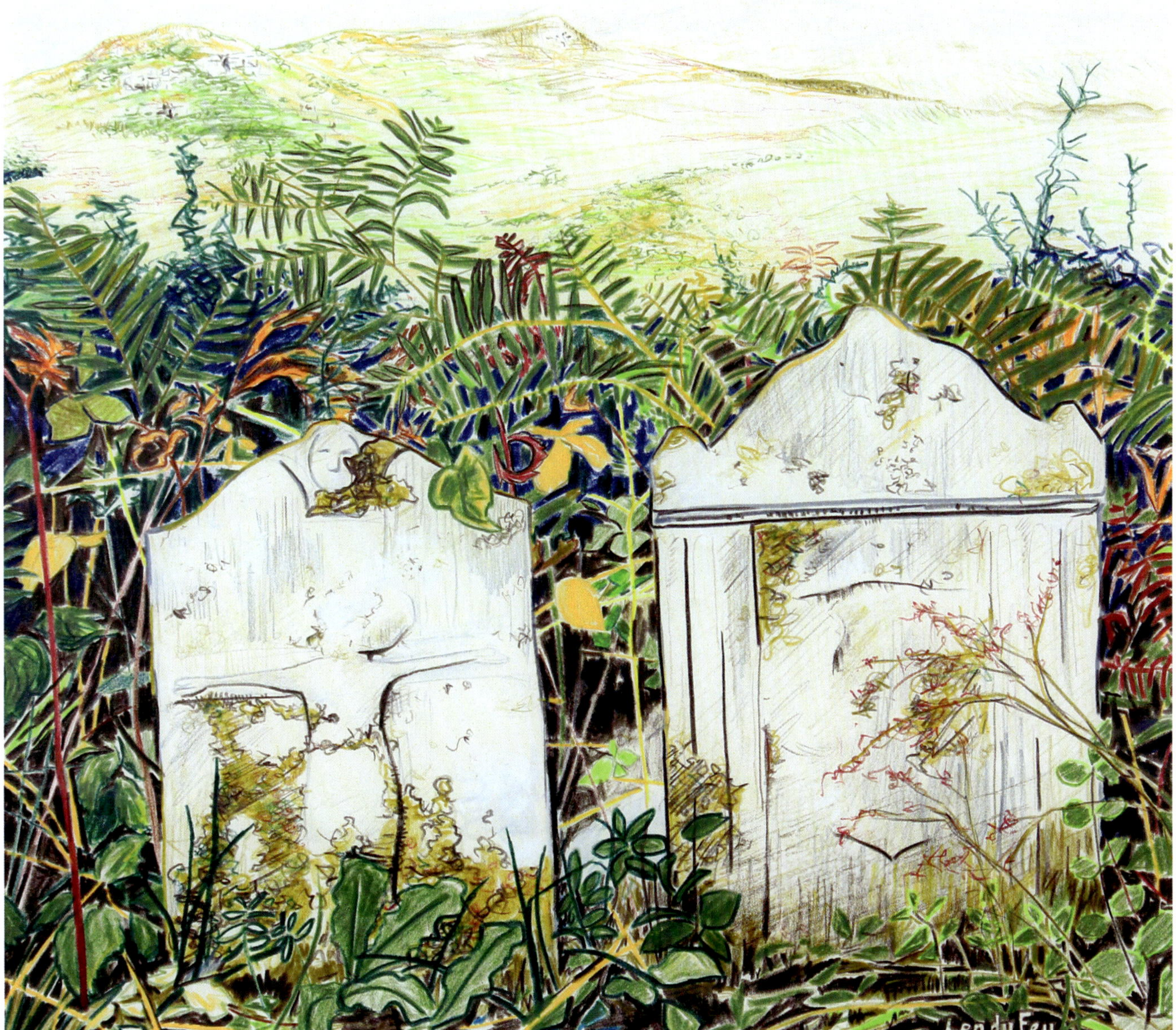

At Sanna Bay the sun burned a small patch of bright through the murky sky and a hare bounded across the white sand beach; exploring rock pools east of Sanna we happened upon a tall narrow slit in a cliff – marked on the map as Glendrian Caves. Inside it opens into quite a substantial space. Lights from our mobile phones and a pocket torch showed carved names and gem-like droplets of water that hung from the walls.

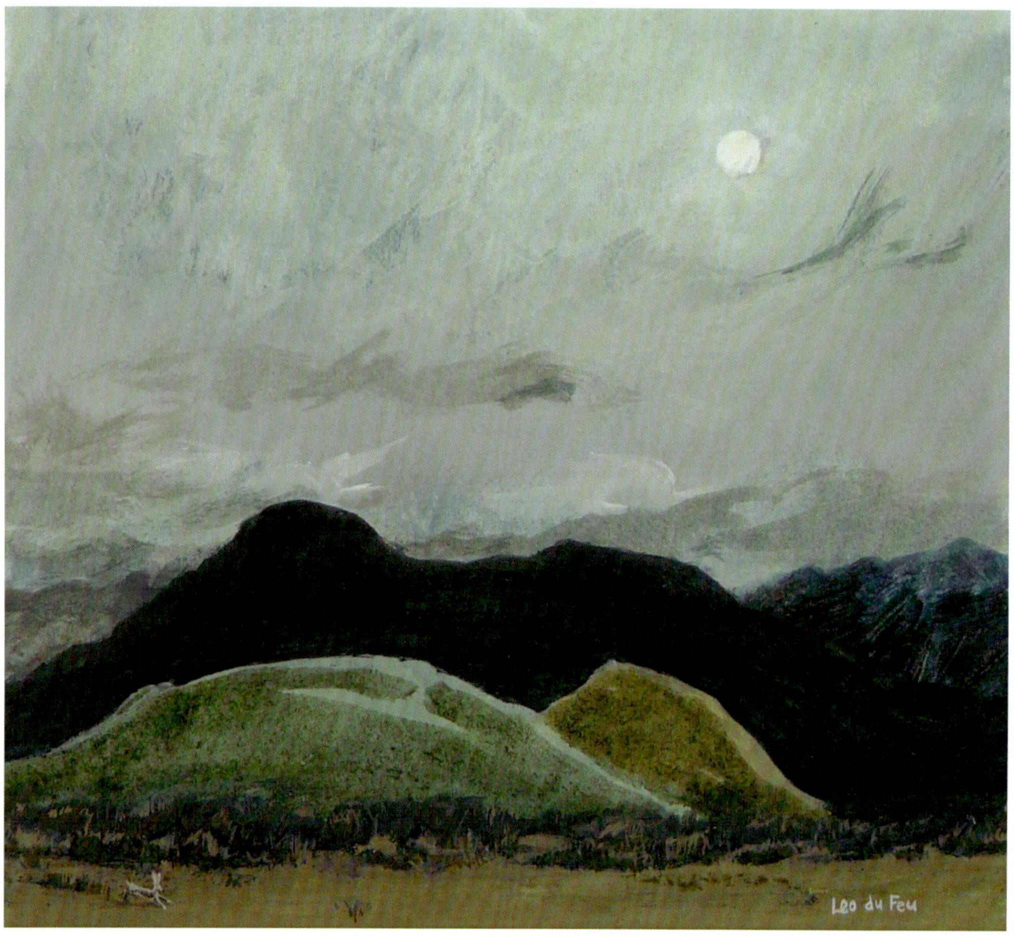

view south with hare,
from Sanna Bay
acrylic
10 x 11cm

deserted cottage at Sanna
acrylic
10 x 11cm

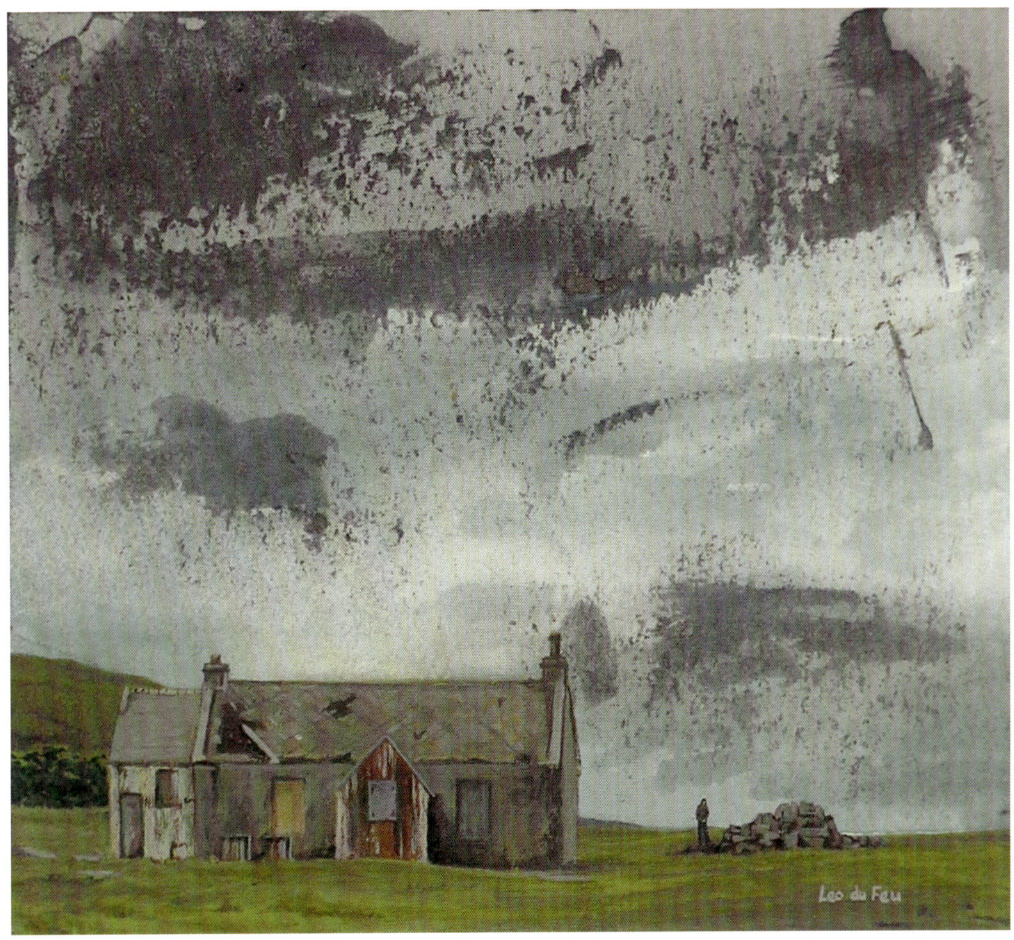

Ullapool

On a 2008 tutoring trip I had a night to spend in Ullapool before catching the morning ferry to Lewis. I loved the look of this dishevelled building on the pier; enticing hills were behind and gulls flocked all around. Look for a lesser black-backed gull floating on the water.

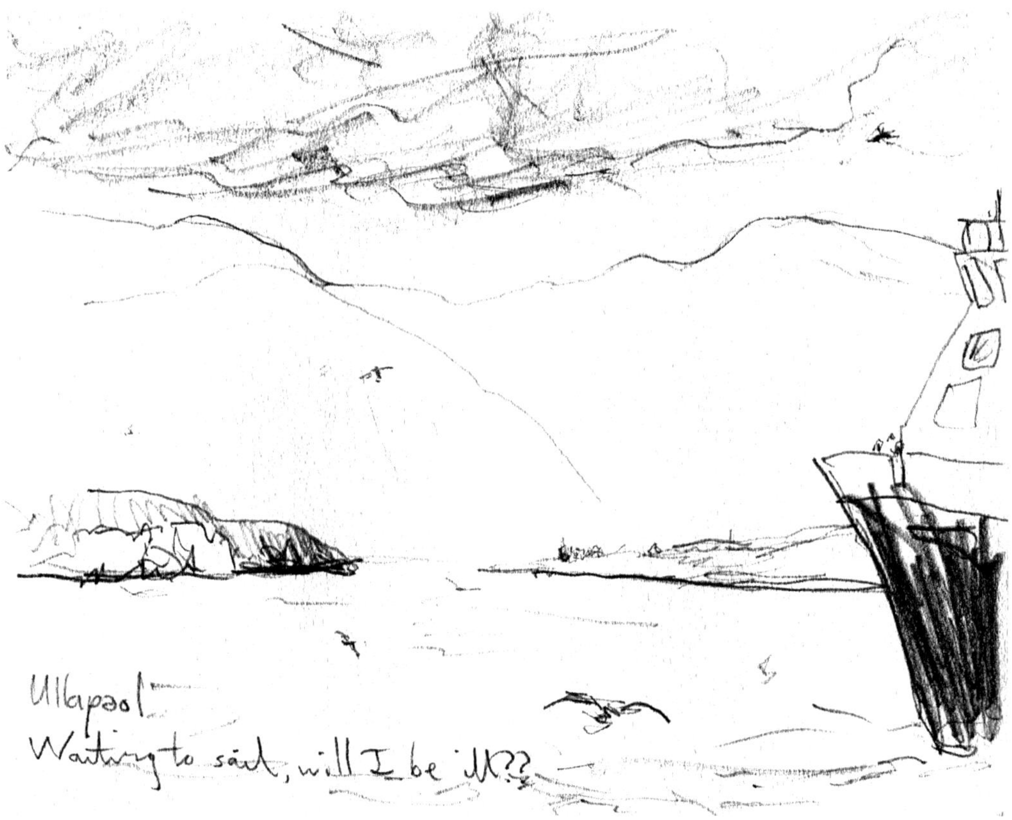

Ullapool ferry
pencil
10.5 x 13cm

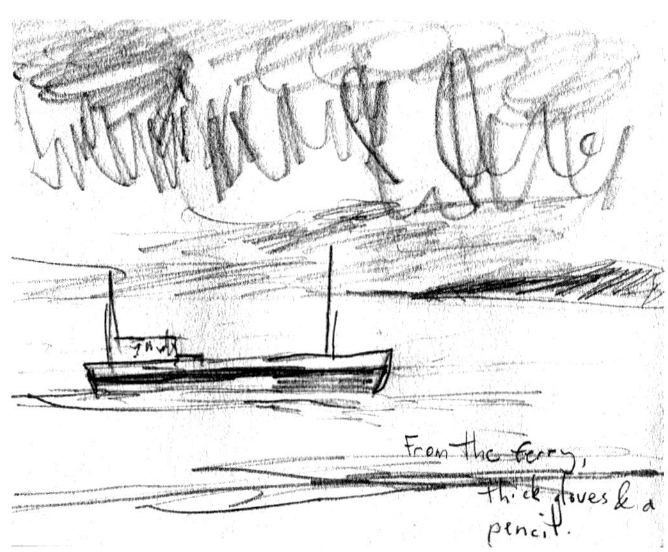

sketching from the ferry
pencil
10.5 x 13cm

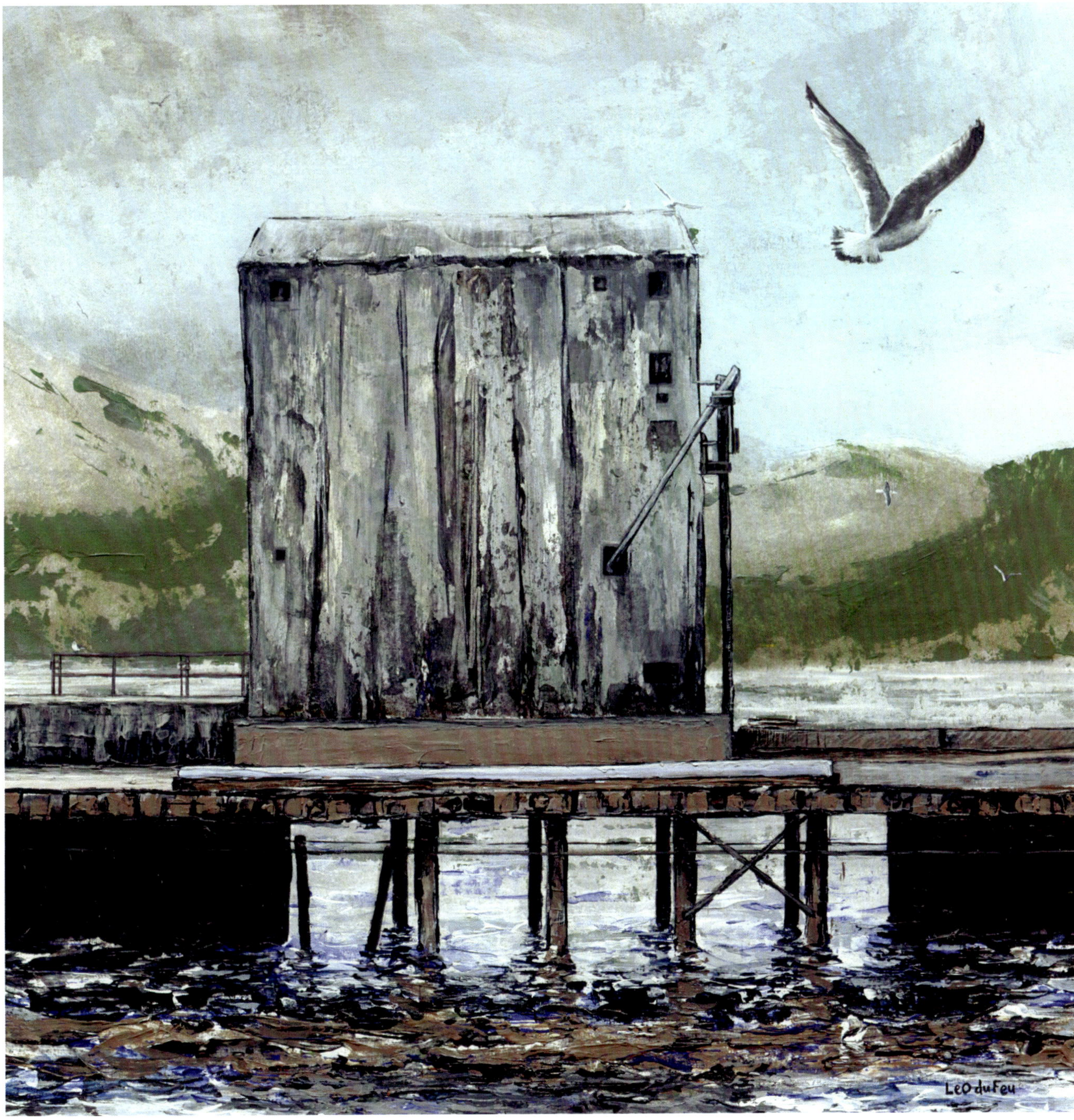

the pier
acrylic
15.5 x 15.5cm

Islands – a chronological account

When I think of Scotland it's the islands that excite me most of all. I hope in time to get to know many more of them.

Rum and Jura

The first island trip I remember was with friends and family in my late school years. We went to Rum in the Inner Hebrides and stayed in hostel accommodation in Kinloch Castle. We walked the width of the island in torrential rain and saw deer through the wet haze. During an afternoon indoors, I sketched the balconies, stags' heads and other ornamentations of the grand hall. The rest of the group played cards and we all chatted; we were even allowed to play the Steinway grand piano. I learned to juggle in our dormitory bedroom.

island lighthouse
pencil

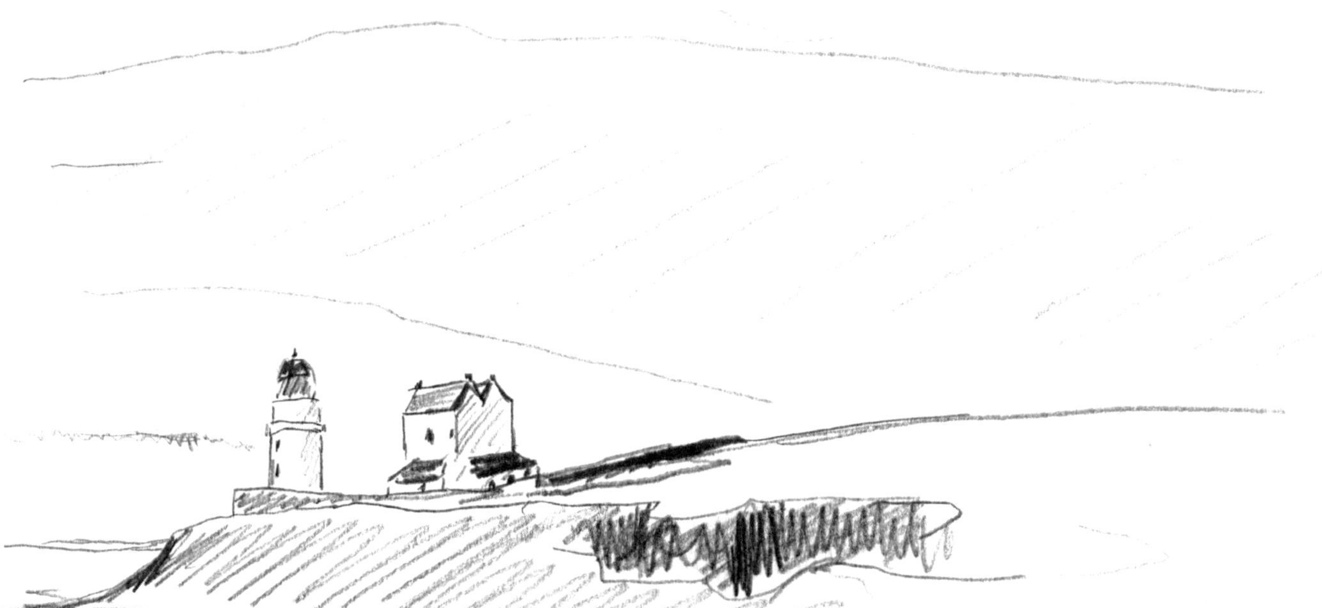

island horizon
pen

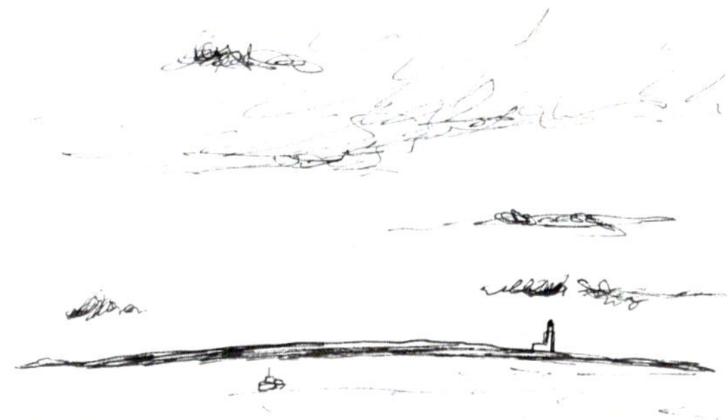

My second island visit was during college days, to Jura, where we stayed in Barnhill farmhouse at the remote north end. Eric Blair (George Orwell) came to this very house in the second half of the 1940s to finish writing his novel *Nineteen Eighty-Four*. Again we walked through rain, as heavy as any I've been in. Once soaked absolutely to the skin we stopped minding and starting jumping: we found puddles that splashed right up above our heads. Back indoors, with an open fire burning, I used an old mirror to paint a rare self-portrait and worked on views of coast and moor as seen through the windows.

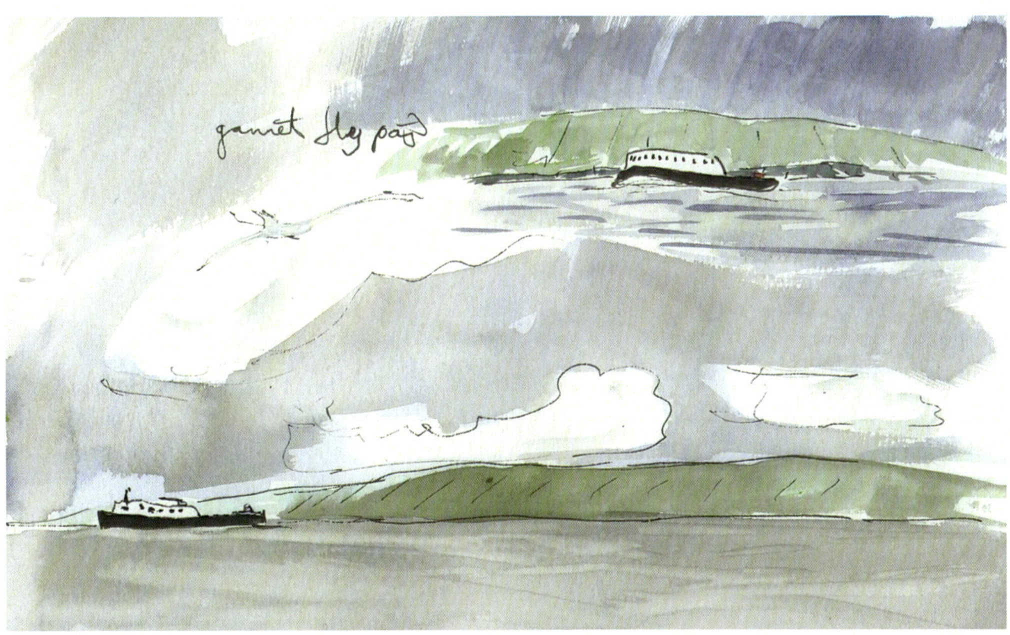

boat sketches
pen & watercolour

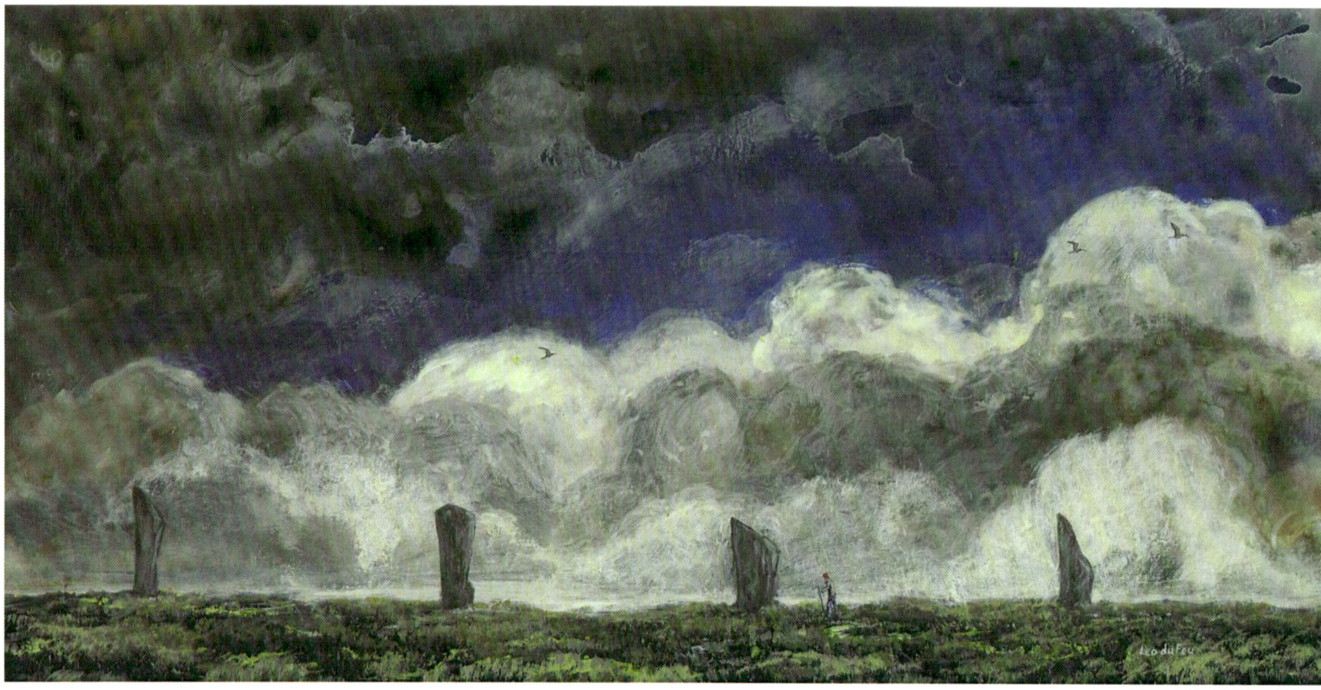

Orkney

Brodgar stones, figure walking, curlews flying
acrylic
11 x 22cm

Orkney was next, a couple of years after college and thanks to my travel scholarship from the RSW. Jennifer and I stayed in a hostel in Stromness and in a self-catering cottage at the Bay of Skaill. We spent a day on the island of Hoy in perfect summer weather; whilst cycling to Rackwick Bay from the ferry, we stopped to visit a huge angular red sandstone boulder that sits alone on the valley floor. The two person-sized chambers carved inside the Dwarfie Stane are around 5,000 years old, and were excavated using nothing but stone or antler or bone. Sounds from outside soften in there and you feel you could be anywhere, any time. Two musicians appeared as we were there; they'd come to sing inside the stone to test its resonance.

boat studies
biro pen

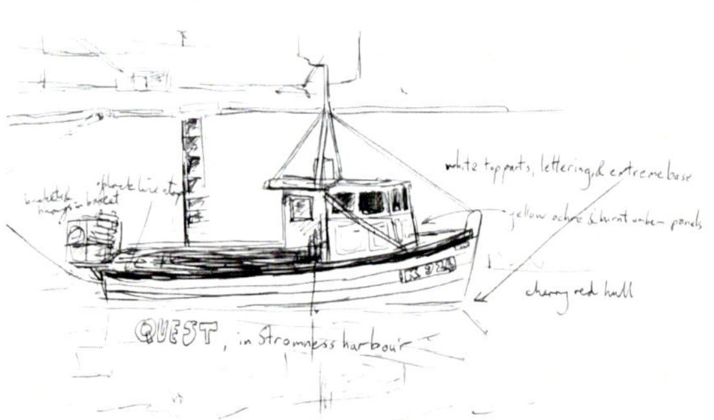

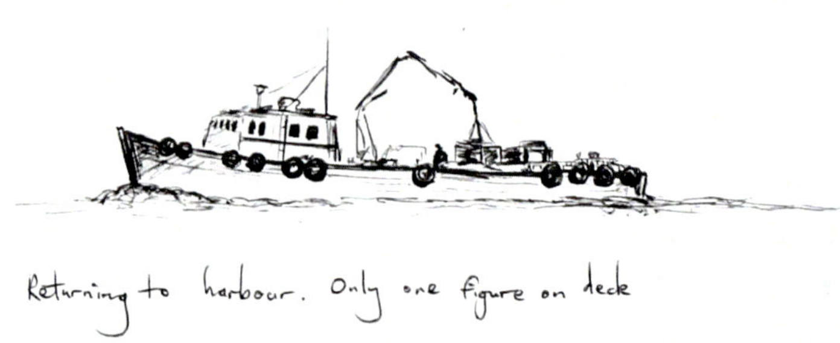

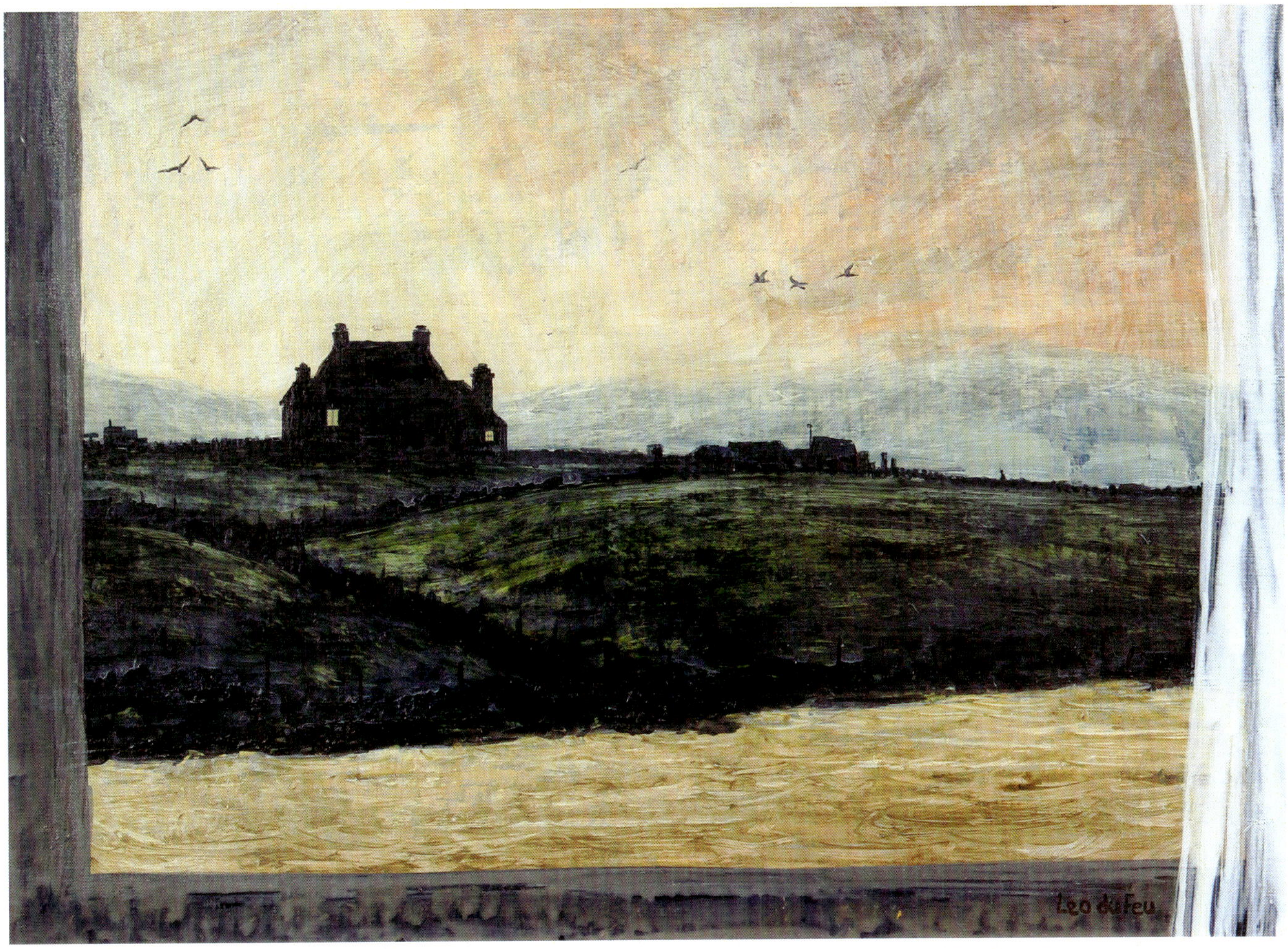

morning view, Stromness
acrylic
15 x 21cm

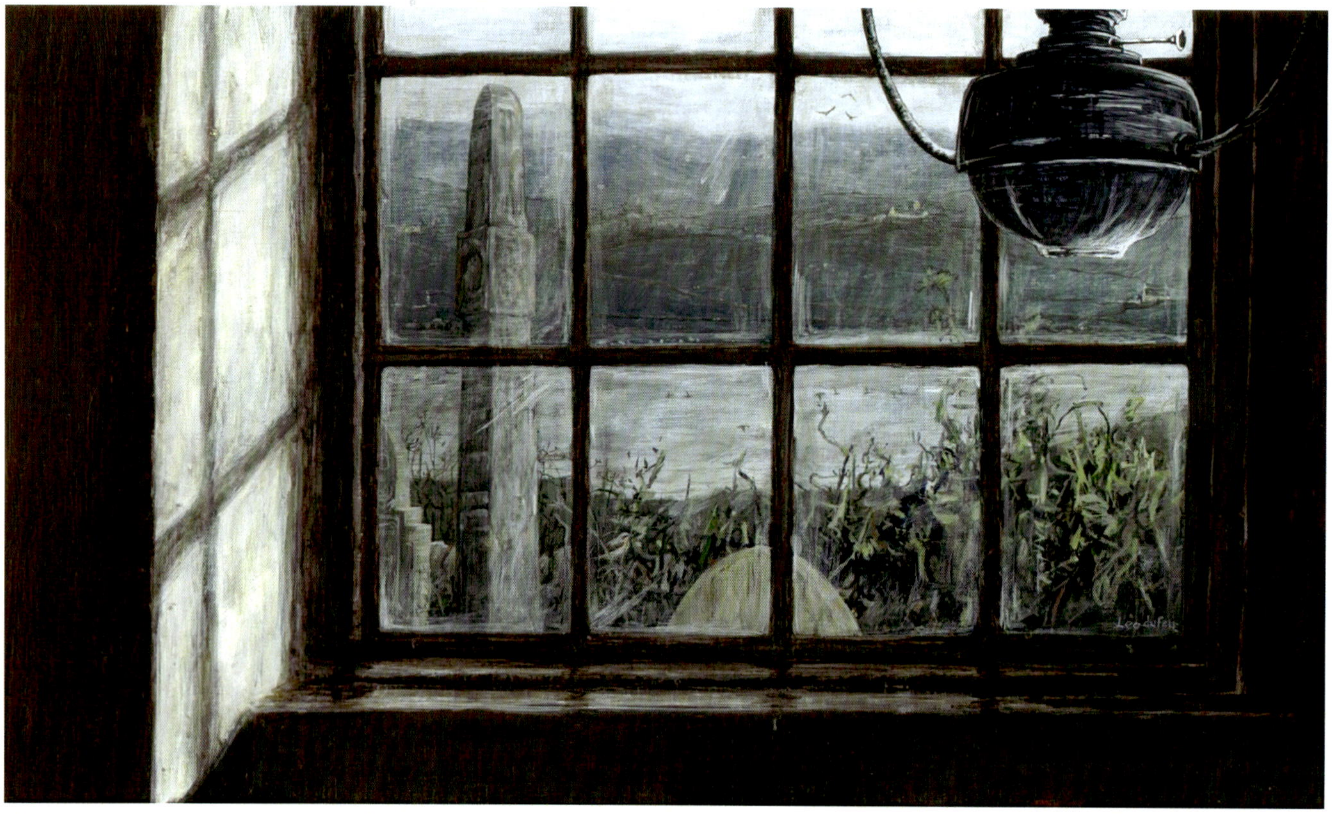

from St. Peter's/Skaill Kirk, Sandwick
acrylic
15 x 25cm

At Rackwick we locked our bikes behind the youth hostel wall and walked across clifftop moorland for a couple of miles to the Old Man of Hoy. Reaching the Old Man we looked across a gulf of nothing at the 449 foot high column of red stone; it's one of the most stunning scenes I've known. Fulmars wheeled curiously below and beside us and bonxies (great skuas) flew powerfully over both moor and waves. In the spring-summer breeding season you risk being dive-bombed by these aggressively territorial birds; keep your scalp safe by waving arms above your head or by walking with a stick poking out from the top of your rucksack – the idea is that the stick gets hit, not you.

Dwarfie Stane, Hoy
pencil
19 x 24.5cm

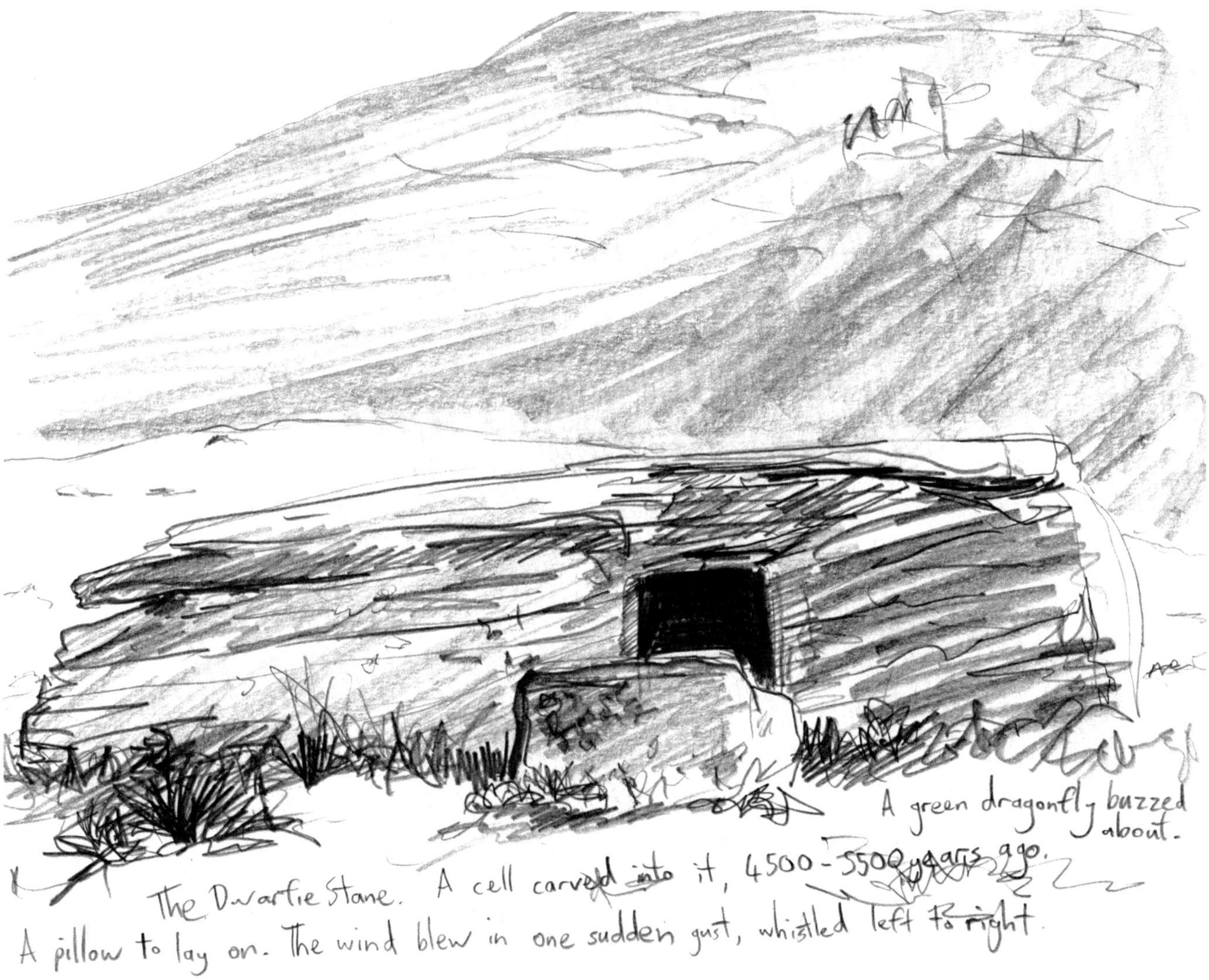

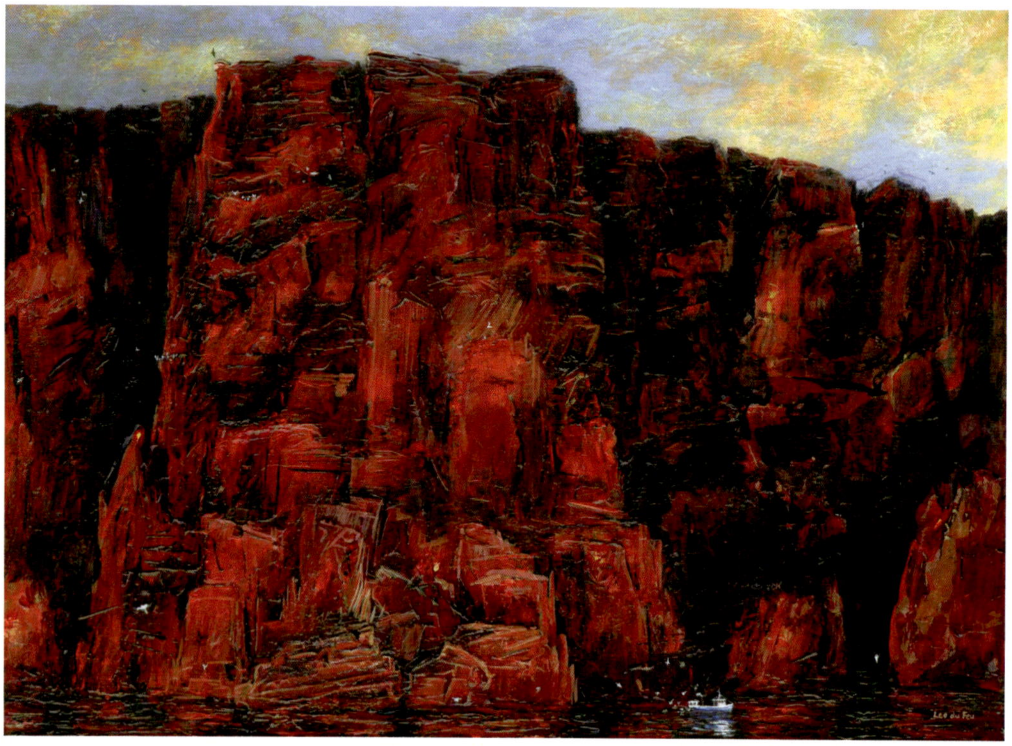

gannets diving,
St John's Head, Hoy
acrylic
15 x 21cm

the old man of Hoy
pencil in sketchbook
19 x 49cm

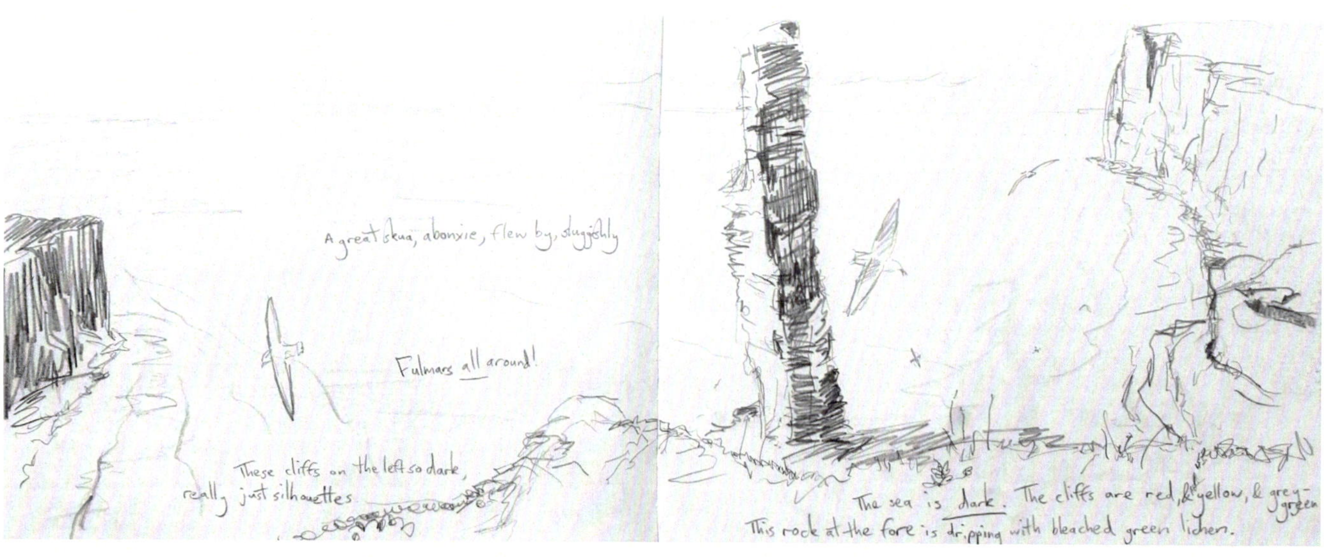

seabird colony,
the old man of Hoy
acrylic
60 x 50cm

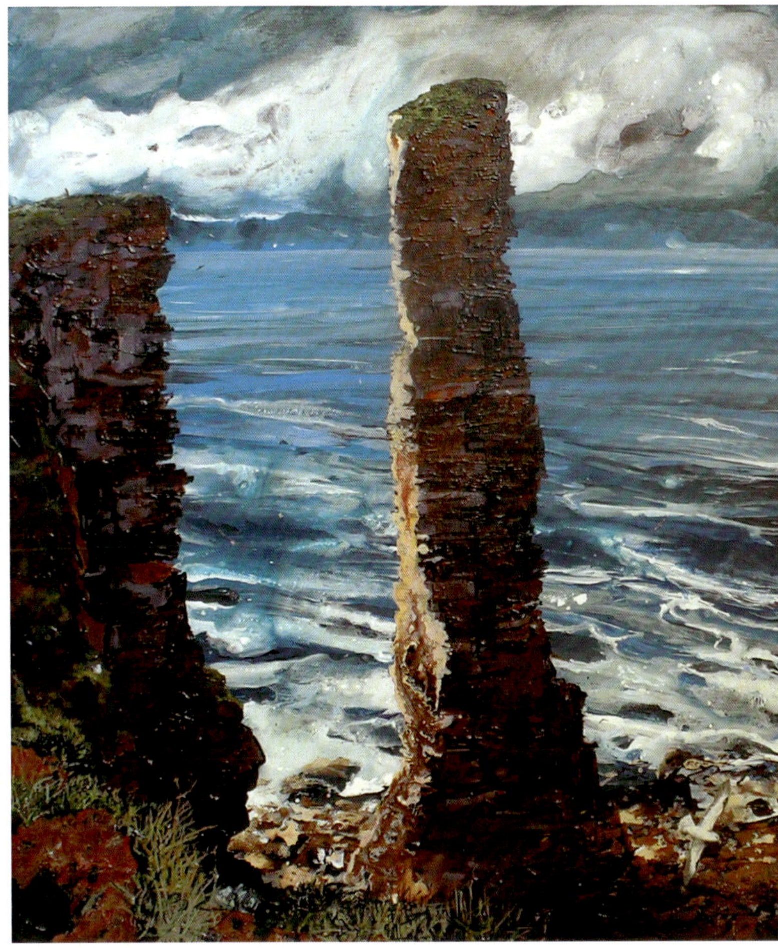

cliffs on Hoy
acrylic
10x11cm

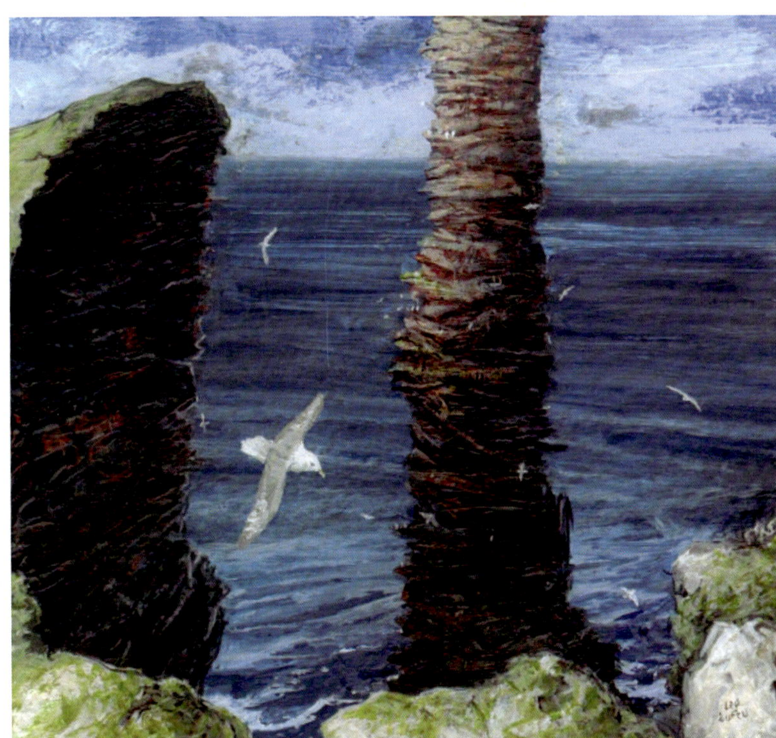

right: arriving in the Orkneys
acrylic
19 x 56cm

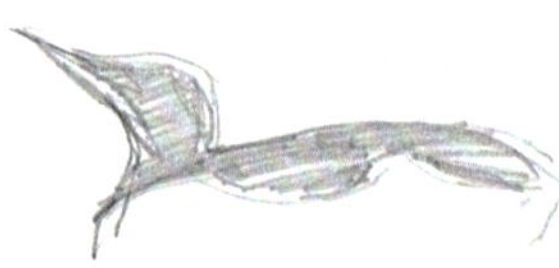

below: on Rousay, Trumland Reserve
pen & watercolour in sketchbook
13 x 41cm

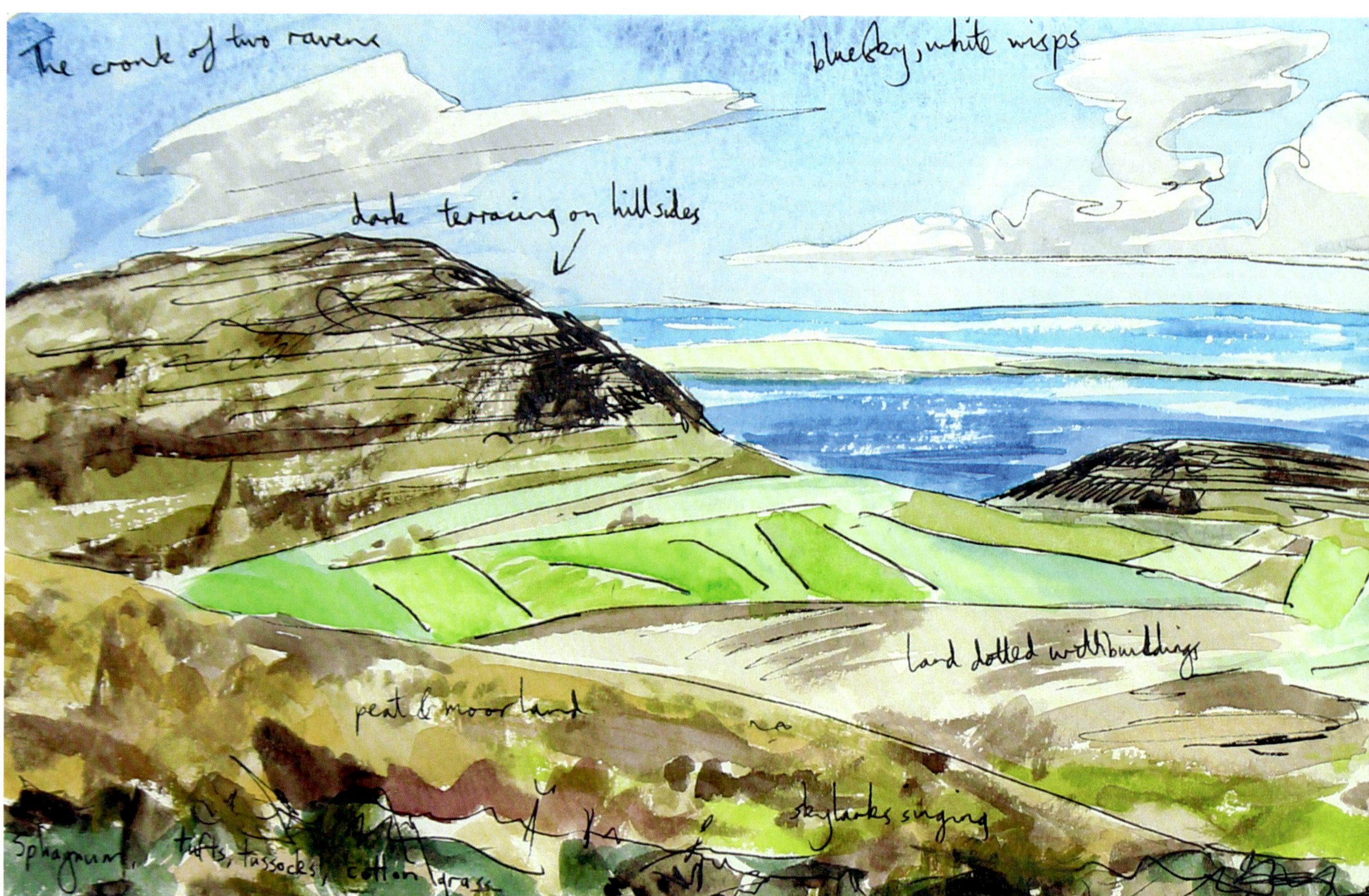

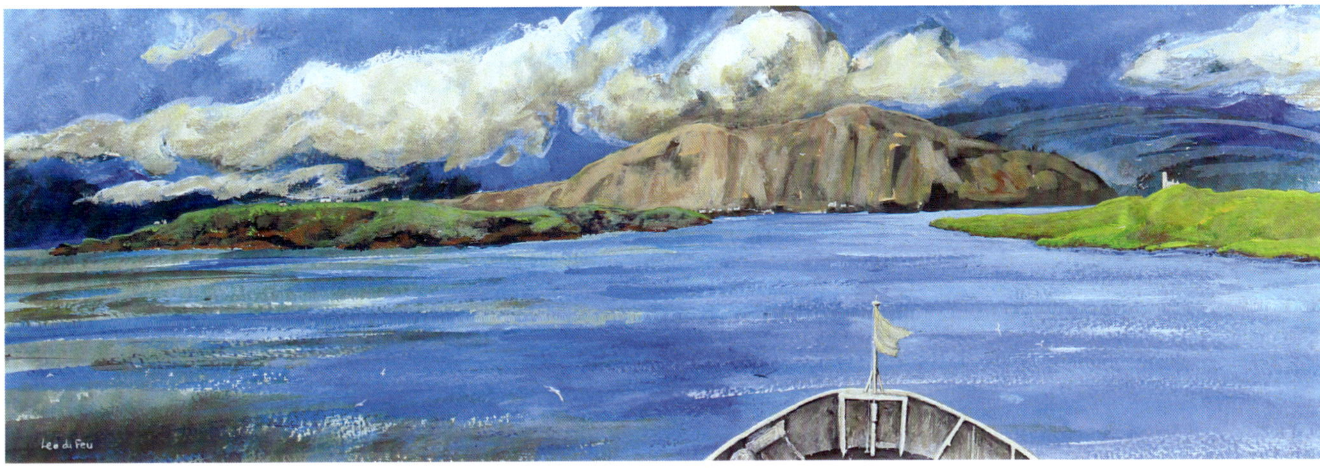
Leo du Feu

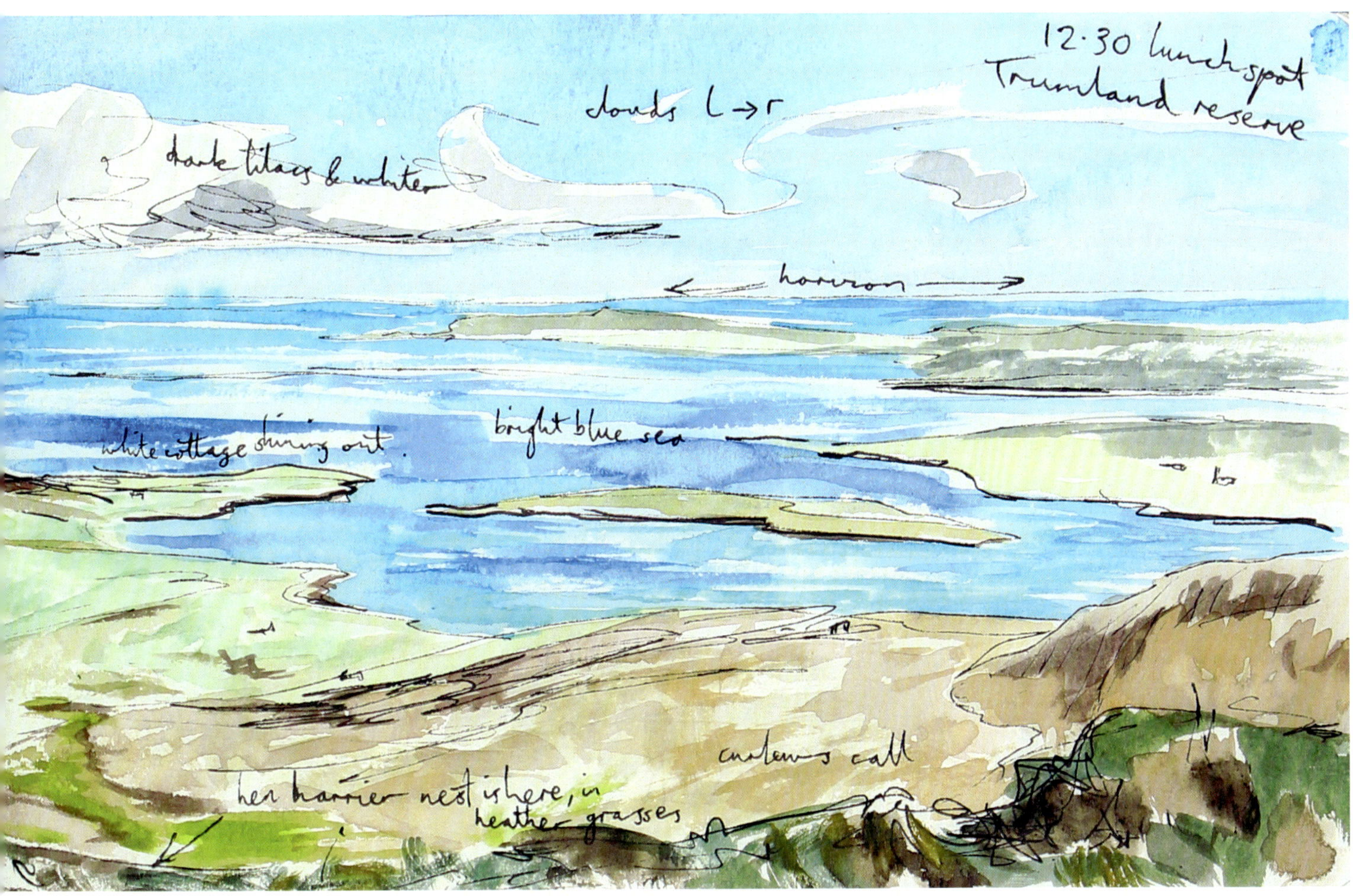
12·30 lunch spot
Trumland reserve
clouds L→r
dark lilacs & whites
horizon
white cottage shining out.
bright blue sea
curlews call
hen harrier nest is here, in
heather grasses

Lewis

In 2008 I was invited to run a two-day painting workshop for the Lewis Arts Club. Their hospitality included taking me all around the island: I saw pristine beaches, cliffs sharply sculpted by the pounding waves of the Atlantic (next stop America!), the standing stones of Callanish and vast expanses of moorland. From the capital, Stornoway, you can walk through the extensive strange rainforest-like grounds of Lews Castle: twisted boughs damply festooned with lichens and mosses; the ground carpeted by ferns and fronds.

I only had a couple of days on Lewis so limited myself to pencil sketches and lots of photos. The trip has resulted in numerous paintings, particularly of a sandy bay north of Tolsta village where I watched a storm blow in as I sheltered in a sea-cave until the rain lessened. Oystercatchers ran the sands and a pair of fulmars circled from their cliffy ledge.

Mousa Broch studies
pencil
each 10.5 x 13cm

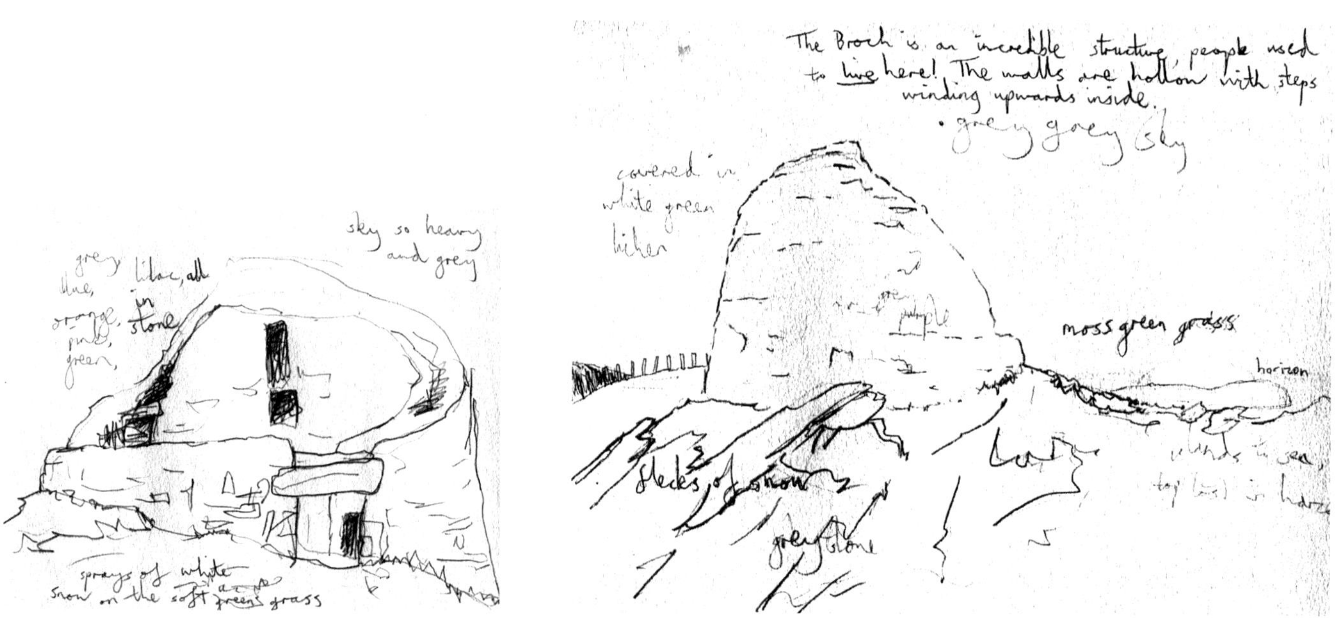

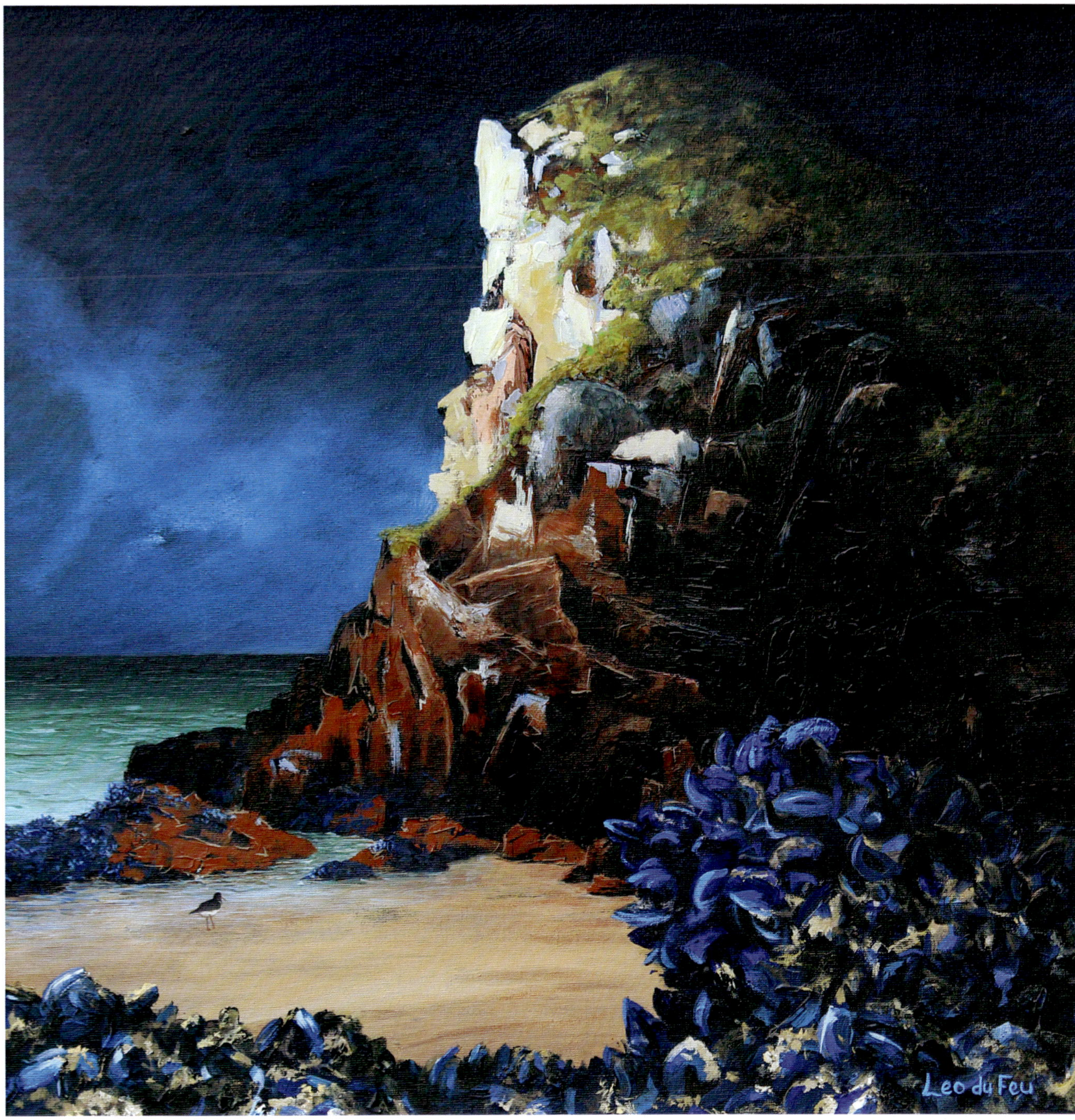

oystercatcher on Lewis
acrylic
50 x 50cm

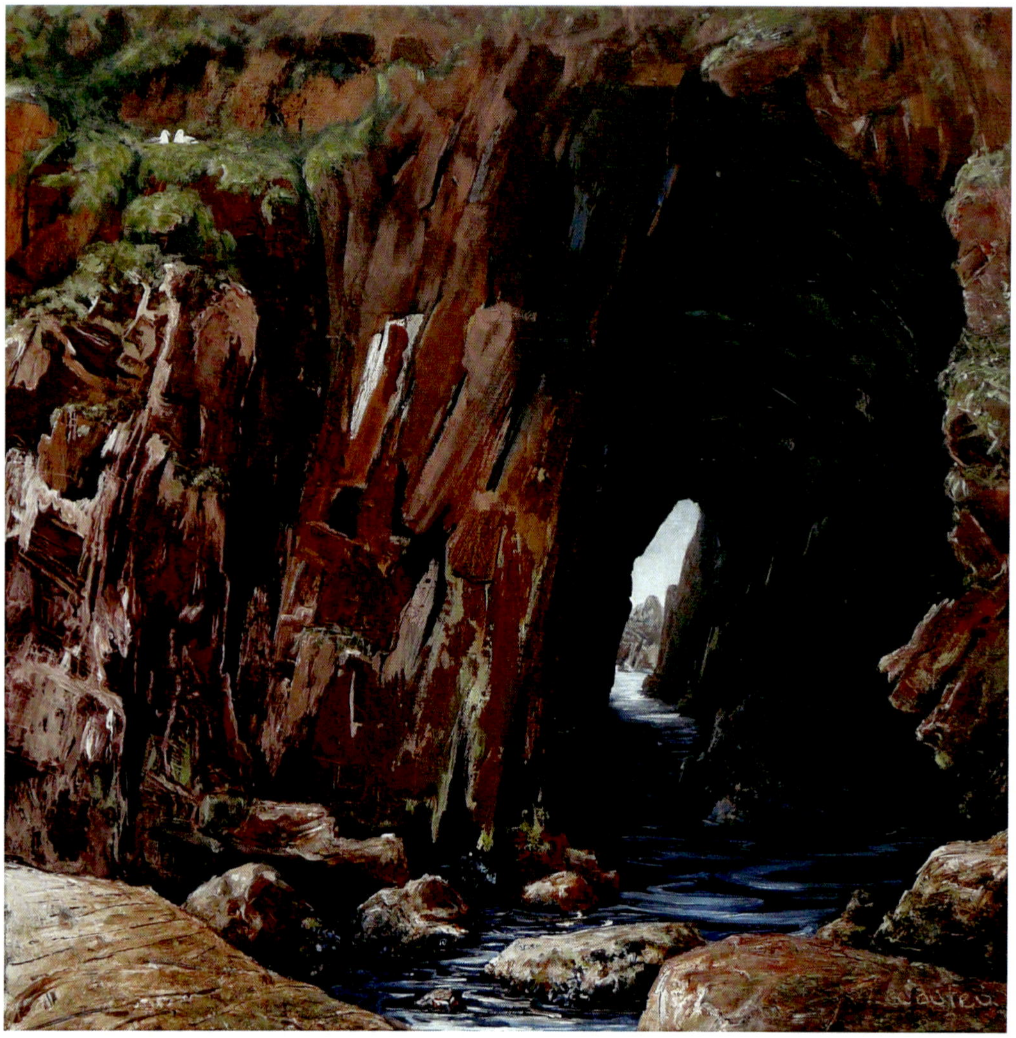

nesting fulmar
acrylic
50 x 50cm

through the sea cave
acrylic
20 x 10cm

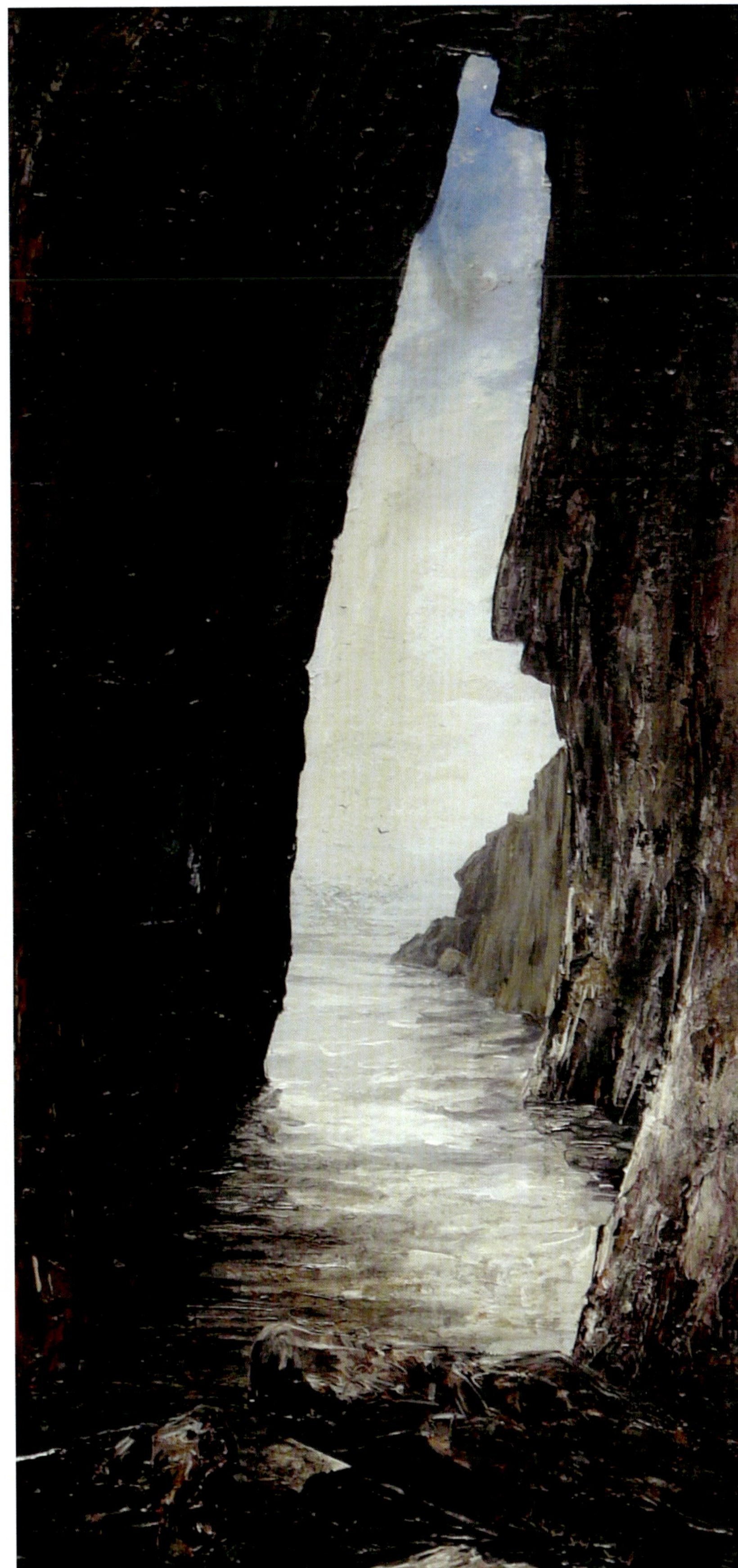

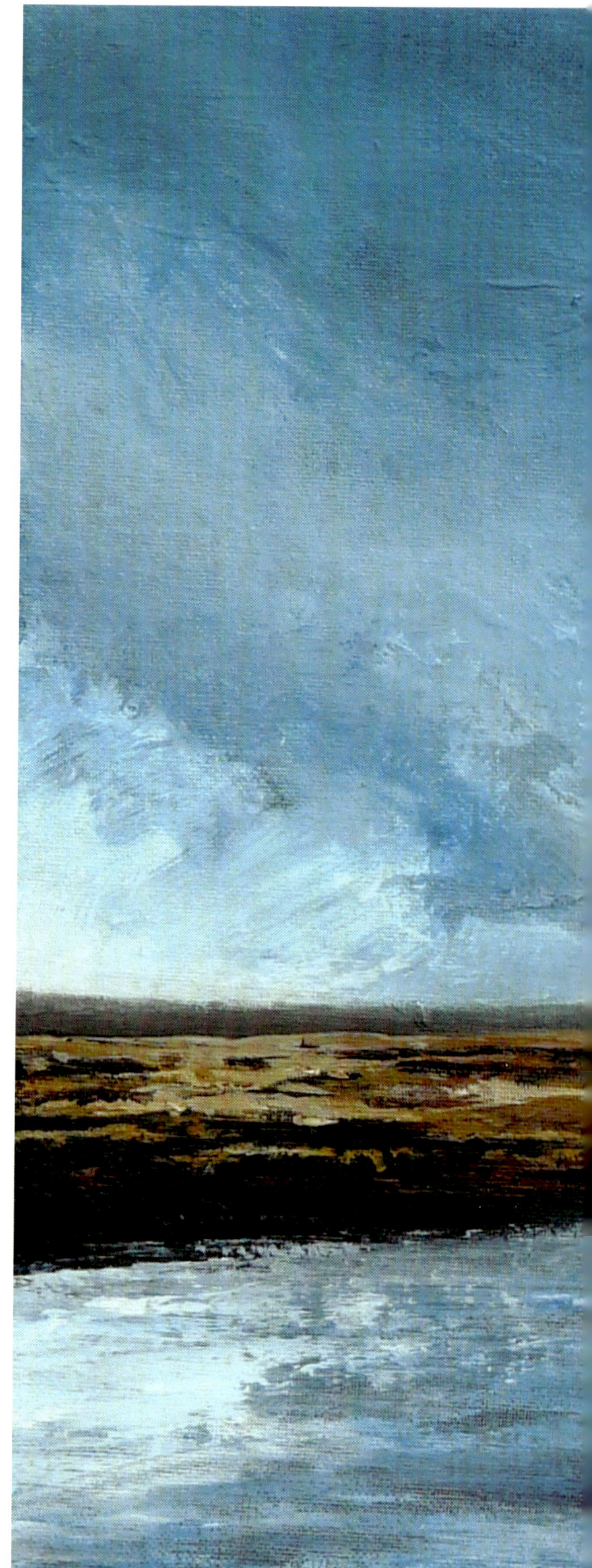

croft on Lewis
acrylic
40 x 50cm

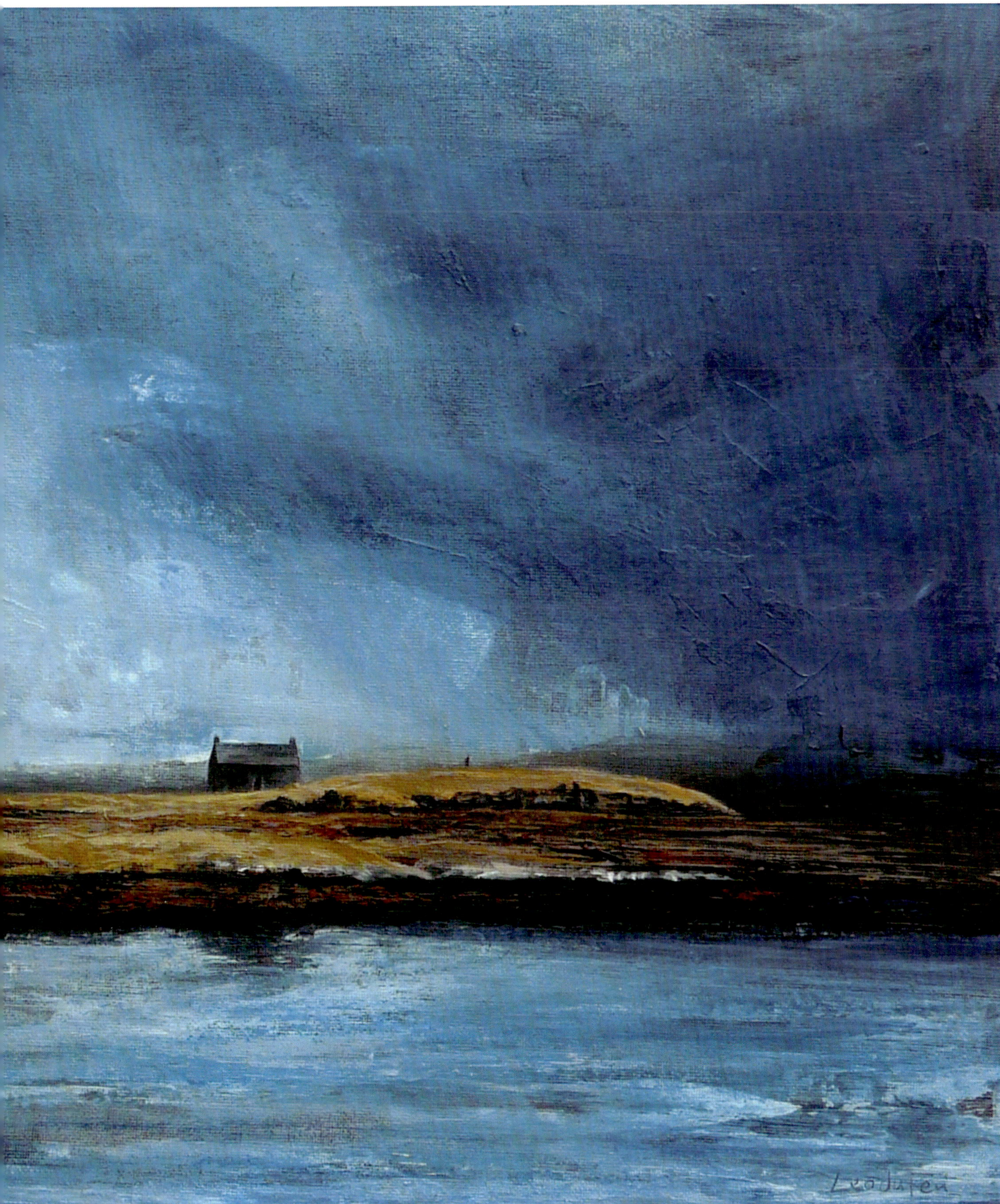

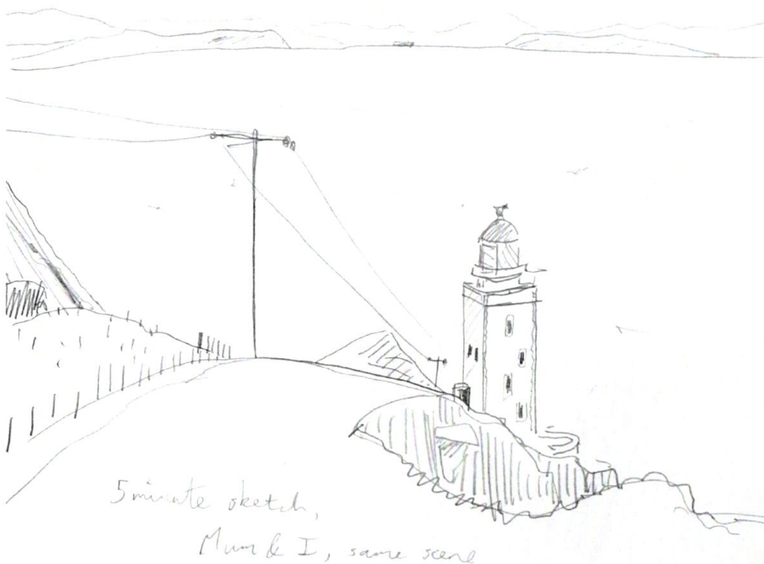

left: the eastern lighthouse, Holy Isle
pencil
19 x 24.5cm

below: Holy Isle cliffs
pencil & watercolour
19 x 24.5cm

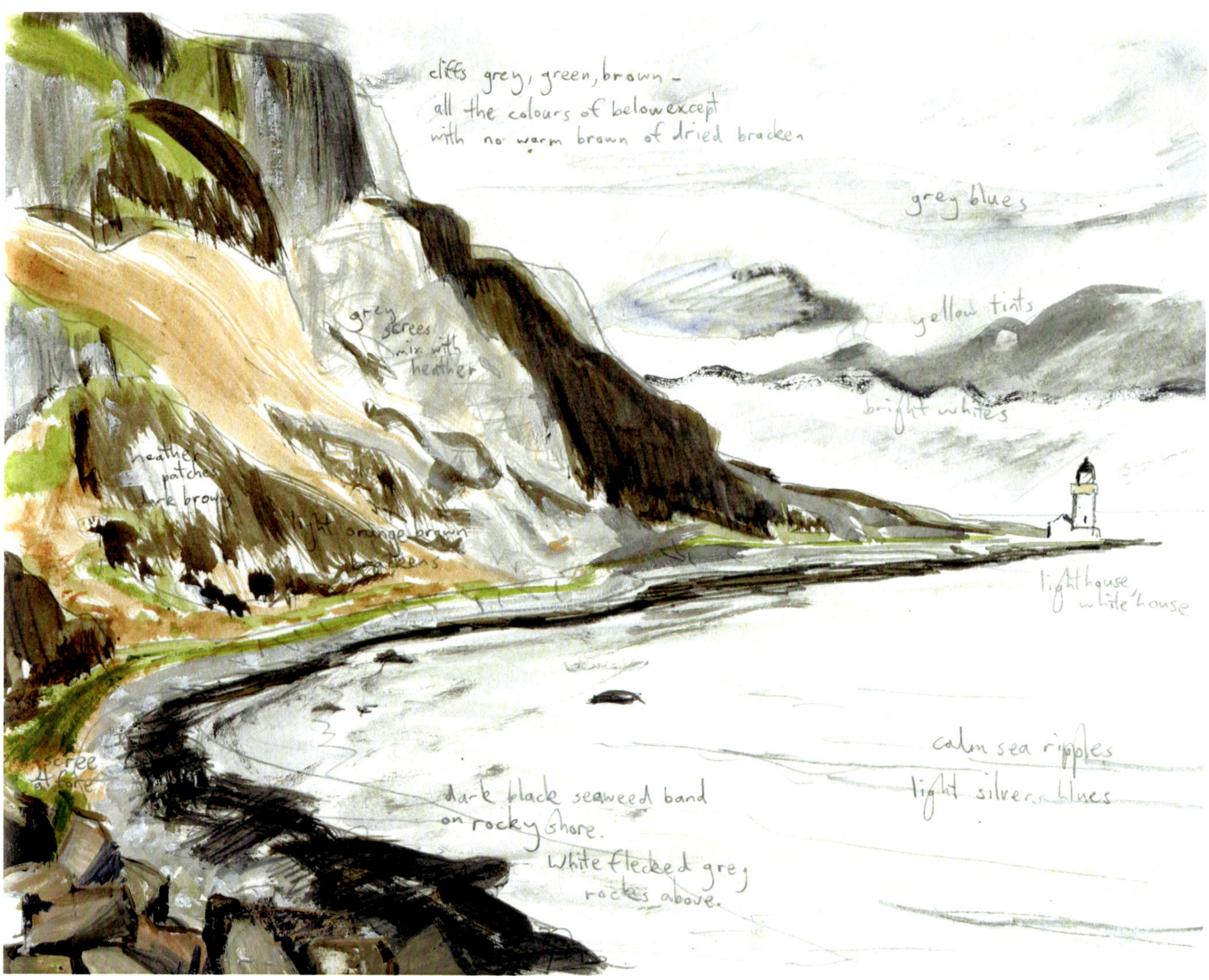

Holy Isle
pen & watercolour
13 x 19cm

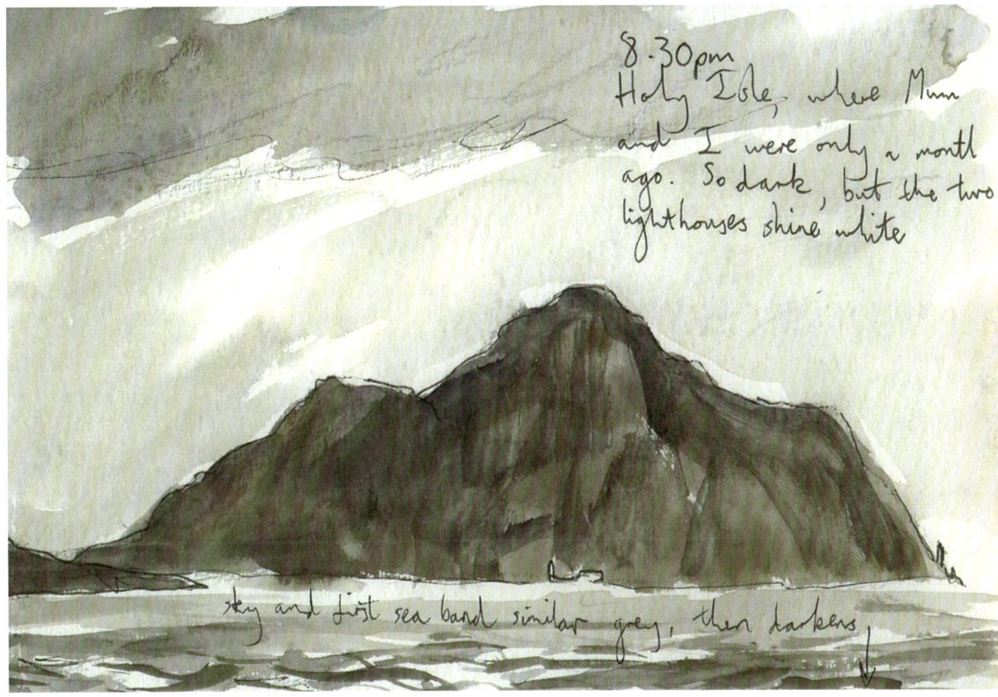

Holy Isle

Holy Isle lies separated from Arran by a mile of protected water called Lamlash Bay. When the weather is suitable a small ferryboat runs out to the island from Lamlash village. The island is small, only two miles long by half a mile wide, but I'd happily spend days there. If you want more than a few hours to explore, book into the Buddhist centre at the island's north end; accommodation is basic but absolutely adequate and includes three delicious vegetarian meals each day. Mum and I came here for four days of art and nature in April 2011.

There's a lot of birdlife; we counted 39 definitely-identified species on our visit. Waders are on the pebble beaches; oystercatchers, turnstones and ringed plover, the latter so camouflaged you can hardly make them out amongst the smoothly rounded stones. Shags and cormorants dry dragon-like wings on the rocks and gulls galore bring constant noise to steep cliffs halfway down the island.

In the spring stonechats perch on gorses and dried brackens; wheatears bounce away as you walk on the shore. Bushes and trees are often alive with the sounds of the smaller 'garden' birds. On our way up Mullach Mor a kestrel darted past us; from the 1,026 foot summit we had clear sunny views for miles all around.

There are also larger mammals on Holy Isle; free-roaming Soay sheep, Saanen goats and Eriskay ponies. All three species beautiful and hardy, and seeming perfectly suited to rugged island life.

A month later I passed the island on a National Trust for Scotland (NTS) cruise, as mentioned in the following pages. From the deck I did a quick sketch painting showing the two lighthouses that guard Holy Isle's southern tip.

Shetland

In 2011 my friend Chris and I went on a National Trust for Scotland cruise of the islands. Extreme stormy weather meant we couldn't land on either Foula or St Kilda, but that didn't matter: we circumnavigated both and got a true sense of how incredibly isolated island life can be.

We spent two days on mainland Shetland where I sketched razorbills diving for small fish in Lerwick harbour; as close as I've seen them. I later made an acrylic painting based on my sketches.

razorbill studies
pencil

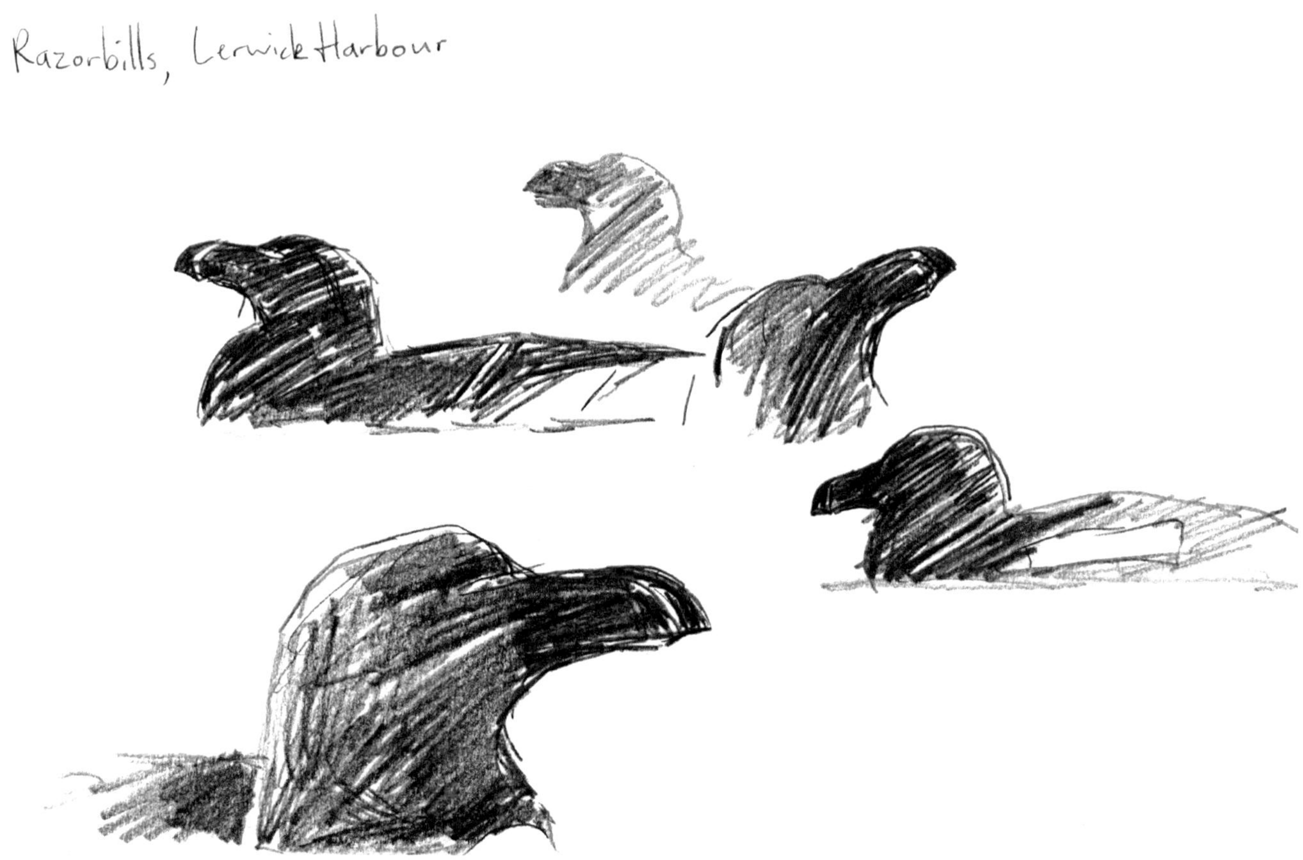

razorbill, Alca torda, Lerwick harbour
acrylic
14.5 x 21cm

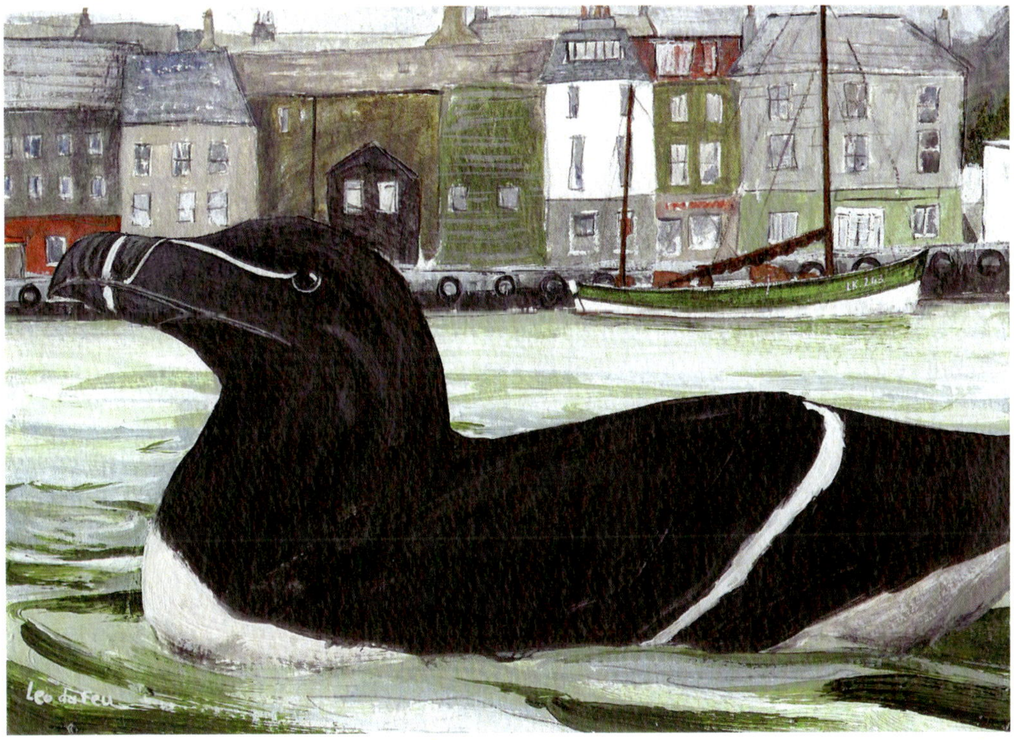

razorbill studies
pencil

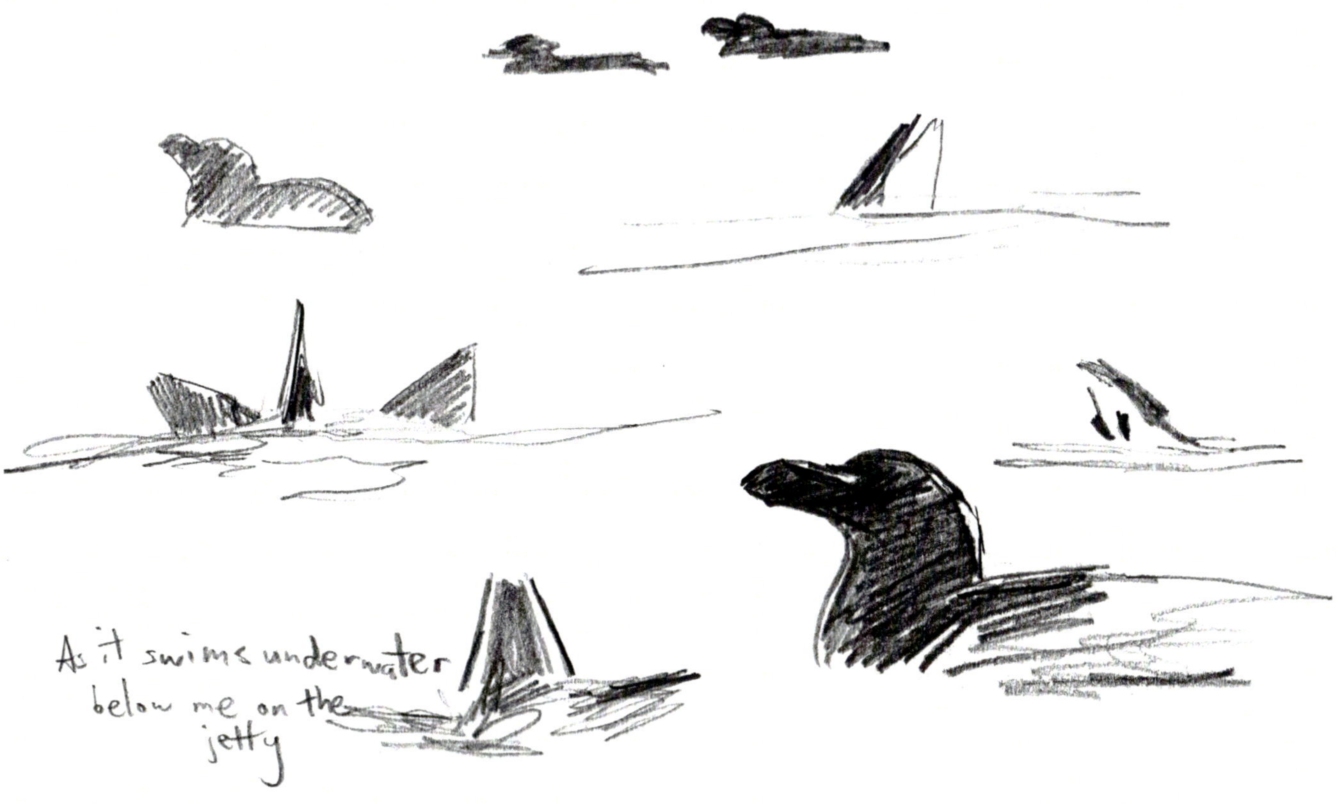

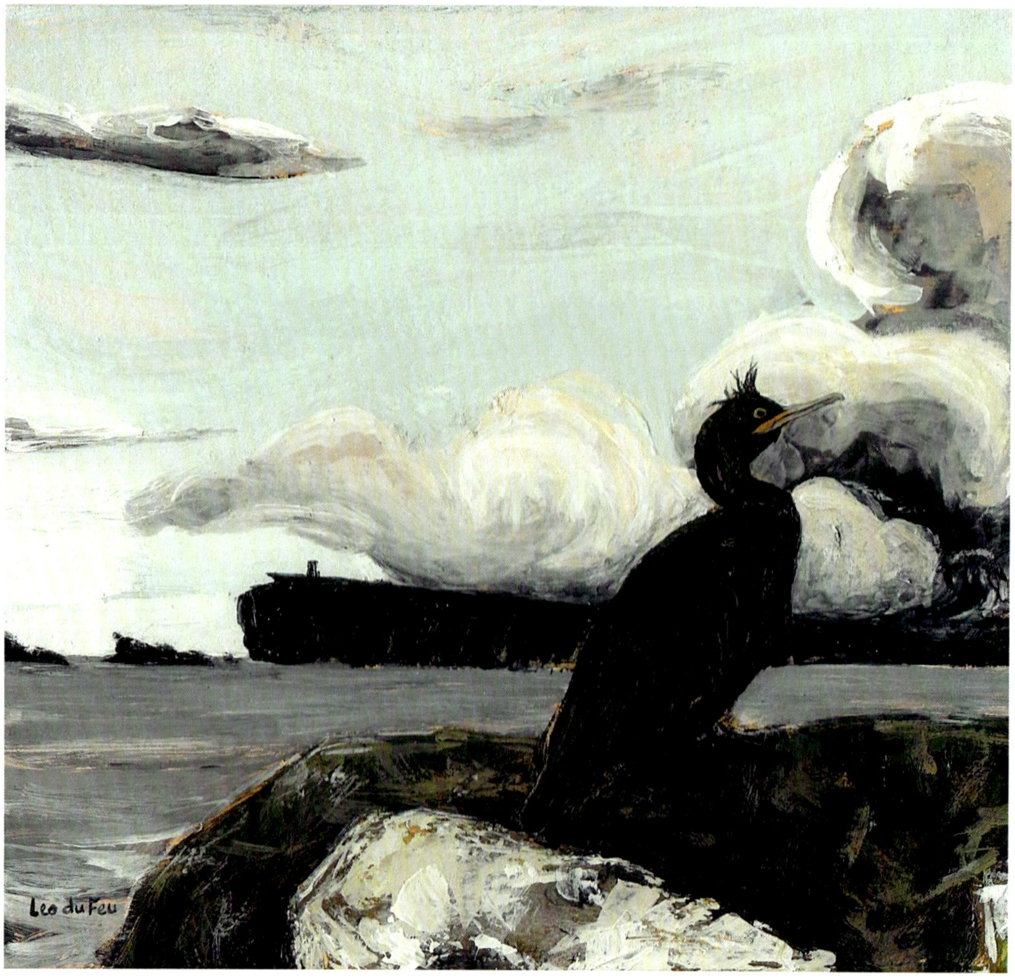

Phalacrocorax aristotelis*, *view to Mousa
acrylic
10 x 11cm

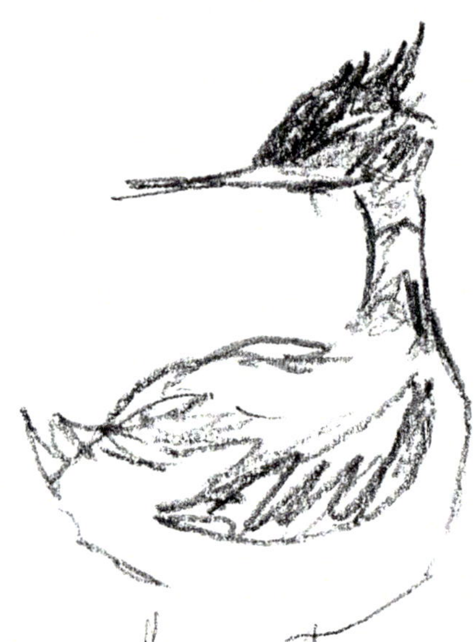

From the mainland some of us visited the small island of Mousa, home to Scotland's best surviving broch, 2,000–2,500 years old. A narrow stair between the double-layered outer walls of this Iron Age conical tower emerges at the top, 13 metres up, to overlook much of the island. Fulmars were all over; on the lush grasses and in the air. A pair of Arctic skuas stood alert and watched me as I watched them. As we arrived, and stepped off the little ferry, an eider mother and her mate bobbed with their fluffy brown ducklings on the choppy waves.

Mousa Broch
pencil & watercolour in sketchbook
13 x 41cm

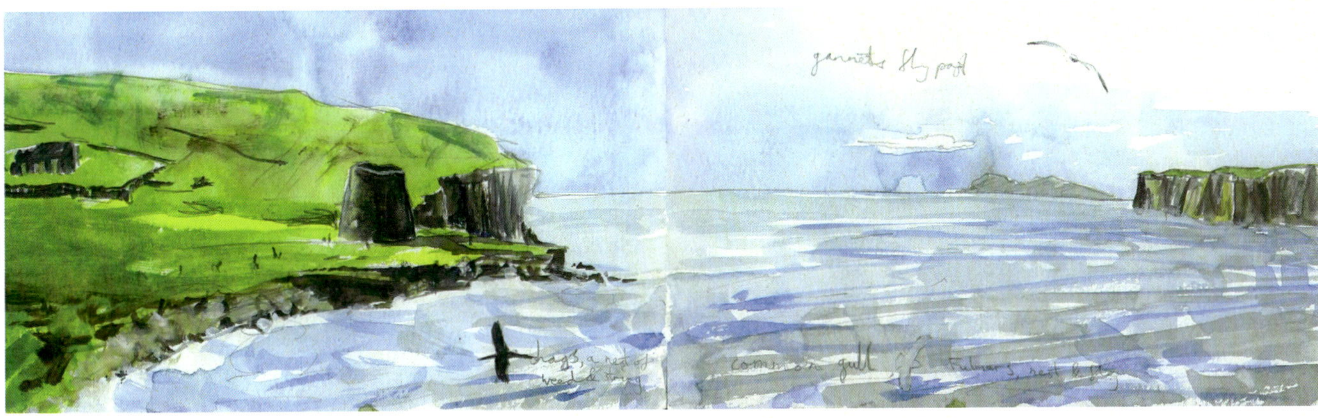

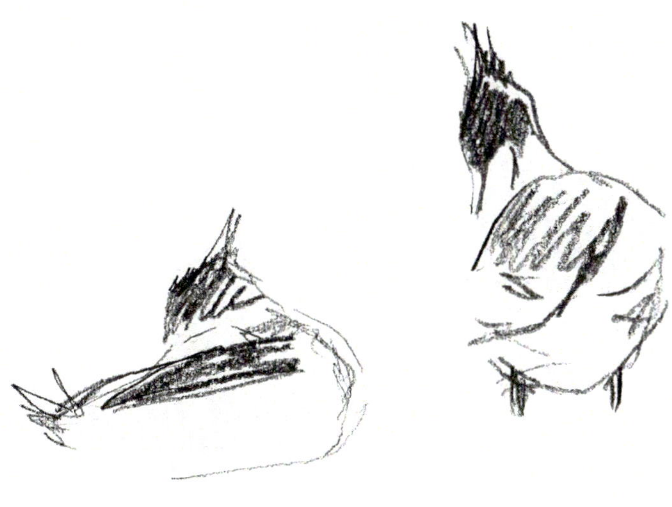

Sketches from trains

At one time train journeys were for me an opportunity to get some reading done. Now that seems impossible; there's too much to be seen out of the windows. Look for things you've never noticed before or keep a list of all the birds and animals that you spot – good activities to try with children?

I like to make small quick sketches of the details that catch my eye: a gnarled tree, a tumbledown cottage, a grand country house. Some of these will be used one day in paintings but many will never make it beyond the confines of my sketchbooks. Here are a lucky few that have managed to escape; records of journeys made, and glimpses of so many places still to explore.

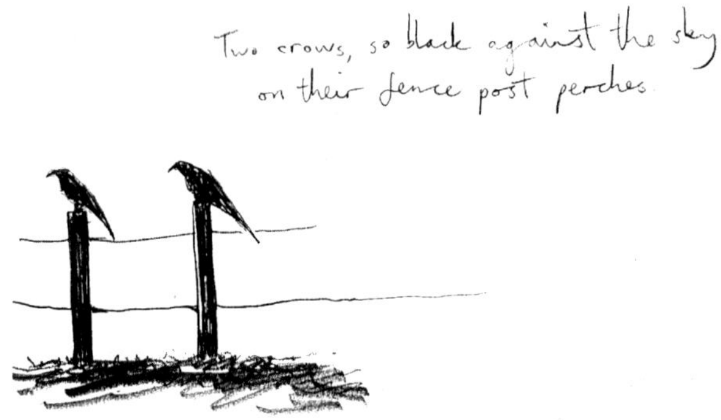

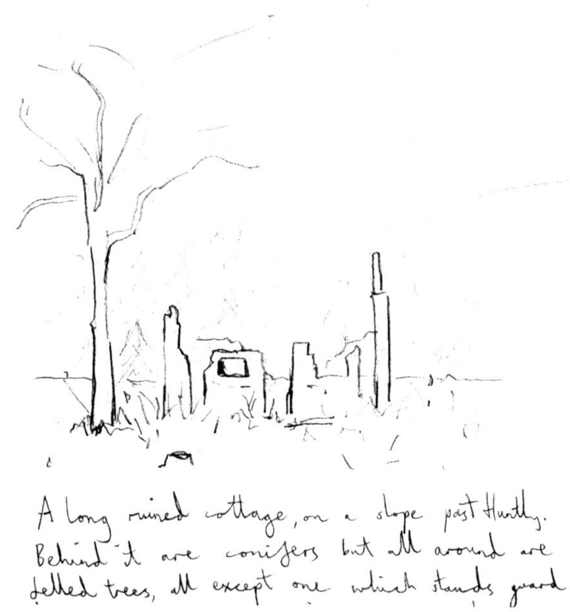

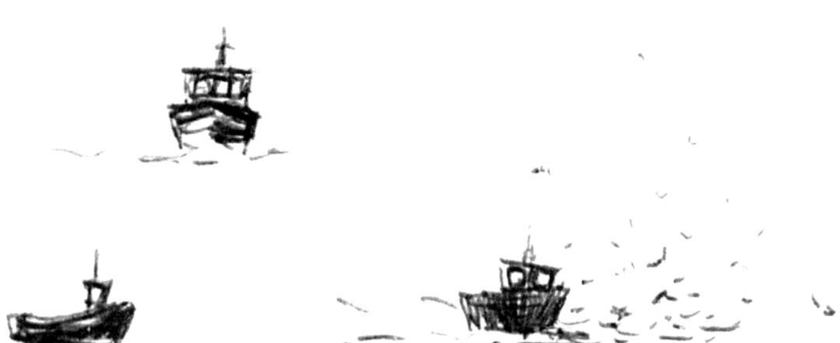

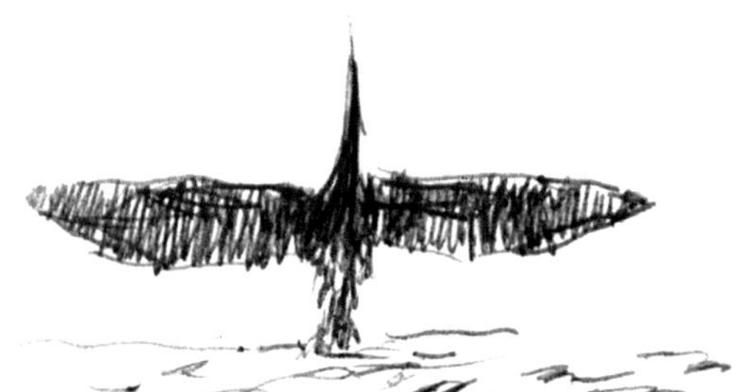

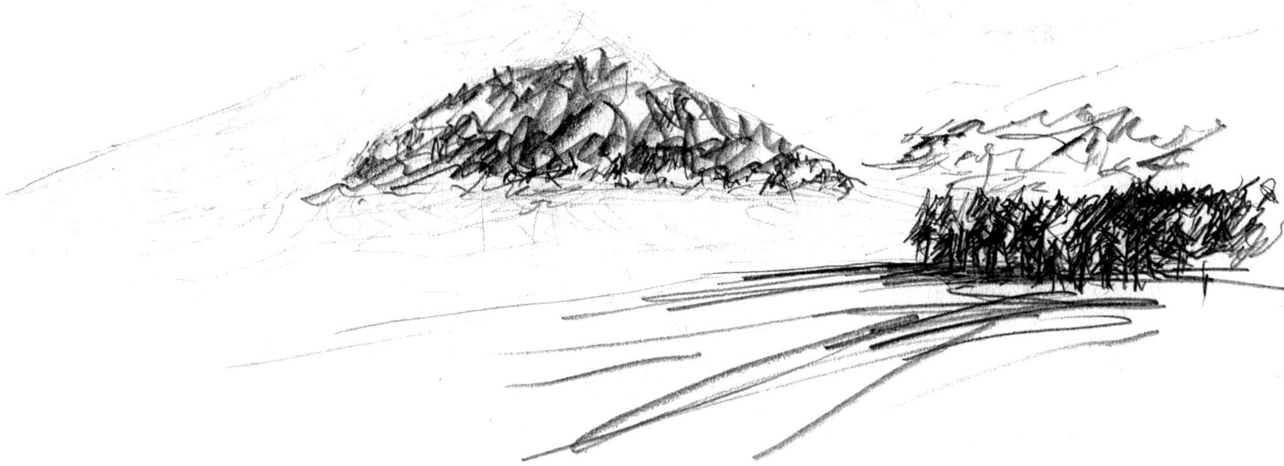

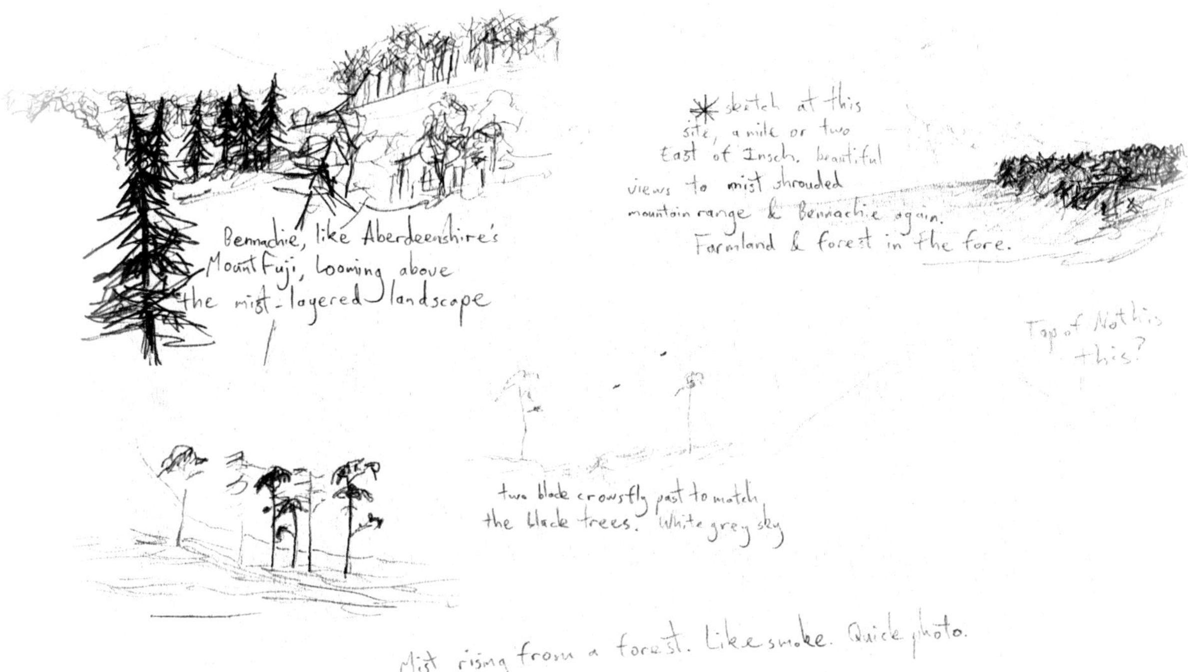
Bennachie, like Aberdeenshire's Mount Fuji, looming above the mist-layered landscape
* sketch at this site, a mile or two East of Insch. beautiful views to mist shrouded mountain range & Bennachie again. Farmland & forest in the fore.
two black crows fly past to match the black trees. White grey sky
Mist rising from a forest. Like smoke. Quick photo.

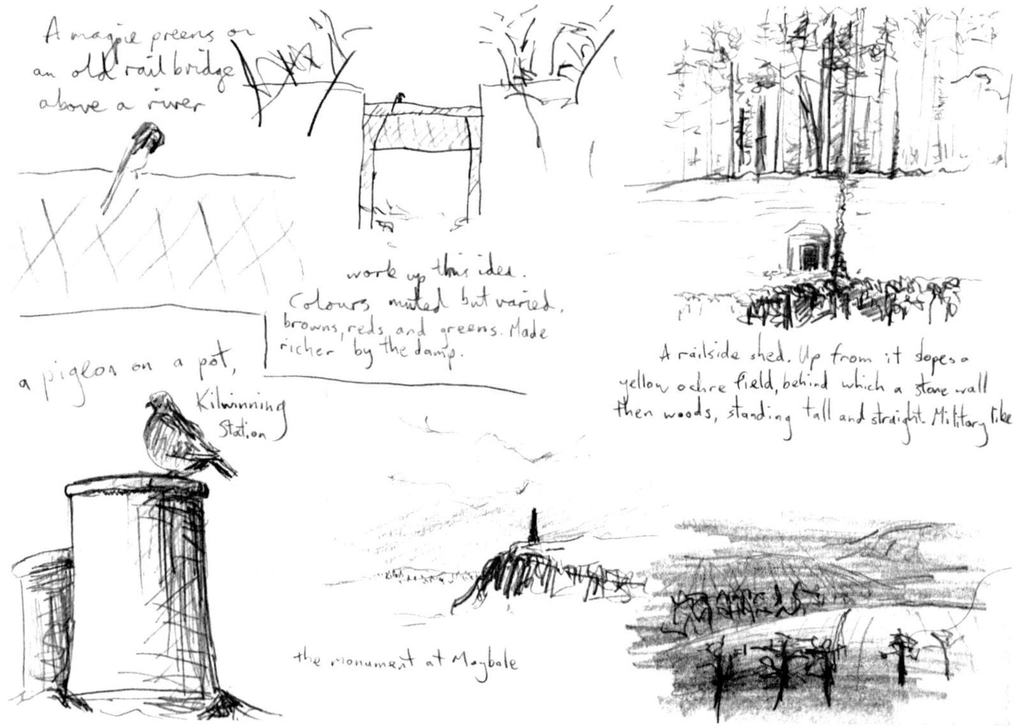

train sketches, Glasgow – Stranraer
pencil

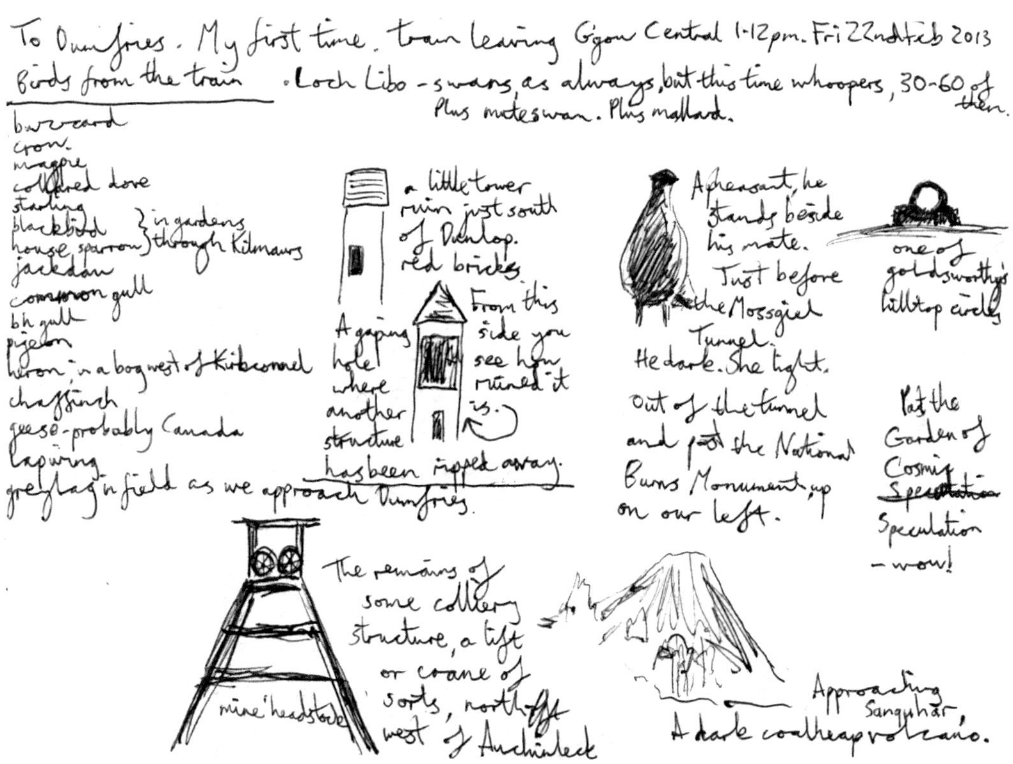

train sketches, Glasgow – Dumfries
biro

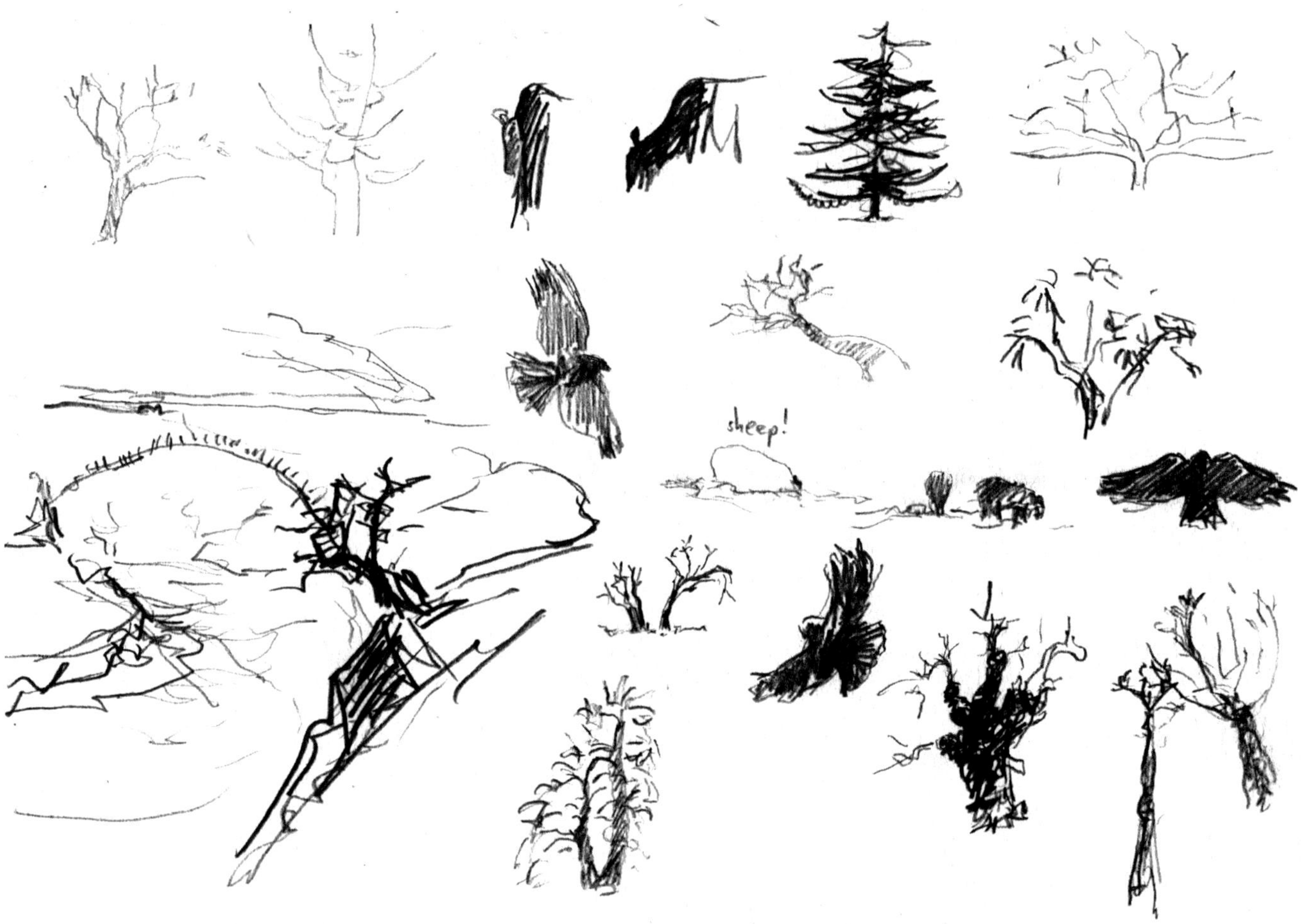

train sketches,
Glasgow – Stranraer
pencil

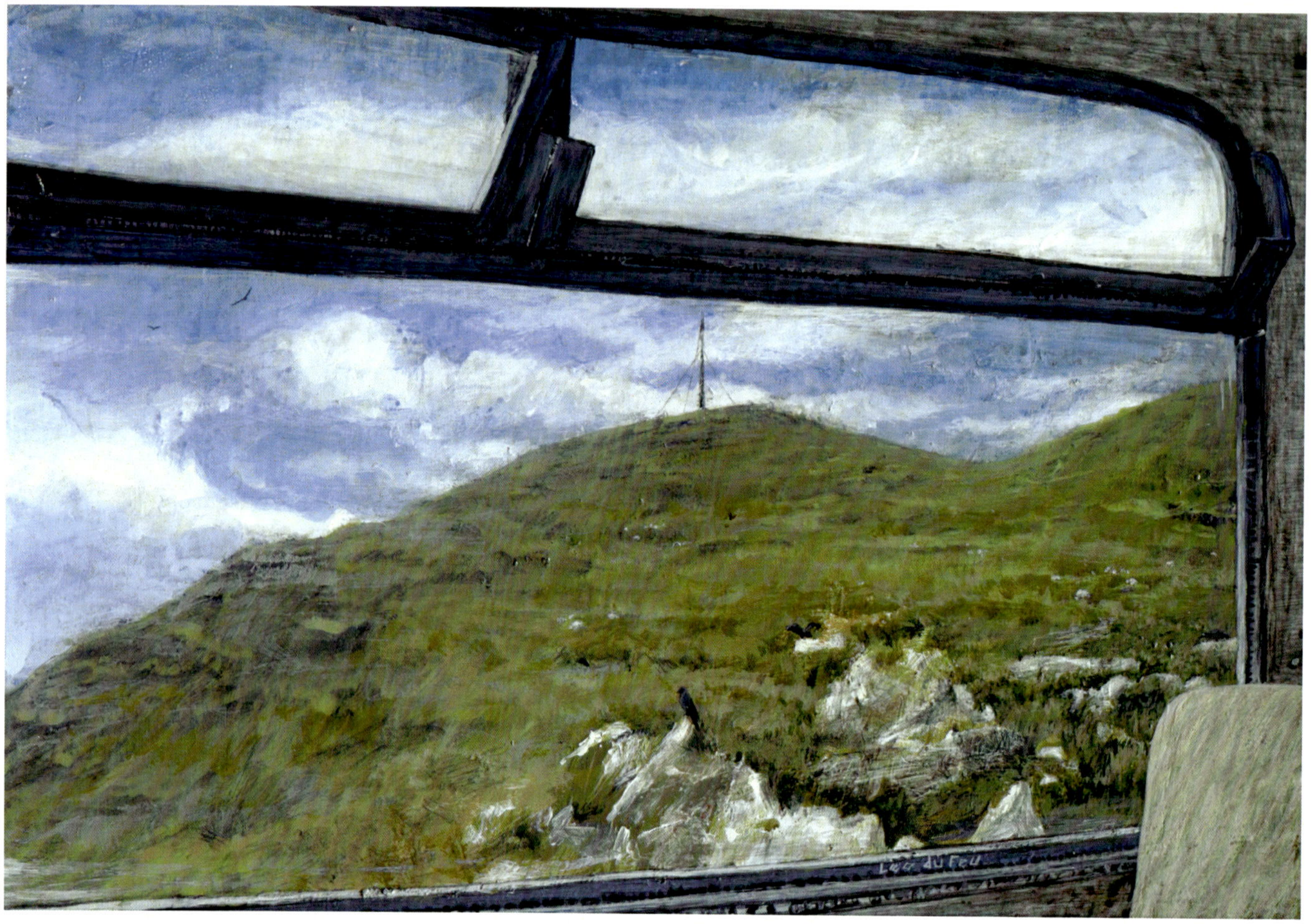

Above: near Girvan, a view to the hills
acrylic
10 x 14.5cm

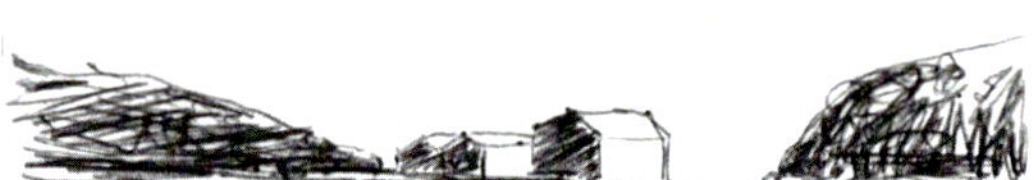

Near Invergordon, metal warehouses, so industrial, on a concrete promontary, contrast against the natural headlands behind. Bright, sunlit, on metal.

There in the grassy dunes past Brora

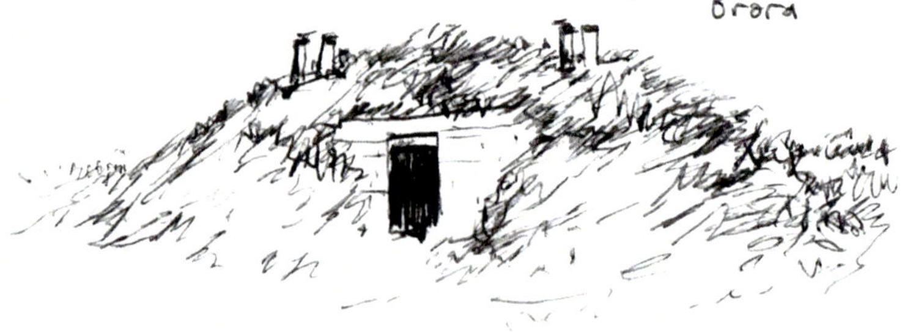

Acknowledgements

In my first book, *Sketches from Canada*, I didn't have any acknowledgements. Partly due to lack of space and partly through the fear of missing someone out. This book is bigger and even more people have played a part.

I'll start with family, so thank you Jennifer for our trips to castles, nature reserves and cafes, for being ever-willing to chauffeur person and paintings, for typing and layout, for fun and oddities. Mum, Dad and Roan for family holidays and walks, countless outdoor hours cementing my love of nature; Mum for sketching trips, for having that caravan, for getting me into this whole art thing; Dad for my studio and stacks of work all over the house; Roan, because he's my brother. Also my Meethill family for all our times in the woods and on the Buchan coastline.

Thank you Michelle and Steve, Ian, Rubina and Fergus, for regular and endless hospitality, lifts, art couriering. Judith for the opportunity to paint in Dumfrieshire. Liz (and her network!) for so much advice and assistance and for always knowing the answers. Kittie for birding sketching trips and for her own inspiring work; Paul for my website and all computer advice; them both for friendship. Chris for knowing everything about birds and for sharing so much of it, for circumnavigating St Kilda and for too much chocolate. Craig for bon mots and art chat over coffee.

Thanks to all who collect and follow my work. The Bet Low Trust, The Royal Scottish Society of Painters in Watercolour (RSW) and the Royal Over-Seas League for recognising and awarding it. Malcolm and the Prince's Scottish Youth Business Trust (now Youth Business Scotland) for helping me set up in the first place. The Royal Glasgow Institute of the Fine Arts (RGI) for my October 2013 solo exhibition, also The Line in Linlithgow and the other galleries across the country.

Thanks to the British Trust for Ornithology (BTO), the Royal Society for the Protection of Birds (RSPB) and the Scottish Ornithologists' Club (SOC) for the inspiring and vital work that they do. Everyone I talk with about nature and birds (those who I listen to and those who patiently listen to me!). Everyone else I haven't named but will wish that I had.

Nearing the end, the Fine Art Department in Edinburgh's Central Library; a favourite place to write. The Linlithgow Bookshop (now Far from the Madding Crowd) and Scottish Youth Hostels Association for support and sponsorship. Jeremy Mills for confidence in my work and for approaching me with this fantastic publishing proposal. Michael Palin, John Busby, Stuart Housden and John Yellowlees for their generous forewords.

And finally, an extra extra large thank you to John and ScotRail for saying yes when I first wrote. It would be impossible to do all this without their support.

LEO DU FEU
JUNE 2013

Influences and Inspirations

Artists

John Busby (1928 –), wildlife artist:
Drawing Birds, Christopher Helm Publishers (2004)
Landmarks and Sea Wings, Wildlife Art Gallery (2005)

Tim Wootton (1963 –), wildlife artist:
Drawing and Painting Birds, The Crowood Press Ltd (2010)

Kate Downie (1958 –), Scottish landscape artist – **www.katedownie.com**

William Gillies (1898–1973), Scottish painter – especially the freedom of his watercolours

The *Group of Seven*, Canadian wilderness painters and explorers, early 1900s – especially their hundreds of outdoor oil sketches

Kittie Jones (1983 –), Edinburgh-based wildlife printmaker painter – **www.kittiejones.com**

Susan Smith (1953 –), Scottish wildlife and landscape printmaker painter – **www.susanmcsmith.com**

Frances Walker (1930 –), Scottish landscape painter and printmaker

Sylvia Wishart (1936–2008), Orcadian painter

Literature

Kathleen Jamie (1962 –), *Findings*, Sort of Books (2005)

Robert Macfarlane (1976 –), especially *The Wild Places*, Granta Books (2007)

George Mackay Brown (1921–1996), Orcadian writer

Hamish Haswell Smith (1928 –), *The Scottish Islands*, Canongate Books Ltd (2008)

Assorted

The British Trust for Ornithology – **www.bto.org**

The Royal Society for the Protection of Birds – **www.rspb.org.uk**

The Scottish Ornithologists' Club – **www.the-soc.org.uk**
Their East Lothian HQ boasts a beautiful gallery exhibiting the UK's top contemporary wildlife artists, and an extremely well stocked ornithological library.

ScotRail – **www.scotrail.co.uk**
Scottish train operator, invaluable to my travels.

Out of Doors, **BBC Radio Scotland**, 6:30–8am every Saturday morning.
Programme covering absolutely anything and everything about Scotland's great outdoors.

BBC Radio 4 – for current affairs, documentaries, nature, comedy, drama. On many days I listen almost constantly.

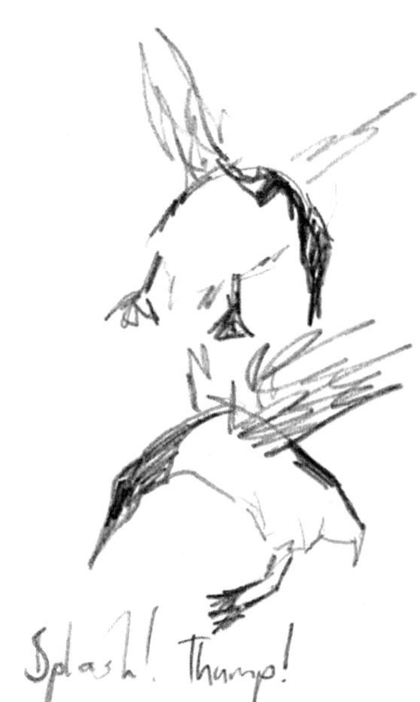